Formative Assessment in the Disciplines

Framing a Continuum of Professional Learning

MARGARET HERITAGE

E. CAROLINE WYLIE

Harvard Education Press
Cambridge, Massachusetts

Paperback ISBN 978-1-68253-466-3

Library Edition ISBN 978-1-68253-470-0

Library of Congress Cataloging-in-Publication Data

Names: Heritage, Margaret, author. | Wylie, E. Caroline, author.
Title: Formative assessment in the disciplines : framing a continuum of professional learning / Margaret Heritage, E. Caroline Wylie.
Description: Cambridge, Massachusetts : Harvard Education Press, [2020] | Includes index. | Summary: "Heritage and Wylie outline a framework for helping teachers develop and extend their competency in enacting discipline-based formative assessment practices across the continuum of preservice and professional learning"-- Provided by publisher.
Identifiers: LCCN 2019054810 | ISBN 9781682534663 (paperback) | ISBN 9781682534700 (library binding)
Subjects: LCSH: Educational evaluation. | Effective teaching. | Teachers--In-service training. | Teachers--Training of. | Professional learning communities. | Student-centered learning.
Classification: LCC LB1707 .H47 2020 | DDC 371.14/4--dc23
LC record available at https://lccn.loc.gov/2019054810

Published by Harvard Education Press,
an imprint of the Harvard Education Publishing Group

Harvard Education Press
8 Story Street
Cambridge, MA 02138

Cover Design: Endpaper Studio
Cover Photo: Jose Luis Pelaez Inc/DigitalVision via Getty Images

The typefaces used in this book are Minion Pro and Myriad Pro.

Contents

Introduction

The idea for this book arose after we had written an invited chapter for the *Handbook on Formative Assessment in the Disciplines* that focused on preparing preservice mathematics teachers to implement formative assessment.[1] In prior work, we had both independently advocated for coherence among preservice, induction, and in-service learning opportunities for teachers.[2] Our coauthored chapter gave us the chance to consider preservice education as the first phase for teachers in beginning to develop knowledge and skills about formative assessment, as well as a basis for continued professional learning throughout their teaching careers. In this book, we expand our thinking and explore more fully what can constitute a professional learning continuum from preservice through induction to in-service that uses discipline-based formative assessment as a critical lever to improve learning outcomes for students.[3]

We have framed our continuum of teacher expertise around three interactive phases, characterized by changes in teacher agency over time.[4] First is the *externally supported* phase, the time in preservice programs when novice teachers are acquiring the initial skills needed for teaching. Second is the *transitional* phase, when the amount of scaffolding from external supports, such as program faculty and mentor teachers, is decreased. In this phase, teachers become more conscious of their practice, are better able to make judgments about what they do in the classroom, and are increasingly equipped to make decisions about how they can improve. The third phase, *self-regulatory*, is when teachers take more control over their own learning and choose the next steps of their development. Across all phases, teachers—whether in training or teachers of record—engage in deliberate practice and receive feedback on their efforts from peers, mentors, and colleagues. This phase corresponds to our notion of continuing in-service, during which teachers never stop learning and continue to hone their expertise over many years.

Our exploration of these three phases is wide ranging, encompassing an in-depth examination of evolving teacher expertise in discipline-based formative assessment. The nature of knowledge and understanding within specific disciplines varies, and we emphasize that formative assessment is shaped and bounded by the discipline in which it occurs. Our premise is that teachers, in order to realize the potential of formative assessment, need not only to know the disciplinary content, but also to be familiar with analytic practices and have an understanding of the development of student learning in the discipline.

We also frame the development of expertise in discipline-based formative assessment in the context of ambitious teaching, which we believe includes formative assessment as an integral component. Ambitious teaching, a relatively recent construct, supports broad goals for student learning to achieve success in school, college, and the workplace. Teachers begin to acquire the practices of ambitious teaching, which we describe in chapter 1, in their preservice programs, and they continue to develop them along our continuum of learning.

In the book, we consider the interconnection of ambitious teaching, formative assessment, and disciplinary knowledge, and we illustrate how this interconnection plays out in practice using examples of actual classroom teaching. The quotations in the book are from actual teachers, unless otherwise stated. Some of the examples of practice are from observations of and interviews with teachers whom we encountered as part of other projects. In other instances, we met teachers who discussed their practice in ways that aligned with the major ideas of this book, and we asked them to supply us with specific examples. Finally, four county-level subject matter experts, who also reviewed the four disciplinary chapters, provided us with examples from their own experiences or observations.

OVERVIEW OF CHAPTERS

In chapter 1, we provide a foundational overview of ambitious teaching, disciplinary knowledge, and formative assessment. Chapter 2 presents the concept of a teacher learning continuum and the three phases that we consider most critical to teacher development: preservice training, induction (the first three years of teaching), and ongoing in-service learning opportunities, which may include teachers assuming a leadership role with colleagues. We then describe the framework we use for each phase of the continuum, containing the essential elements for cultivating teachers' formative assessment expertise: formative assessment practices; disciplinary knowledge, including content pedagogical knowledge; and habits of practice. We also describe our approach to professional learning at all phases of the continuum.

Chapters 3 through 6 explore the implications for formative assessment in the context of specific disciplines: mathematics, English language arts, science, and social studies. These chapters focus primarily on the intersection between formative assessment and the disciplinary knowledge aspect of the framework presented in chapter 2.

In chapter 7, we take the three elements from the framework introduced in chapter 2—formative assessment practices, disciplinary knowledge, and habits of practice—and describe a set of knowledge representations and experiences that establish the groundwork for preservice teachers to begin developing expertise in discipline-based formative assessment. In this phase of the continuum, we examine learning opportunities through the lens of representations, decompositions, and approximations of practice.

Chapter 8 follows the extension of these elements into a teacher's induction period and describes how new teachers, through mentor-mentee relationships, can build on their preservice learning once they have classes for which they are fully responsible. We explore the characteristics of effective induction programs and how they can support beginning teachers to integrate classroom management skills and instructional routines with formative assessment, and to continue on a trajectory toward ambitious teaching practices. We describe the components of a high-quality induction program that can support teacher engagement with formative assessment specifically at this phase of the professional learning continuum.

In chapter 9, we consider how more experienced teachers can develop their learning beyond the induction phase, focusing primarily on peer-to-peer relationships as a means of developing collective expertise. The nature of the proposed learning experiences differs from both the preservice and induction phases to reflect the ongoing learning needs and increases in expertise of in-service teachers. We examine environments in which teachers work that enable their ongoing professional learning, and we describe the opportunities that teachers can avail themselves of in such environments as they develop formative assessment expertise.

Chapter 10 is where we advocate for teacher leaders to support the professional learning of their colleagues, and we specifically address capacity building, distributed expertise, and the benefits to teacher leaders of assuming this role. We describe the qualities needed for effective teacher leadership and how teacher leaders can support their colleagues' continued learning. We end with a consideration of the need for teachers to engage in continued learning, increasing their expertise to meet the challenges entailed in educating today's students in a rapidly changing world.

WHO SHOULD READ THIS BOOK?

We believe the book will be valuable for those planning professional learning for teachers at any stage along the continuum (teacher educators, professional learning providers, teacher leaders), and particularly for those working to develop more coherent approaches to teacher learning, but also useful to teachers themselves.

We hope, however, that readers of this book will not be working in isolated groups according to the phase of the professional community that they are responsible for. Rather, we hope to motivate conversations and collaboration among all levels of professionals who support teacher learning, with the goal of developing a more coherent professional learning continuum.

There is limited value in defining the knowledge and experiences that preservice teachers are expected to have if those expectations differ from the expectations of the principals, grade-level team leaders, or department chairs who are working with those novice teachers. If school leaders incorrectly assume knowledge and skills that novice teachers do not have, students will likely suffer, as the novice teachers may not receive the support they need. On the other hand, if school leaders assume that the novice teachers know less than they do, they might provide too much support and frustrate the beginning teachers.

We would be delighted to learn that this book was being used to promote conversations among schools of education, other preservice providers, and school district personnel to create the necessary support for teachers at all stages of the continuum to develop and deepen their formative assessment practices. We hope that whatever your role in education, you will find value in our book.

CHAPTER 1

Ambitious Teaching, Disciplinary Knowledge, and Formative Assessment

Schools are places where students come to learn. This has been the case right from the beginning of schooling, in the US and everywhere else, but what students learn and how they learn it changes over time, because the world of today and tomorrow does not stay the same. Andreas Schleicher, director of education and skills at the Organisation for Economic Co-operation and Development (OECD) points to this situation in a recent paper, *Educating Learners for their Future, Not Our Past*, in which he notes the social pain that occurred when people were left behind during the Industrial Revolution as technology raced ahead of education, and calls on present-day societies to "imagine the type of education that will help people take advantage of our times."[1]

The imperative for educational change is underscored by Heather McGowan, an expert on the future of work. Contrasting the current era with other periods in history, she observes that at the same time the pace of change is accelerating, people's work lives are getting longer. When the steam engine was developed, the average life expectancy was thirty-seven years, and steam remained the driving force in business and industry for about one hundred years. When the combustion engine and electricity were introduced, life expectancy was roughly forty years, and those technologies continued to dominate the work force for nearly a hundred years, too. In both time periods, several generations absorbed a single big change in the workplace, whereas today there are multiple changes in the nature of work within a generation.[2] So in the past, it was possible to educate people for a lifetime. Not any longer. Education in the past was about received wisdom; education in the future is about user-generated wisdom.[3] Put another way, education that helps students "take advantage of our times" requires them to think for themselves, critically, creatively, and metacognitively, instead of simply learning about and reporting someone else's thinking.[4]

Along the same lines, a recent position paper published by the OECD advances broader educational goals to support individual and collective well-being in our rapidly and profoundly changing societies. Among these goals are the requirement for students to: exercise agency, understood as setting goals and taking actions to achieve them; develop disciplinary knowledge, along with the capacity to think beyond disciplinary boundaries and apply their knowledge to novel situations; develop social and emotional skills such as empathy, self-efficacy, and collaboration; and acquire the attitudes and values to mediate their knowledge, for example, motivation, trust, and respect for diversity.[5]

For teachers who still subscribe to a transmission model of teaching, one in which they transmit learning to students by disseminating information with little to no opportunity for student talk, achieving these broader education goals is likely to require a rethinking of the work of teaching. They will need to reconceptualize the nature of learning tasks, of classroom questioning and discussions, and of opportunities for students to reason and explain their thinking. Similarly, when teacher practices change, students who have been on the receiving end of a transmission model will need to rethink their work as learners, moving from being passive recipients of information to active participants in the learning process and engaging in the social aspects of learning. To accomplish this change, students will need structures and supports to learn through discussion and collaboration and to engage in metacognitive thinking, which requires the student to understand both the purpose of the learning and the criteria for achievement, and also to engage in self-assessment.[6]

A model for pedagogy that exemplifies the changes in teaching practices to realize the goals we have just described is that of *ambitious teaching*. The research literature on ambitious teaching emerged several years ago, primarily in the area of teacher preservice preparation, to ensure that beginning teachers developed the knowledge and skills necessary to support achievement of the demanding goals reflected in the college- and career-ready standards adopted by most jurisdictions in the US.[7] Broadly, ambitious teaching is grounded in a deep understanding of subject matter; it entails teaching practices that are interactive and discourse-based, and which enable students to make sense of what they are learning.[8] Ambitious teaching is also adaptive to students' needs, so that teachers are consistently working on the edge of students' current understanding. To work on the edge, teachers need to recognize whether their students' understanding is emerging, partially formed, fragmentary, or at the point where it can be consolidated. Based on this recognition, teachers can adapt their teaching to continuously keep learning moving forward.[9] Adaptive teaching is, to a great extent, dependent on formative assessment, which is itself a high-leverage practice that is integrated into ambitious teaching.

We frame our consideration of a continuum of expertise in discipline-based formative assessment from preservice through induction to in-service in the context of ambitious teaching because such teaching represents the idea that "rigorous and equitable teaching is within the grasp of most practitioners, even those just entering the profession."[10] The seeds of ambitious teaching are sown in preservice and continue to grow as teachers progress through their careers. In this chapter, we describe foundational ideas about ambitious teaching and the connection with formative assessment and disciplinary knowledge, and we tie these ideas together in examples of practice. Let us first go deeper into what we mean by ambitious teaching.

AMBITIOUS TEACHING

Our consideration of ambitious teaching is grounded in three core ideas: shared understanding of learning goals, eliciting student thinking, and disciplinary discourse practices.[11]

Shared Understanding of Learning Goals

College- and career-ready standards (CCRS) lay out the discipline-based goals that students need to meet throughout K–12 schooling. The CCRS comprise disciplinary content knowledge and the analytical practices of the discipline, for example, reasoning and justifying claims with evidence. As we shall see through the chapters in the book that are devoted to formative assessment in specific disciplines, ambitious teaching involves an integration of content learning and analytic practices so that students are acquiring both the knowledge of the discipline and the ability to adopt each discipline's particular methods of working. In this way, students are apprenticed to the discipline, participating in activities that are similar to the everyday activities of professionals who work in a specific discipline.[12] For example, mathematicians make sense of problems and persevere in solving them, scientists plan and carry out investigations, and historians analyze primary source material. Some analytic practices cut across disciplines; for instance, constructing viable arguments, critiquing the reasoning of others, and engaging in argument from evidence are common to many disciplines. Both long-term (a course or a unit of study) and short-term (a lesson) learning goals embody the content learning and analytic practices of the discipline and are made visible to students. For example, in a lesson focused on mathematical content, conjecturing about functions, the teacher asked students to consider which mathematical practices they were engaged in to make their conjectures, and they noted they were using mathematical structures that helped them apply functional relationships to solve real-world problems.[13] Their use of structures will not be confined to conjecturing about functions, and building awareness of this mathematical practice helps students develop a repertoire of strategies that they can employ in other mathematical contexts.

When students have a shared understanding of the learning goal with their teachers, they are better able to engage in metacognitive thinking; they understand where they are headed in their learning and can be supported to assess their own learning status. Self-assessment is a facet of self-regulated learning that was identified by the National Research Council Committee on Defining Deeper Learning and Twenty-First Century Skills as important to developing intrapersonal competencies, a category of skills needed for success in school and beyond.[14] In today's world, learning goals are expanded to include these intrapersonal competencies (for example, responsibility, self-evaluation, self-direction, metacognition, and flexibility), which students acquire as they learn disciplinary content and practices. It is worth reiterating that these expanded goals are for all students, not just a select few, so that each one has the opportunity to receive "rigorous and equitable teaching."

Eliciting Student Thinking

A key tenet of education reform is that teachers make pedagogical decisions in the midst of instruction.[15] In ambitious teaching, teachers elicit student ideas and respond to their emerging ideas as the lesson unfolds. This requires teachers to plan learning activities and tasks which enable students' inquiry and permit them to surface and build on the ideas they generate with support from their teacher and peers. For example, in a middle school science class on photosynthesis, the teacher presented a narrative of the ideas that students were generating and encouraged students to contribute additional ideas as they developed their understanding of this topic:

> Richard and Dean think the plant's getting more food. Susan . . . and Stacey as well? Yes. Susan thinks it's because this plant is getting more light. What do others think? Tariq?

Later in the lesson, the teacher helped the students compare and draw together the ideas that had surfaced in the discussion:

> What do others think about Carolyn's idea? (Many students nod.) Yes? It's bigger because it has more light and can photosynthesize more. So, Richard and Dean, how does your idea fit in with this?[16]

Ambitious teaching centers on assisting students' active construction of knowledge, rather than "telling," which is the primary emphasis of the transmission model of teaching. Active construction of knowledge is consistent with contemporary perspectives on learning.[17] In particular, the sociocultural perspective, while emphasizing knowledge construction, highlights the collaborative nature of learning. Lev Vygotsky's work is foundational to the sociocultural perspective, since he articulated that knowledge appears first on the social level between people before it is internalized at the individual level.[18] In this situation, the role of the teacher is to elicit students' thinking and provide scaffolding that assists them to build on their initial ideas in collaboration with the teacher and their peers as they individually advance to a more complete understanding of a concept.

An example of this kind of scaffolding occurs in a second-grade lesson on how poets use specific devices to supply rhythm and meaning in a poem. During independent reading time, the teacher sat with a student who was reading a poem in which the poet uses different typography to evoke the sounds and movement of a school bus. As the teacher interacts with the student, she scaffolds his thinking with questions in ways that help him pin down the relationship between the typography and the poetic intent:

> "So what do you think this is doing?" The teacher points to the bold text. "As you were reading aloud, I noticed you extended the 'o' sound in slow. Why did you do that?" Answer: "there was space between the letters."
>
> "What is it that the poet wants the reader to do by putting in the spaces?"
>
> Finally, to help the student connect the typography to the rhythm and meaning of the poem, the teacher asks, "Why do you think it's important for the author that you read the poem in a certain way?" To which the student replies, "Well . . . because it makes it sound better . . . and makes it . . . makes it sound like what the poem is describing."[19]

Through the scaffolding the teacher provided, the student has reached an understanding of the goal of the lesson, and he has done this on his own and in his own words.

In the excerpts above, we see teachers adapting their pedagogical responses to their respective students' thinking and assisting them to make sense of what they are learning. The teachers are not pronouncing judgment on the correctness of students' responses, nor simply telling students what they ought to observe or appreciate. Rather, these teachers used students' initial and evolving ideas to support their incremental sense-making about what they are learning, which ultimately will result in deeper disciplinary understanding. In such instances, students are guided toward understanding through sensitive teacher scaffolding. The ability to elicit and engage with students' thinking is made possible when teaching and learning are characterized by disciplinary discourse practices.

Disciplinary Discourse Practices

Students' engagement in disciplinary discourse as a means to learning is a feature of the CCRS and of calls for reforms in disciplinary learning.[20] This emphasis reflects a growing body of research that indicates a clear relationship between students' opportunities to reason dialogically with others and the development of durable understanding.[21] However, many studies have investigated the type of talk that occurs in classrooms, and they make clear that the teacher is responsible for most of what is said.[22] Ambitious teaching reduces the predominance of teacher talk, instead emphasizing student talk.

When considering how discourse is stimulated in classrooms, it is instructive to examine the work of UK researcher Robin Alexander, who has coined the term *dialogic teaching*, in which teachers energize their own and their students' talk. In so doing, they harness the power of discourse to stimulate and extend students' thinking and advance their learning and understanding.[23] Alexander stresses that dialogic teaching is not just any talk in the classroom. It is rooted in the discipline and is characterized by:

- *interactions* that encourage students to think, and to think in different ways
- *questions* that invite much more than simple recall
- *answers* that are justified, followed up, and built upon rather than merely received
- *feedback* that informs and leads thinking forward
- *contributions* that are extended rather than fragmented
- *exchanges* that chain together into coherent and deepening lines of inquiry
- *discussion and argumentation* that probe and challenge rather than unquestioningly accept
- *professional engagement with subject matter* that liberates classroom discourse from the safe and conventional
- *classroom organization, climate and relationships* that make all this possible

From Alexander's criteria, it is apparent that students' thinking is elicited and built on through discourse practices in the classroom. Moreover, through discourse and sharing thinking, knowledge becomes public and students can become learning resources for one another.[24] The public nature of thinking elicited through discourse has been referred to as "interthinking" because, nested in collaborative learning, it provides a rich mixture of ideas that can be drawn on by students and their teacher, enabling them to consider a greater range of ideas and engage in social relationships to learn together.[25]

The willingness of students to share their thinking will be determined by the nature of the relationships in the classroom. Students must feel safe to express their ideas in different stages of development without fear of ridicule or sanction from either their teacher or their peers. Feelings of safety are established when teachers create a classroom climate in which each learner's contribution is valued, the expectation that students listen to each other and build on one another's ideas is clear, and diversity in the rate and pace of learning is accepted.

Alexander notes that teachers' engagement with subject matter liberates classroom discourse from the safe and conventional. If teachers are to elicit student thinking through discourse and build on that thinking to advance learning, they need sufficient disciplinary knowledge for them to feel secure in engaging with students' developing ideas and to be released from the narrow confines of teaching what comes next in a textbook.

Throughout this section we have seen that ambitious teaching is grounded in disciplinary knowledge, from shared understanding of learning goals to eliciting student thinking to the use of disciplinary discourse practices. In the next section we introduce what disciplinary knowledge consists of, which we will develop further in chapters 3 through 6.

DISCIPLINARY KNOWLEDGE

Every discipline has its own epistemic knowledge, the distinctive nature of the thinking processes and beliefs specific to that discipline. Epistemic knowledge can be stimulated by questions such as: "What am I learning in this subject and why?" "What can I use this knowledge for in real life?" and "How do professionals from this disciplinary field think?"[26] To take the idea of disciplinary epistemic knowledge a little further, let us consider the case of argumentation, a cross-disciplinary process through which students learn to reason, draw logical conclusions, and present an argument. Yet the nature of the formation of an argument varies according to specific disciplines. In mathematics an argument is developed through a sequence of logical statements, with the aim of demonstrating whether a claim is true or false. In science, an argument requires the existence of a scientific idea, expectations generated as a result of that idea, and observations to test out the idea. To marshal an argument in English language arts (ELA), students are required to clearly state the claim they are making, provide textual evidence from a source or sources, and help the audience understand how that evidence is supportive of the stance being taken. Argumentation in history requires students to support a claim with primary or secondary historical sources, which they critique in terms of how the perspective, reliability, and bias of the sources influences the argument.

Across mathematics, science, ELA, and history, while there are similarities in terms of the use of a logical process to support claims, each kind of argument draws on a different evidentiary base, and the specific nature of the argument varies. Such differences in argumentation will require teachers to understand the nature of argumentation within their specific discipline so that they are able to set clear and relevant learning goals and respond to student thinking while it is in development.

In addition to understanding how a particular discipline is structured and what is valued in that discipline, a teacher also needs to know how to effectively teach students about the discipline. Three main types of knowledge are needed for this purpose: knowledge of students and how they learn disciplinary content, so that they can recognize student errors, justifications, misconceptions, and developmental sequences; knowledge of appropriate disciplinary strategies in order to identify appropriate ways in which to develop emerging student ideas; and horizon knowledge in a discipline so they can understand how topics or ideas are connected over the span of the curriculum.[27] With horizon knowledge, teachers may be better able to respond to emerging ideas in ways that ultimately provide a grounding for ideas that come later in the curriculum. In this way, teachers are able to connect the "here and now" of a specific student's learning with the longer-term goals that are for all students.

These types of knowledge are part of the more broadly defined pedagogical content knowledge (PCK), a necessary foundation for formative assessment, as it enables teachers to access and interpret information about student learning and to orchestrate appropriate and immediate actions intended to advance learning.[28]

To successfully implement formative assessment, teachers must become familiar with the progress of inquiry and the terms of discourse of a discipline, understand the relationship between information and concepts that organize that information in a discipline, and have a grasp of the growth and development of students' thinking about these concepts.[29]

Let us now turn to formative assessment, which is an integral part of ambitious teaching.

FORMATIVE ASSESSMENT

There are many research- and practice-based definitions of formative assessment in the literature. For this book we have adopted the definition developed by a consortium of states, the Formative Assessment for Teachers and Students (FAST) State Collaborative on Assessment and Student Standards (SCASS) from the Council of Chief State School Officers, established to promote formative assessment across member states.[30] We chose the FAST SCASS definition because it represents a professional view from state-level personnel of their expectations for teachers' implementation of formative assessment and for what preservice teachers ought to be learning about in their preservice programs and beyond.[31]

FAST SCASS Definition

> Formative assessment is a planned, ongoing process used by all students and teachers during learning and teaching to elicit and use evidence of student learning to improve student understanding of intended disciplinary learning outcomes and support students to become self-directed learners.

This definition has been revised from an earlier one created by the FAST SCASS in 2006 to include the "planned" nature of formative assessment—it is not something that happens serendipitously in the classroom; make clear that formative assessment occurs in the context of disciplines, which shapes how the practice is implemented; and emphasize "students becoming self-directed learners," a necessary attribute of lifelong learners and a key outcome of K–12 schooling.[32]

In common with many others, the FAST SCASS definition characterizes formative assessment as a set of practices that engage both students and teachers in a process of eliciting evidence of learning related to specific goals and acting on that evidence to advance learning. While there are generalizations to the practice of formative assessment at a high level, essentially formative assessment is rooted in the discipline in which it occurs. Teachers plan situations, activities, tasks, or questions in the course of teaching and learning that generate observable evidence, and to do this effectively requires sufficient disciplinary knowledge to know what constitutes evidence. They must also interpret the evidence, and such evidentiary reasoning presumes a grounding in disciplinary content.[33] Once teachers have interpreted the evidence, they make a pedagogical decision about how to respond to a student's current learning status—otherwise it is not formative assessment—which also presumes both disciplinary knowledge and PCK.

The FAST SCASS members elaborated the definition, noting a set of key practices in formative assessment.

> Effective use of the formative assessment process requires students and teachers to integrate and embed the following practices in a collaborative and respectful classroom environment:
>
> - Clarifying learning goals and success criteria within a broader progression of learning
> - Eliciting and analyzing evidence of student thinking
> - Engaging in self-assessment and peer feedback
> - Providing actionable feedback
> - Using evidence and feedback to move learning forward by adjusting learning strategies, goals, or next instructional steps

Taken together, the definition and its elaboration highlight the integrated and embedded nature of the practices of formative assessment, indicating that they are not a set of discrete steps, but rather are interdependent elements of ongoing classroom teaching and learning. While a novice in formative assessment may focus on a specific practice for the purpose of developing fluency, it is the integration of all of them that leads to effective enactment of formative assessment.[34] The continuum that we describe across the chapters of the book will illustrate how sophistication in integrating the practices develops as teachers' knowledge and skills increase over time.

The key practices elaborated in the definition are synergistic with significant elements of contemporary learning theory and research, several of which we referenced previously in the context of ambitious teaching.

Table 1.1 identifies a number of these elements and their connection with formative assessment.

TABLE 1.1 Contemporary learning theory and research connections to formative assessment

ELEMENT	CONNECTIONS TO FORMATIVE ASSESSMENT
Goals (the standard of performance that a learner is consciously trying to accomplish) inform and motivate learning and play a critical role in directing attention to learning behaviors.[35]	A key practice in formative assessment is ensuring that students have clear learning goals and criteria for goal achievement; teachers either coconstruct the goals with students or communicate them directly so that students understand what their learning entails. Students can also set their own goals through self-assessment.
Individuals come to new learning with a range of prior knowledge, skills, beliefs, and concepts, including funds of knowledge from their homes and communities, which significantly impact their ability to acquire new knowledge, remember, reason, and problem-solve.[36]	Teachers use formative assessment to draw out students' initial conceptions, creating classroom environments and conditions under which student thinking can be revealed. They build on students' initial conceptions in their pedagogical responses.
Knowledge is actively constructed within social contexts through interactions with others.[37]	Providing opportunities for students to collaborate and engage in discourse in support of learning is a key strategy for gaining insights into student thinking that teachers can respond to. Feedback from teachers and peers assists students in understanding where they are in relation to learning goals and what they need to do to improve/move forward; students are actively involved in the learning process.
Successful learning requires coordination of multiple cognitive processes. To be able to coordinate these processes, individuals need to be able to monitor and regulate their own learning.[38]	Students develop the skills to assess their own work/learning and make decisions about what they need to do to improve/move forward. In this way, they are engaged in regulating their own learning.
Developing strong metacognitive skills (thinking about one's thinking) enhances achievement and develops abilities in learning independently.[39]	Students learn the skills of self-assessment and develop the capacity to engage in an internal dialogue about how their learning is progressing relative to goals. Teachers ensure that students understand goals and criteria for successful performance, and students use them to assess how their learning is progressing.
Effective feedback that is specific, clear and focused on improvement is often essential to acquiring new knowledge and skills.[40]	Teachers' pedagogical responses to elicited evidence includes providing feedback to students that helps them consider how to improve/advance their learning. The process of peer feedback, with appropriate structures and supports, can help students improve their work, both as givers and as receivers of feedback.

Not surprisingly, given the connection between formative assessment and cognitive theory and research, evidence of the benefits of formative assessment has been steadily accumulating over the past two decades.[41] Ample evidence suggests that considerable improvement in student achievement, even when measured by end-of-year summative assessments, is possible when teachers implement formative assessment routinely and frequently.[42] In addition, elsewhere we have argued that effective formative assessment contributes to the development of students' positive identities as learners.[43] Students are supported to see themselves as effective and capable learners because teachers are consistently working on the edge of learning, assisting students to advance from where they are to where they can successfully go next. Also, there is emerging evidence that formative assessment has a beneficial impact on achievement gaps, reducing the gap between the performance levels of poor and more affluent students, and between African American and white students.[44] For these reasons, we regard formative assessment as a critical part of every teacher's toolbox. Indeed, distinguished assessment expert Jim Popham has expressed the view that "teachers' failure to employ formative assessment borders on the unethical."[45]

In the next section, we look at the ideas we have examined so far with respect to ambitious teaching, disciplinary knowledge, and formative assessment in the context of two contrasting examples of actual practice.

EXAMPLES OF PRACTICE

History Class Example

The first example is taken from Mr. Wilson's fourth and fifth grade combination class.[46] Notice how he engages students in thinking like historians throughout this lesson. Also notice the multiple ways in which he collects evidence of student learning (listening to students' discussions, observing their notes, and making his own notes).

Previously, in history/social studies lessons, Mr. Wilson's students had studied California's geographical regions, and now he was ready to move the students on to an inquiry of the patterns of movement and changes in the people of California over time. The standards he planned to address in the lesson (three class periods) were:

- Dimension 1. Constructing Compelling Questions
- Dimension 2.10.3-5. Compare information provided by different historical sources about the past
- Dimension 4.1.3-5. Construct arguments using claims and evidence from multiple sources

Mr. Wilson shared with the students that they were going to act like historians and explore primary source material. They were going to build on their previous studies of geography in California with the goal of connecting primary sources related to the people of California with ideas of patterns, perspectives, and change. He provided several success criteria for this learning goal:

- Make inferences about the time, place, and lives of the people in the sources
- Describe the perspectives of the people in the sources
- Explain how the sources connect—the patterns, perspectives, and changes
- Generate questions that are applicable to all the people in the primary sources

After discussing the goal and success criteria with the students and making sure they understood the focus of their learning for the lesson, the students moved into small groups to examine four different primary sources selected from a group of ten. Sources included the following images.

- *Images from Manzanar* by Ansel Adams, 1943
- *Welcome to Lakewood* from *Life* magazine, 1953
- An idealized portrait of the first Christian baptism in California, San Juan Capistrano Mission, by Engelhardt Zephyrin, 1922
- A circa 1860 portrait of an unidentified pair of prospectors by an unknown photographer from the collection of the Canadian Photography Institute.

First, the students examined one of the sources individually and recorded their thinking, as they had previously done with primary source material, using a graphic organizer:

- What do you observe?
- What do you think you know?
- What do you want to find out?

Next, they discussed their responses with the other members of the group. During this time, Mr. Wilson observed and made notes on what the students were writing on their graphic organizers and what he heard them say in their discussions. He noticed that students were helping each other corroborate and confirm their inferences about the source. For instance, one student said, "I agree that this is in Manzanar, because I saw pictures like that before in a book in our class." In a different group, a student commented, "I disagree, I don't think that is from the Gold Rush, because I see electricity poles and modern cars in the background, so it can't be that long ago." Mr. Wilson asked questions to probe their thinking: "What convinces you the inference you are making is appropriate?" and "What makes you say that the person in this source is experiencing problems?" Their responses helped him steer the students toward meeting the first two success criteria.

The final part of the group discussion was to generate a question that they could ask of anyone represented in the primary sources. He heard a student in one group suggest the question "Why did you move to Lakewood?" to which another student responded that questions were supposed to be ones you could ask any of the people in the other primary sources, not just in Lakewood, and suggested a revised question, "Why did you move, or why did you move to this place?"

At the end of the group time, students were brought together for a closing debrief conversation. Mr. Wilson recorded the conversation to use the transcriptions for later lessons. He guided the conversation, using what he had heard during the group work time, to focus around the ideas of change, movement, patterns, perspectives, and connections.

Below is an excerpt of the conversation Mr. Wilson had with his students:

MR. W: So what connections were you making among the primary sources?

FINLEY: I think they are different times and places in California?

MR. W: Did anyone else think that? Petar, you want to add on?

PETAR: I think all the pictures connect.

MR. W: Connect how?

PETAR: In different ways. Let's say someone is coming here and the other person in the picture is coming here, too.

MR. W: Tell me more.

PETAR: Well, if someone's in the state, like for us, it was someone biking. The other people were mining. And then other people were doing other things.

MR. W: So you said it was about people and how they came here? And they connect by?

PETAR: By moving.

MR. W: Paloma, did you want to add on? (She was raising her hand.)

PALOMA: Well, I think it is also about people coming to California.

MR. W: OK, does anyone else have that same kind of connection?

Next, the whole class discussed the questions the students had generated in their groups.

MR. W: So now here is my question: What are your questions? What questions do you have? What are some of your questions that you have, that you could ask anybody in any of these primary sources? Sanjaya?

SANJAYA: Well, a questions that you could say for either one is maybe . . . "Where did you come from?" or "Where are you going?"

MR. W: I love that, "Where did you come from? or Where are you going?" It sounds almost like the beginning of a poem. "Where did you come from?" "Where are you going?" Anything else you would add?

DANICA: I think, "What problems are you working through?" Because a lot of them don't seem very happy. Other than the beach primary source, everyone else looks like they are having a problem.

MR. W: Other than the beach one, everyone else looks like they are having a problem. So, "What problems are you going through?" Interesting. Ooh, that's like Abel's ships with the waves in the provocation. Some were ups and some were downs. In a lot of your provocations

> you talked about life's bumps and journeys. So that idea of "What problems are you going through?" Is that a pattern? That there are problems over time that people face?

Through this debrief on the primary sources, the students came to consensus on four questions that would guide their subsequent exploration of people who settle in California:

- Where are you going?
- Where are you coming from?
- Why are you moving or changing?
- What problems are you working through?

Mr. Wilson concluded the discussion by restating the four questions and wondering how the students could use them to further study California. He invited them to think about that and said they would be returning to the questions in the next class period. Finally, Mr. Wilson asked the students to do an individual assessment of how well each had worked that day by responding in writing to these prompts:

- How well did I work as a historian today?
- I know this because . . .
- Something I might do differently the next time is . . .

The students kept their responses in their social studies folders, and Mr. Wilson planned to review these with the students during independent work time on subsequent days.

Analysis of history class example In this example of practice, we see ambitious teaching grounded in disciplinary knowledge and integrated formative assessment. Mr. Wilson planned his lesson to address specific history/social studies standards and analytic practices. He invited his students to apprentice to the discipline by acting like historians, analyzing and drawing inferences from primary source material. He used his disciplinary knowledge to develop a shared understanding of learning goals, and he also provided the students with success criteria so they knew where they were headed in the lesson. His disciplinary knowledge played a role in the careful selection of material to stimulate the students' inquiry about the movement of people. Mr. Wilson scaffolded their analysis of the primary sources by providing a graphic organizer with clear guiding questions, which became the basis for their individual inquiry and group discussions.

Throughout the lesson, he engaged in formative assessment, listening to students' discussions, observing their notes and making his own, and probing their thinking so that he could respond pedagogically to advance them toward the lesson goal. He also included an opportunity for student self-assessment at the end of the lesson so that students could reflect on their learning and behavior as historians. Student self-assessment would also become a source of evidence for Mr. Wilson.

Disciplinary discourse practices were evident throughout the lesson. For example, Mr. Wilson engaged students in discussion from which he could obtain evidence of learning; he responded to student ideas in the whole class sessions, guiding them to make connections among the primary sources they had examined and discussed in their groups; and through discourse he steered students to generate questions that could direct their further study, finally inviting them to consider how they might use the questions to investigate the movement of people in California.

It is also evident that Mr. Wilson has created a safe environment for students to share ideas and build on each other's thinking. Students were comfortable suggesting and taking up revisions to a question, for example, and were willing to share their thinking in small groups and in the whole class discussion and build on what their peers had shared.

Science Class Example

Let us now contrast the example from Mr. Wilson's class with a published example of teaching from a science class with seven-year-old students.[47] The teacher began her lesson by explaining to her students that they were going to be learning about adaptation with the goal of answering the question, "Why do animals live where they live?" The starter activity was a small-group discussion stimulated by four pictures and the question, "Which is the odd one out: bird, cat, fish, or elephant?" After the students had spent time in discussion, the teacher asked each group to offer their answers. The first group answered, "Elephant," to which the teacher responded, "No," and moved on to another group for an answer. None of the groups offered the teacher's expected answer, "Fish," which was the premise on which she had based her lesson plan. When the children were later asked by a researcher why they had said elephant, they responded, "Well, your mum and dad would let you have a bird, fish or a cat as a pet but never an elephant." Clearly, the students had a reason for their answer, but the teacher did not take up the opportunity to learn about their thinking, and in the process likely diminished students' enthusiasm for learning.

Analysis of science class example The teacher's learning goal for seven-year-old students was a demanding one, and she had set up group discussions with an effective stimulus for students to generate their initial thinking about why animals live where they do. However, when eliciting students' thinking about which creature they thought was the odd one out, she did not use their responses to explore the students' reasoning and ultimately bridge their initial ideas to one of the big ideas in science, adaptation; for instance, she could have pursued their preliminary responses with follow-up questions designed to elicit students' ideas of how various features of the elephant, cat, and bird helped them survive in their environments, and then asked the students to think about the physical attributes of the fish, in contrast.

Although the teacher had set up the opportunity for disciplinary discourse very effectively in the task she provided, she did not make use of the students' group discussions and their follow-up, whole-class discussion as formative assessment opportunities to understand their thinking. Instead, she engaged in *evaluative listening* rather than *interpretive listening*, focusing only on the "right" or "wrong" answers, and moving through the planned lesson without reference to the students' thinking.[48] As a result, she did not gain insights that she could build on and was unable to help her students examine their knowledge; nor did she use sensitive responses to direct them to fruitful avenues for constructing their own understanding.[49] Furthermore, if the teacher had considered the funds of knowledge students bring to their learning from their lived experiences, she could have asked them to justify their choices in terms of what they knew about the four creatures, and consequently understood that their reasoning stemmed from their everyday experiences that fish, cats, and birds can be pets, but elephants are not generally pets.[50] Her response could have been to help them consider a scientific way of understanding the differences, thereby engaging them in the practices of the discipline.[51]

In his influential paper, Swiss scholar Philippe Perenoud distinguishes between sequences of activities in lessons that only allow for the remediation of prescribed concepts and those in which tasks can be adjusted once the learning has been initiated.[52] In the history lesson, the teacher was listening for the sense the students were making and had the opportunity to adjust the course of the lesson in response to their ideas—the task could be adjusted once the learning had been initiated. In the science class, although the teacher had ostensibly created a task to elicit student thinking, her response was more in line with a prescription—the students were expected to get the "right" answer, the predetermined one she had in her head. In this instance, assessment could only be a procedure used to determine a correct or incorrect answer, and in the event of its being incorrect, respond with remediation—the teacher tells the students the correct answer.

CHANGING PRACTICE

We began this chapter with a discussion of education that takes "advantage of our times," highlighting that much of the status quo in teaching and learning cannot persist in the interest of individuals and societies. Student memorization and reproduction of explanations found in textbooks needs to be replaced by teachers mediating "increasingly sophisticated forms of academic conversation and activity by the students."[53] We have seen how this replacement teaching and learning can be achieved through ambitious teaching centered on the practices of shared understanding of learning goals, eliciting student thinking, and disciplinary discourse. We have also pointed to the importance of teachers' disciplinary knowledge and to formative assessment as a lever for improved learning when integrated with ambitious teaching.

For many teachers, moving their practice to reflect more ambitious teaching grounded in disciplinary knowledge with integrated formative assessment will be a challenge, but one that is well worthwhile, given the benefits to their students. Both the change and the challenge are well summed up by this teacher:[54]

> I am learning how to teach in a new way. In the past, I did a lot more presentation style teaching where I talked a lot more and did a lot more of the intellectual work in the classroom. But now I am learning how to hand the reins over to the students so that they

> are the ones doing the intellectual work, they're the ones doing the heavy lifting.
>
> My planning has changed a lot. Instead of being focused on the activity and what I am going to say, I'm focusing on what are the students learning and what are they doing with the learning, and then me thinking through what they might not understand and how could I question in a way to help push them towards understanding as opposed to me presenting information and students passively consuming it.
>
> So, I've seen a lot of great things in my classroom, but it is a little bit outside my comfort zone in a productive struggle, positive kind of way to help kids learn this way and for me to learn to teach this way.[55]

Despite this practice being currently outside her comfort zone, this teacher is willing to stretch herself and stay the course because she has seen the value to her students: they are actually doing the learning.

SUMMARY: THE BIG IDEAS OF CHAPTER 1

- Given the ever-increasing pace of technological innovations, students increasingly need to learn to think for themselves, critically, creatively, and metacognitively, instead of simply receiving content to be memorized.
- Ambitious teaching (developing students' deep understanding and flexible knowledge), is grounded in three core ideas: shared understanding of learning goals, eliciting student thinking, and disciplinary discourse practices.
- Disciplinary knowledge includes familiarity with the progress of inquiry and the terms of discourse of a discipline, an understanding of the relationship between information and concepts that organize that information in a discipline, and having a grasp on the growth and development of students' thinking about these concepts.
- Formative assessment is a multifaceted, evidence-based process that focuses on the use of evidence of student learning to inform next steps. Formative assessment can be described in general terms, but these practices need to be particularized within each discipline.

- Ambitious teaching, disciplinary knowledge, and formative assessment practices are intertwined. Teachers' disciplinary knowledge supports their capacity to engage in ambitious teaching and to use formative assessment as the fuel to ensure their students' continuous progress toward college- and career-ready goals.
- The formative assessment practices are synergistic with significant elements of contemporary learning theory and research.

CHAPTER 2

A Framework for Professional Learning

Teachers do not become competent overnight, and they certainly do not become experts in a short space of time. There is no quick route to expertise in teaching, nor is there a shortcut to effective formative assessment practice.[1] Teacher expertise is developed over an extended period of time through continued engagement in professional learning. At the preservice level, support for teachers is built in, and it usually continues during their first year or so of teaching through induction programs. However, while teachers generally make rapid gains in effectiveness early in their careers, additional experience is often associated with more modest improvements in practice.[2] From this finding, one conclusion we can draw is that improvements in teachers' classroom practice, to a very large extent, will be shaped by the contexts in which they work. In this regard, it is disturbing that a primary reason that teachers cite for leaving the profession is lack of school-based support.[3] A goal of this book is to offer suggestions for how teachers can experience continued professional learning in their workplace settings and receive the support they need to develop their knowledge and skills toward increased expertise, specifically in formative assessment, over the course of their careers.

We expect that, on exiting a preservice program, beginning teachers will have a baseline competence in ambitious teaching and integrated formative assessment from which they can continue to grow professionally through induction and in-service learning opportunities. We do not anticipate that all teachers will necessarily reach the status of expert (see chapter 9), but we think it is perfectly possible for many teachers to reach high levels of competency and for some to become teacher leaders, supporting their colleagues' professional learning in their own contexts (see chapter 10).

As we noted in the book's introduction, we propose that teacher expertise in discipline-based formative assessment can take place across three main phases of development: *externally supported*, *transitional*, and *self-regulatory*.[4] Teachers in preservice programs are engaged in the externally supported phase of developing expertise while they acquire the minimum competencies they need in order to take responsibility for a class of students. During this time, they receive a great deal of external support from both program faculty and cooperating teachers in their practicum experiences.

The transitional phase is the period of induction when teachers build on their preservice learning, and in the process transition from their novice status to a position of increased experience and skill. During the transition period, early career teachers are often provided with additional supports, such as a school-based mentor or a district-provided coach to assist with the transition to all the responsibilities that having their own classrooms entail. However, in comparison with teachers' preservice experience the amount of external support is reduced during the transitional phase. During induction, teachers become more aware of their own teaching practices and begin to make decisions about priorities for improvement.

The third phase in the development of expertise is self-regulatory, the time when teachers take much more control over their own in-service learning. They decide what they want to target for their own professional growth and how they will achieve their targets, including seeking support from others, such as peers and school leaders.[5] We regard teachers becoming leaders in their schools and districts as an extension of the self-regulatory in-service phase; they have made their own determination to adopt a leadership role, which, of course, does not mean that they stop learning. Instead, as they support their colleagues' improvement, they continue to learn from that experience, while also learning to take on new responsibilities.

In this chapter, we lay out our overall approach to teacher professional learning in discipline-based formative assessment across these phases of a continuum of developing expertise. We also describe the general content of each phase. The specific content for each phase of professional learning is outlined in chapters 7, 8, and 9, which address preservice learning, induction, and in-service respectively.

We begin with a discussion of sociocultural theory, which is our framing approach to teacher learning. Next, we introduce four ideas extending from this theory: scaffolding, communities of practice, apprenticeship, and legitimate peripheral participation. Finally, we discuss the general content of the professional learning that occurs within the sociocultural framework.

SOCIOCULTURAL APPROACH

Our approach to professional learning is grounded in sociocultural theory, which stems from Lev Vygotsky's view that learning is socially constructed in the context in which it occurs, whether that is society, the family, or school, for example.[6] Vygotsky's emphasis on the social construction of learning is based on two related perspectives. First, he viewed language as the ultimate collection of tools and symbols within a culture that enables its members to communicate with others and to construct meaning. The learning process, therefore, is one in which language is used in meaning-making activities. Second, Vygotsky did not regard individuals as isolated entities; instead, he stressed that individuals acquire knowledge and skills with and from others who are situated within a particular culture and societal context.[7] For instance, children who live in rural areas are likely to have more resources to understand texts and underlying concepts connected with farming than children who live in an urban, car-manufacturing community, who in turn may have more opportunities to learn about technology in the workplace. Indeed, children from each community will tend to bring sets of taken-for-granted assumptions, language, and know-how to new learning activities.

Although Vygotsky's intent was primarily to understand development and learning in children, his ideas have significant implications and practical applications for learners of all ages, which are reflected in our approach to professional learning for teachers.[8] At each phase of our continuum, teachers are engaged in interaction with others who are situated in the context of schooling and teaching. In this vein, a comment from an elementary teacher about how she is learning to implement formative assessment underscores the value of interacting with others in a similar situation: "I think that having that person or a team of people that you can share with, give and receive feedback, is really a critical part of taking that first step to implementing formative assessment practices."[9]

At different phases of the professional learning continuum, teachers participate with others in the context of classroom practice to enhance their knowledge and skills in formative assessment. Preservice teachers engage with program faculty, cooperating teachers, and their peers to acquire knowledge and skills; teachers in induction programs are mentored by colleagues; and during in-service, teachers learn through interactions with peers and teacher leaders.

SCAFFOLDING

Another concept in Vygotsky's theory is the idea that learning occurs within the zone of proximal development (ZPD).[10] Vygotsky conceptualized that a child's development takes place in the ZPD through engaging in processes of problem-solving that are slightly beyond the child's competence, but facilitated through the guidance of a more skilled partner, such as a parent, caregiver, teacher, or peer. The role of the more skilled partner was further conceptualized by others as "scaffolding," the graduated assistance routines that are set up for novice learners by more accomplished experts.[11] The more skilled partner motivates and guides the learner by providing just enough assistance with questions or prompts; highlighting features of the task, such as drawing attention to the nature of the problem to be solved; adjusting supports as necessary, including decreasing assistance as the learner demonstrates a grasp of the problem; and offering the learner opportunities for reflection about the learning.

Our approach to professional learning is characterized predominantly by scaffolding and reflection on practice rather than by instruction or transfer of knowledge. However, we do not exclude instruction and knowledge transfer, for example, preservice teachers will have opportunities to examine standards and progressions which represent consensus views about what students should learn, and they and their seasoned teacher colleagues may profitably attend lectures from experts or read about research and theory. The knowledge gained from these experiences needs to be translated into classroom activity. We view this process of applying and refining the knowledge and skills needed for formative assessment as best accomplished through guidance and reflection on teachers' own practice.

Preservice teachers' learning can be supported through scaffolding within their ZPD by more skilled professionals. For example, cooperating teachers may guide their analysis and reflection on a lesson plan that incorporates formative assessment with questions such as, "In what ways do you think that your learning goals and success criteria guided your lesson and helped you obtain evidence of students' understanding of the concept you wanted them to learn?" Similar scaffolding can be used at the induction stage through questions and prompts and by drawing attention to key features of the task, such as the need for clearer alignment between learning goals and success criteria. The preservice or externally supported phase requires the most scaffolding, with the level of scaffolding reducing through the induction or transitional phase. At the in-service phase, scaffolding takes the form of peers collaborating in joint inquiry about their classroom practice so that they are able to coconstruct knowledge about teaching and learning, develop new ways of teaching and assessing, and critically reflect on their practice.[12] A teacher working with peers to refine their formative assessment practices expressed how the group coconstructed knowledge. The teachers developed a routine of trying things out in their respective classrooms after their monthly meetings, then reconvening and "questioning each other, kind of like saying, did you try this, do you try that, how about this?"[13]

As this teacher makes clear, learning through scaffolding is not a passive undertaking, but rather requires active involvement to develop new ways of understanding the world of teaching and learning, and it progresses through critical reflection on practice.[14] To promote these forms of learning, we adopt the idea of a *community of practice*, beginning at the preservice phase and becoming self-sustaining as teachers move into the self-monitoring, self-regulation phase.

COMMUNITY OF PRACTICE

The term community of practice refers to an age-old phenomenon: the formation of groups organized around the use of a common set of practices, procedures, and standards deployed in pursuit of some goal.[15] Any context is potentially a community of practice, which is constituted through a set of relations between participants who share a concern, a set of problems, or a particular interest in something, and who deepen their knowledge and expertise by interacting on an ongoing basis.[16] In this situation, learning is not focused on receiving a body of knowledge, but rather is an "integral part of generative social practice in the lived world."[17] When teachers participate in a community of practice, their "generative social practice" centers on teaching, learning, and assessment, and their activities are directly linked to increasing expertise in those areas.

At any phase of our professional learning continuum, participants in a community of practice come together in a continued effort to enhance their knowledge and skills, although the nature of participation changes depending on the specific phase. At the preservice phase, teachers have access to learning opportunities about formative assessment through participation in discussions about practice with their mentors and peers. The responsibilities of teachers at the induction phase differ significantly from the practicum experiences in preservice, because they are now responsible for classes of students. Support for teachers at this phase continues in the setting of the workplace and can be provided through specific district or school induction programs and from assigned mentors within their schools. At the in-service phase, teachers depend on their peers and school and district leaders for continued support, regularly participating in groups to discuss ideas, solve problems of practice, and provide feedback to one another.

One experienced teacher, Olivia Lozano, reflecting on how she had been able to develop formative assessment expertise, explained that she benefits "from having a partner, someone that I can bounce ideas off of, someone I can go to for advice, someone who can give me feedback."[18] With this statement, Ms. Lozano calls attention to the nature of a community of practice as a forum for people with shared concerns who deepen their knowledge and expertise by interacting on an ongoing basis. A community of practice can be as simple as "having a partner" or can be constituted more formally through having a team of people that comes together on a regular basis and is guided by shared protocols, agendas, and routines.

Whether constituted as a partnership or a team, a community of practice invests in the growth of all participants through collaboration and interaction, leading to a form of collective capital that each member can leverage for their individual professional growth, particularly at the self-regulation stage of the continuum, in which they increasingly take control of their own learning.[19]

Two additional concepts are associated with the idea of a community of practice—apprenticeship and legitimate peripheral participation. The first concept, apprenticeship, can be characterized as a mostly nondidactic way of teaching and learning, grounded in a local context and dependent on participation in work-related activities. The acquisition of skills during an apprenticeship involves social participation and interaction, observation, and imitation.[20] During their preservice programs, teachers begin an apprenticeship to teaching, engaging in the activities of apprentices such as observation, interaction, and imitation. In chapters 7 and 8, which focus specifically on preservice and induction programs, we describe how teachers can participate in these kinds of activities, commensurate with the phase they have reached, to begin developing expertise in formative assessment.

The second concept is legitimate peripheral participation. When teachers join a community of practice as apprentices, they are legitimate peripheral participants who are striving to become full members and adapt their identity to that of the other members of the community.[21] They are "legitimate" because they are recognized by group members as valid participants in activities, and are "peripheral" in the sense that they are not yet full and autonomous members of the community they have joined. Gradually, as they participate in work or other activities, they become less peripheral, until they are recognized as full members of the group. There is no set time for this to happen, but likely toward the end of their induction period. As full members of the group, they have a responsibility to continue their own professional learning through participation in the community of practice, and to support new members who join as apprentices. Chapter 9 focuses on the opportunities available to teachers during their in-service phase as fully fledged members of the community of practice. Chapter 10 addresses the final phase of the continuum, when teachers take on leadership roles within their schools and districts and continue to participate in a community of practice in a leadership capacity.

The sociocultural approach characterized by communities of practice provides the context for engaging with the content of professional learning. In the next section, we present an overview of the general components of professional learning across the continuum of expertise.

COMPONENTS OF PROFESSIONAL LEARNING

Figure 2.1 represents the content framework for the professional learning continuum for discipline-based formative assessment.[22] The approach to teacher learning is a sociocultural one, which embraces communities of practice as a lynchpin. Ambitious teaching, discussed in chapter 1, is placed at the center, signaling that it grounds all professional learning. Recall that ambitious teaching entails a deep understanding of subject matter, teaching practices that are interactive and discourse-based, and support for students to make sense of what they are learning.[23] The framework comprises three main components: formative assessment practices, disciplinary knowledge, and habits of practice. Teachers acquire knowledge and skills in formative assessment that are necessarily integrated with disciplinary knowledge. Both elements, in turn, reciprocally inform ambitious teaching and are consolidated and boosted by its enactment. Acquiring the requisite knowledge and skills for discipline-based formative assessment is motivated by several habits of practice that teachers begin to develop in preservice programs and that are amplified and sustained over the course of their teaching careers. The framework's three components are not treated as separate entities but rather are intertwined to form the content of professional learning across all the phases of the continuum.

Let us now consider the framework's components in more detail.

FORMATIVE ASSESSMENT PRACTICES

Formative assessment is a set of practices that encourage both teachers and students to seek evidence about how students are developing their knowledge, skills, and understanding with the intention of using the evidence to inform learning. Assessment opportunities are embedded into the ongoing learning activities and interactions in the classroom, and the evidence generated from these classroom activities is used by both teachers and students to keep learning moving forward.[25] In chapter 1, we presented a definition elaborating the practices of formative assessment. These are:

- establishing clear learning goals and success criteria,
- obtaining and using evidence of learning while learning is taking place,
- providing feedback to students, and
- engaging students in self-assessment.

Professional learning for formative assessment involves supporting teachers in acquiring the knowledge and skills necessary to implement these practices into teaching and learning with increasing sophistication.

FIGURE 2.1 Framework for the development of formative assessment expertise[24]

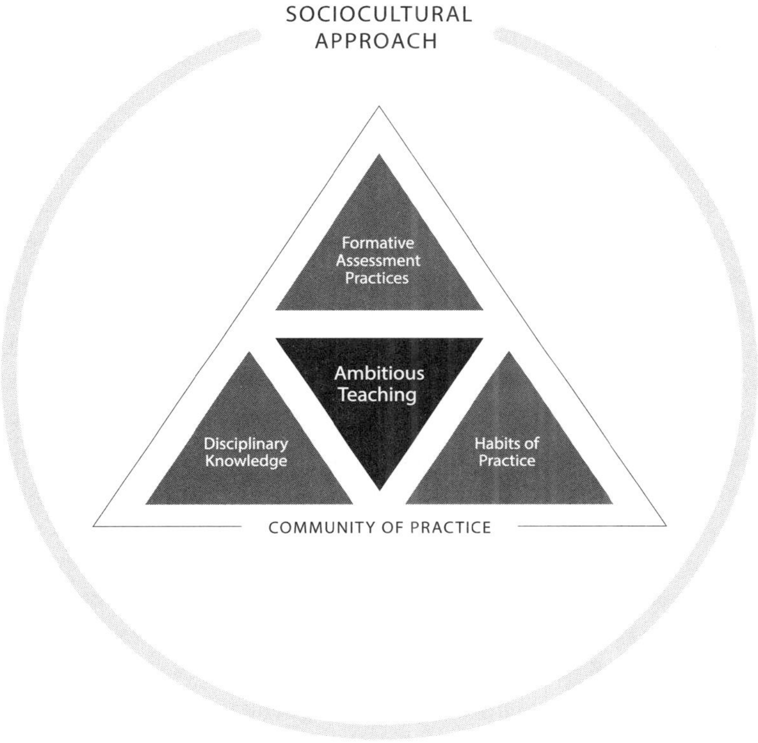

Establishing Clear Learning Goals and Success Criteria

Any type of assessment begins with clear goals, and formative assessment is no different. Teachers' skills in establishing learning goals within a larger span of learning, such as a learning progression or a unit of study, along with indicators of what meeting those goals entails—success criteria—are foundational to both teaching and assessment. With clarity about the intended learning goal and the performances of learning that show achievement of the goal, teachers know what they are looking and listening for while students are engaged in their learning tasks and interactions. The clarity and depth of learning goals and success criteria are synergistic with teachers' disciplinary knowledge. As teachers expand their knowledge of specific disciplinary content and practices as well as their understanding of how students learn within the discipline, there is generally a commensurate increase in their ability to create substantive goals and criteria within a broader progression of learning.

Obtaining and Using Evidence While Learning Is Taking Place

The learning goals and success criteria generate the purpose of the lesson that enables teachers to construct the lesson's organization, tasks, activities, and interactions. When these aspects of the lesson are clear, teachers can then be aware of where the formative opportunities lie in their lesson and plan to make good use of them while the students are engaged in learning.[26]

As they obtain evidence of the current status of students' knowledge, skills, and understanding, teachers' skills in drawing inferences from it are pivotal to the effectiveness of formative assessment. Whatever the source of the assessment evidence during the lesson—observation, dialogue, demonstration, written response—teachers must have the skills to interpret the evidence from the perspective of what it shows about students' conceptions, misconceptions, skills, and knowledge. Interpretation involves a careful analysis of the students' responses in relation to the criteria for success, which leads the teacher to draw inferences about the current status of learning in relation to the intended lesson goal, and then to make decisions about how to respond pedagogically to keep learning moving forward.[27] Often teachers' pedagogical actions are immediate, taking place while students are engaged in their learning activities. Teachers may also decide to use the evidence obtained in a class period to inform the subsequent one. The important point here is that the action is taken while student learning is still in development.

Providing Feedback to Students

When a teacher provides feedback to students based on the evidence analyzed, the purpose is not to "fix" or "correct" a problem but rather to engage students' thinking and provide sufficient guidance, without offering a total solution, for the students to take the next steps in learning on their own.[28] Teachers need to understand how feedback can support students' learning, and when it is appropriate to provide feedback rather than taking other forms of pedagogical action, such as modeling, explaining, or prompting. Teachers also require the skills to provide clear and descriptive feedback to students to help them understand the discrepancy between where they are currently in their learning and the intended goals of the lesson, and to provide them with a course of action to consider for improvement. Students need opportunities to use the feedback to advance their learning, and teachers need to build in time for them to do this.

Increasingly, peer feedback among students is regarded as important to the formative assessment process, and so teachers must become skilled in supporting students to acquire peer feedback skills through modeling effective feedback, teaching the specific skills of feedback, and monitoring how students' feedback skills are developing.

Engaging Students in Self-Assessment

In addition to gaining information about how their learning is progressing as a result of teacher and peer feedback, students engage in their own self-assessment to reflect on where they are relative to the goal and success criteria, and then to make determinations about what they need to do to move forward. Often students' self-assessment leads them to request feedback from either the teacher or their peers so they can obtain guidance about their next steps. Self-assessment promotes students' engagement with the core processes of self-regulated learning, including self-monitoring and goal setting.[29] Among the teacher competencies for student self-assessment are an understanding of the purpose of self-assessment and its contribution to self-regulated learning, skills to ensure that students fully understand the learning goal and success criteria and what meeting them entails, and the ability to support students in acquiring self-assessment skills and in using the evidence they have generated through the process.

DISCIPLINARY KNOWLEDGE

As we shall see in chapters 3 through 6, teachers' formative assessment knowledge and skills are inextricably connected with their disciplinary knowledge, and therefore in our framework the development of teachers' formative assessment practices occurs in the context of specific disciplinary content and analytical practices. This is not to say that formative assessment strategies cannot be generic. For example, preservice educators Brent Duckor and Carrie Holmberg advocate for preservice teachers to acquire a series of moves for formative assessment—priming, posing, pausing, probing, bouncing, tagging, and binning—that they can immediately utilize during teaching practicum. These moves contribute to a preservice teacher's ability to appropriately set up a discussion (priming), engage all students in a meaningful discussion (posing, pausing, probing, bouncing), and make sense of the evidence of student thinking that arises in the discussion (tagging, binning) to inform the next instructional steps.[30] However, the utility of these moves will be considerably enhanced when they are underpinned by disciplinary knowledge. As Ms. Lozano observed,

> As a new teacher, it was really hard for me to draw from experience, my content knowledge that wasn't fully developed yet. That happened with time, and as I became a more experienced teacher, I became more familiar with the standards; then I was able to draw from that knowledge in order to provide my students with in-the-moment, on-the-spot instruction that would help them to meet the learning goal for that class.[31]

Disciplinary knowledge for formative assessment encompasses several aspects. First, teachers need content knowledge of the discipline they are responsible for teaching. This includes an understanding of the knowledge, concepts, skills, and analytical practices that characterize the discipline, as well as an understanding of how to teach these disciplinary elements. In this regard, distinguished scholar Lee Shulman identified a particular kind of knowledge that teachers need for teaching, which he referred to as "pedagogical content knowledge" (PCK), "the special amalgam between content and pedagogy" needed for teaching a particular subject.[32] Building on Shulman's ideas, researchers have since elaborated the concept of PCK and shown how teaching demands a simultaneous integration of key ideas in the discipline with the ways in which students understand them.[33] With this form of disciplinary knowledge, teachers are equipped to understand what constitutes evidence of learning in relation to key ideas, and to know how student learning can be advanced toward a deep understand of these key ideas.

Second, teachers need to understand how learning progresses in a discipline, so that when they plan learning goals and success criteria, they place them in a larger trajectory of learning, connecting current learning to previous and future learning. When teachers understand the connections and progression of ideas within a discipline, they are better able to respond to evidence in ways that move learning forward from its current status, including providing feedback that guides students in taking the next steps in their learning.[34]

Third, teachers need knowledge of the forms of disciplinary thinking and the challenges and misconceptions students typically experience in relation to particular topics. With this specific disciplinary knowledge, teachers are better able to anticipate and recognize student errors, justifications, and misconceptions, and to orchestrate appropriate and immediate actions intended to advance learning.[35] For instance, by understanding that students developing proportional reasoning may incorrectly assume additive relationships when comparing ratios (incorrectly assuming that 2:3 is equivalent to 3:4), a math teacher will be better positioned to recognize the error and take appropriate pedagogical action.[36] Similarly, a science teacher needs to realize that understanding gases can cause special difficulties for students because those they commonly experience, like air, are invisible. As a result, the students may have naive ideas about gases based on their experiences of the world, for example, associating gases only with the use and function of objects such as footballs and tires.[37] With this knowledge, teachers are more equipped to address these ideas in their teaching and to attend to them should they arise.

A further advantage of this kind of disciplinary knowledge is that teachers are able to pose questions which are broad in nature and permit them to explore the full range of student thinking during the course of productive dialogue.[38] This knowledge also supports teachers' engagement in interpretive listening during dialogue in order to understand students' partially formed or not fully articulated explanations.[39]

HABITS OF PRACTICE

Habits of practice refer to the specific dispositions and patterns of behavior that incline teachers to ongoing professional learning.[40] Our continuum of professional learning for discipline-based formative assessment is premised on the idea that these habits of practice are inculcated during teachers' preservice experience and are sustained and consolidated by teachers throughout their careers. Specifically, we focus on three habits of practice: an inquiry stance, deliberate practice, and critical reflection.

An Inquiry Stance

Inquiry is a process of examining professional practice to inform decision-making for action. It can be undertaken individually, but it is most powerful when it is collaborative.[41] In advocating for collaborative teacher inquiry in a community of practice, New Zealand scholar Helen Timperley stresses that improved student outcomes will only be achieved when the teachers are focused on becoming increasingly responsive to their students.[42] In this regard, the common threads of an inquiry stance across the phases of the professional learning continuum are that teachers are focused on identifying what is successful for their students, considering the impact of their practice on student learning, and making decisions about how they can improve their practice for the benefit of each one of their students.

At the preservice and induction phases, inquiry might center on an analysis of how a lesson with integrated formative assessment went, including considerations of the clarity of learning goals and success criteria for students, the actionable quality of the evidence obtained, and the degree to which the teacher's pedagogical action resulted in improved student learning. Even though the sophistication of their formative assessment practice will have increased during the in-service phase, these same considerations will likely characterize teachers' inquiry, as illustrated by this veteran teacher's comment, "To this day we feel like we still need to share our learning goals and success criteria with one another and get feedback because they're not always one hundred percent."[43] Teachers' inquiry during in-service might center on how well the students are involved in formative assessment, including their abilities to self-assess, develop their own learning goals, and provide peer feedback, and what could be done to support their improvement in these areas.

An inquiry stance to practice will only flourish in conditions that promote it. Since inquiry involves collaborative analysis of established practices and routines, it presumes a schoolwide environment of trust in which teachers feel that they can explore their practice and express ideas without fearing that they will be sanctioned or demeaned.[44] In this regard, it is instructive to recall John Dewey's thoughts on the dispositions for reflective action:

- *open mindedness:* giving full consideration to different perspectives and alternative possibilities
- *responsibility:* the capacity and commitment to carefully consider the personal, academic, and social consequences of actions
- *wholeheartedness:* a willingness to critically examine one's assumptions and beliefs, as well as the results of actions, always with the intention of learning something new[45]

Deliberate Practice

Deliberate practice is practice that is purposeful and designed to maximize improvement. In particular, five principles of deliberate practices are relevant to the development of teachers' skills:

1. Presenting challenges that push practitioners just beyond their current abilities
2. Setting goals that are well defined and measurable
3. Making a conscious effort to improve practice
4. Receiving high-quality feedback and adjusting in response to feedback
5. Developing mental models to guide decisions[46]

During preservice programs, faculty and cooperating teachers will likely guide teachers to incrementally move beyond their current capabilities in a purposeful trajectory, whereas once teachers are beyond the induction phase, they will make their own determinations, often with support from administrators and peers, of what is just beyond their current capabilities.

Goal setting and measuring achievement of goals are characteristics of each phase of the continuum. Rather than focusing on broad, general improvement, it is more effective to target specific aspects of formative assessment for deliberate practice, in the same way that an orchestra violinist might practice specific sections of a piece of music to improve the overall performance. Along these lines, Ms. Lozano made the following suggestions when asked for advice about deliberate practice:

> Pick one area. You might want to start with the learning goal and the success criteria because that will be the most important thing

> that you share with the student at the beginning of a lesson. Then you might decide you want to start incorporating some peer feedback or really thinking about how you will be recording the students' growth towards meeting that learning goal. How you're documenting learning using conferencing notes.[47]

At the preservice phase, teachers will most likely set goals based on the program's design with foundational skills preceding more sophisticated ones. For instance, teachers might focus on setting a clear purpose for a lesson before they think about the specific learning goals and success criteria to achieve the purpose. They may be videotaped during their teaching placements and review the target of their deliberate practice with cooperating teachers to set new goals. A similar process might occur during the induction phase, while during in-service, teachers take more responsibility for setting goals and self-monitoring for improvement, although many teachers also seek support from peers and school leaders.

At all phases, teachers make a conscious effort to improve their practice. Beyond their preservice and induction programs, during which improvement is a given, teachers' habits of practice motivate their commitment to continuously improving their knowledge and skills. High-quality feedback from program faculty, mentors, and peers is instrumental to improvement.

Finally, teachers gain in sophistication across the stages of the continuum in their mental models of how students learn. This model is, of course, connected to their disciplinary knowledge, and it assists their instructional decision-making in response to formative assessment evidence. This view of mental models is confirmed by Ms. Lozano who, reflecting on her experience of formative assessment for several years, noted:

> My greatest challenge in implementing formative assessment has been to really develop the content knowledge sufficiently enough to be able to provide that on-the-spot, on-the-fly instruction for my students. As a novice teacher it was really hard because there were so many areas that students needed support with, but I had to make that decision in the moment as to what their next step might be or what that in-the-moment instruction would be.[48]

The more teachers understand how students learn within a discipline and what constitutes evidence of learning, the more robust their mental models will be, strengthening their capacity to respond to evidence during the course of student learning.

Critical Reflection

Critical reflection is a response to past experience; it involves conscious recall and analysis of the experience as a basis for evaluation and decision-making and as a source for planning and action. Teachers who explore their own teaching through critical reflection develop a keen awareness of their practice and determine what can benefit their own professional growth and the support they provide to their students.[49]

Although critical reflection is inherent in inquiry and many aspects of deliberate practice, we call it out as a habit of practice for two reasons. First, because of its importance for the development and maintenance of professional expertise. Second, because critical reflection amounts to far more than thinking about how a lesson went or the success of a particular strategy; it requires teachers to move beyond the "how to" questions to asking "what" and "why" questions that are part of a broader purpose. When teachers critically reflect on these questions, they exercise control over their own actions for improved classroom practice.[50]

There is a range of approaches to supporting teachers' critical reflection, including peer observation and discussion on the feedback from the observer; teachers' analysis of videos of their formative assessment practice, as well as analyzing others' videos to prompt reflection on their own practice; and self-assessment using structured protocols to capture details of the practice. In chapters 7, 8, and 9, we illustrate how such approaches can be employed across the professional learning continuum.

We began this chapter with the notion that learning to implement formative assessment is not achieved overnight—teachers do not accelerate from zero to perfection in one move. Instead, they incrementally develop their knowledge and skills along a continuum of professional learning, by collaborating with others in a community of practice in a process of inquiry and critical reflection, and by engaging in deliberate practice. At the different phases of the continuum, they are likely to encounter bumps along the way, but their commitment to doing the very best they can for their students will undoubtedly sustain them. Summing up the "journey" she has taken with her colleagues in formative assessment, one teacher characterized it as "one of learning, one of trial and error, one of determination and perseverance," and she stressed the importance of not giving up "when it gets hard."[51]

SUMMARY: THE BIG IDEAS OF CHAPTER 2

- There is no quick route to effectively implementing formative assessment practices.
- Teacher expertise in discipline-based formative assessment can take place across three main phases of development: externally supported, transitional, and self-regulatory.
- This book's approach to professional learning is grounded in sociocultural theory and is characterized by interaction with others in a community of practice.
- The apprenticeship model provides a lens for examining how scaffolding by various people supports teachers' learning as they move from legitimate peripheral participation to full members of the community of practice.
- The content of the professional learning continuum comprises three overlapping components: formative assessment practices, disciplinary knowledge, and habits of practice.

CHAPTER 3

Formative Assessment in Mathematics

Robert Moses, a civil rights organizer in the nineteen sixties and the creator of the Algebra Project, has repeatedly championed the idea that mathematical literacy—the ability to problem-solve, reason, and analyze information using mathematical representations—like reading and writing, is necessary for full citizenship.[1] In his memoir he notes, "The political process has been opened—there are no formal barriers to voting, for example—but economic access, taking advantage of new technologies and economic opportunity, demands as much effort as political struggle required in the 1960s."[2] More recently the need for mathematical literacy, combined with the ability to engage in lifelong learning, was underscored by a 2017 special issue of the *Economist* which argued that these capacities will permit workers of the future to keep up with the rapidly changing landscape of jobs in the twenty-first century.[3] In particular, students who leave school behind their peers in mathematics are much less likely to be able to gain the ground needed for them to get high-paying jobs in the future.

Along similar lines, American historian Lynn Arthur Steen has argued that quantitatively literate citizens need to understand and be able to do more with mathematics than a mere rote application of formulas and equations.[4] For example, they need to be able to look at problems from a mathematical perspective and understand why thinking quantitatively can help them understand the problem, be able to apply careful reasoning to complex problems, be confident in their ability to apply mathematics to a situation, have access to a range of mathematical tools to explore a problem, and develop appropriate questions to ask about a particular situation. Steen further proposes that the domain of quantitative literacy embodies a set of elements, among which are confidence with mathematics, the ability to interpret quantitative data and engage in logical thinking, using the appropriate mathematical tools in context, and having number sense to support estimation.[5] These elements require students to have both conceptual and procedural fluency, and also the ability to apply mathematics to problem situations. Mathematics teachers play a critical role in supporting student learning of this type, integrating formative assessment into ambitious teaching and learning opportunities so that teachers can be adaptive to emerging student ideas in order to keep learning moving forward.[6]

The focus of this chapter is on the nature of the discipline of mathematics and how teachers can use formative assessment to support students in acquiring the mathematical literacy needed for success in the twenty-first century. We begin by considering the *Common Core State Standards for Mathematics* (CCSS/Math), which outline what K–12 students are expected to achieve in school, and their connections to prior guidance for mathematics.[7] As the college- and career-ready standards in most states are similar to the CCSS/Math, we will use them as the main point of reference for mathematics outcomes in K–12 schooling. We turn then from the *what* to the *how* of supporting students learning to think and act like mathematicians, drawing on a National Research Council publication, *How Students Learn Mathematics*, to consider some critical actions for mathematics teachers.[8] Next, we focus on the intersection between formative assessment and disciplinary knowledge, providing vignettes of practice by way of illustration. Finally, we consider the implications that are raised by the chapter's content for teacher learning.

WHAT MATHEMATICS STUDENTS NEED TO LEARN

The National Council of Teachers of Mathematics (NCTM) published the *Principles and Standards for School Mathematics* in 2000 to outline the critical components of a high-quality mathematics education to which all students, not just a select few, should have access.[9] NCTM authors articulated both content and practice standards and described how they supported each other. They call out five particularly important aspects of mathematical practice that are in line with desirable mathematics teaching, shifting away from the rote application of algorithms: (1) problem solving, (2) reasoning and proof, (3) communication, (4) connections, and (5) representation.[10]

The following year another publication, *Adding It Up*, discussed five interwoven strands of mathematical proficiency that combine content and practice:

1. *Conceptual understanding:* comprehension of mathematical concepts, operations, and relations
2. *Procedural fluency:* skill in carrying out procedures flexibly, accurately, efficiently, and appropriately
3. *Strategic competence:* ability to formulate, represent, and solve mathematical problems
4. *Adaptive reasoning:* capacity for logical thought, reflection, explanation, and justification
5. *Productive disposition:* habitual inclination to see mathematics as sensible, useful, and worthwhile, coupled with a belief in diligence and one's own efficacy[11]

The ideas from *Principles and Standards* and *Adding It Up* are reflected in the 2010 CCSS/Math. They define the content (the mathematics that students should know) and practices (the ways in which students should go about doing and understanding mathematics) to be learned by students from kindergarten through high school.

The CCSS/Math focus on fewer topics than most prior state standards, with more explicit linking of topics across grade levels and a more balanced emphasis across conceptual understanding, procedural skills and fluency, and application. The content categories of the CCSS/Math include: counting and cardinality; operations and algebraic thinking; number and operations; measurement and data; geometry; ratios and proportional systems; the number system, equations, and expressions; statistics and probability; and functions. Not all categories are relevant for each grade band.

In addition to defining specific content for each grade level, the CCSS/Math outline eight standards for mathematical practice that apply to all grade levels:

1. Make sense of problems and persevere in solving them
2. Reason abstractly and quantitatively
3. Construct viable arguments and critique the reasoning of others

4. Model with mathematics
5. Use appropriate tools strategically
6. Attend to precision
7. Look for and make use of structure
8. Look for and express regularity in repeated reasoning

These practices should be applied to the grade-level content, providing opportunities for, say, an elementary student to justify why her approach to finding the area of an irregular shape is valid, or to critique a peer's justification, or for a middle school student to use functions to develop mathematical models to represent a problem situation, and use the model to make predictions. Clearly, the mathematical practices cannot be considered separately from mathematics content, which is underscored in this statement from the writers of the CCSS/Math:

> Students who lack understanding of a topic may rely on procedures too heavily. Without a flexible base from which to work, they may be less likely to consider analogous problems, represent problems coherently, justify conclusions, apply the mathematics to practical situations, use technology mindfully to work with the mathematics, explain the mathematics accurately to other students, step back for an overview, or deviate from a known procedure to find a shortcut. In short, a lack of understanding effectively prevents a student from engaging in the mathematical practices.[12]

In summary, the CCSS/Math are innovative in some ways, particularly as they foreground the mathematical practices, while reflecting prior thinking from the NCTM standards and quantitative literacy frameworks such as Steen's.

To support students' development of mathematical thinking and reasoning, teachers need to help them simultaneously develop flexibility and fluency with key mathematical content. For many mathematics teachers, the CCSS/Math, and in particular the practice standards, have represented a significant shift in teaching and learning from their own experiences of learning mathematics in school as students.[13] In chapter 1, we discussed formative assessment and the role of teachers' disciplinary knowledge, referring to both the knowledge that a teacher needs to have about the substance and syntax of their particular discipline, and their understanding of the development of students' understanding of disciplinary ideas. In the next section, we consider how students learn mathematics and the implications for formative assessment.

HOW STUDENTS LEARN MATHEMATICS

As noted earlier, the CCSS/Math represent *what* students should learn throughout their K–12 experience, but do not describe *how* they should learn it. To understand more about how students learn mathematics, we turn first to the landmark publication, *How People Learn* (*HPL*).[14] In this volume, the authors presented three research-based principles to guide the design and support of meaningful learning experiences:

1. Students come to the classroom with preconceptions about how the world works. If their initial understanding is not engaged, they may fail to grasp the new concepts and information, or they may learn them for purposes of a test but revert to their preconceptions outside the classroom.
2. To develop competence in an area of inquiry, students must (1) have a deep foundation of factual knowledge, (2) understand facts and ideas in the context of a conceptual framework, and (3) organize knowledge in ways that facilitate retrieval and application.
3. A "metacognitive" approach to instruction can help students learn to take control of their own learning by defining learning goals and monitoring their progress in achieving them.[15]

In a companion volume, *How Students Learn: Mathematics in the Classroom* (*HSLM*), several experts in the field of mathematics explored these three principles in the specific context of students learning mathematics.[16] We now explore each principle and provide one or more examples of the principle in practice to illustrate how it connects to formative assessment and student learning in mathematics.

Principle One: Engaging Student Preconceptions

The first principle requires that teachers engage students' mathematical preconceptions and build on existing knowledge that they bring with them to the new learning. Formative assessment plays a critical role in understanding students' starting points for learning. Teachers can gain insights into what students bring to the table for new learning, including their preconceptions, in several ways. For example, they can support the exploration and use of multiple strategies and encourage students to talk about their mathematical thinking. Through discourse, the teacher can help students move from informal approaches and ways of thinking about mathematics that may not be efficient to more formal mathematical approaches. Using these methods to elicit evidence requires a learner-focused classroom, as opposed to a teacher-focused one, in which the teacher's voice is not the only one heard, and students feel safe sharing their ideas, even when those ideas may be only partially correct or even incorrect.

Putting* HPL *principle one into action Formative assessment experts Mike Askew and Dylan Wiliam found that "learning is more effective when common misconceptions are addressed, exposed, and discussed."[17] As an illustration of how teachers can be supported in uncovering and addressing misconceptions, we describe a research project conducted by the second author in collaboration with colleagues.[18]

The project drew on existing research, teaching resources, and experienced practitioners' knowledge to develop a bank of mathematics misconceptions linked to standards. Using these misconceptions as a starting point, the research team generated questions that could be used to spur classroom discussions during which misconceptions might surface. The teacher materials for each question described the targeted misconceptions. The misconception questions were primarily in the form of multiple-choice questions that incorporated several misconceptions into the possible answer choices. The project employed multiple-choice questions because it reduced the burden on teachers to process the information. To support classroom discussions about misconceptions, students used whiteboards or lettered cards to show their answer choice. The teacher could then scan the room to get a sense of how many students selected each answer, rather than having to try to review up to thirty different answers and group like responses on the fly. The example in figure 3.1 illustrates the kinds of questions to elicit student misconceptions that were developed in this project.[19]

The correct answer to this question is option C. Option A is the mode of the dataset, which some students might confuse with median.

FIGURE 3.1 A misconception-focused question that addresses the mathematics topic of central tendency

What is the median for the following data set?

38	74	22	44	96	22	19	53

A. 22
B. 38 and 44
C. 41 *
D. 46
E. 70
F. This data set has no median

* Correct answer

Some students believe that the median must be one of the numbers in the data set, so options B or E are attractive distractors to students with that belief. Option D is the mean of the data set, which some students will also confuse with the median. Option E is the midpoint between 44 and 96, which students might select if they fail to order the numbers first. The teacher notes included with this question provided explanations for each answer choice.

Teachers were encouraged to ask students for explanations of their answer choices, rather than assuming they always selected an answer based on the reasoning that the writers had presumed. Rich conversations among students about their thinking could often help students recognize and change thinking that was initially influenced by a misconception. The project team also proposed a way of characterizing sources of student misconceptions to help teachers anticipate the ways in which students might think about a new topic and, as a result, be prepared to respond when misconceptions arose.[20] Table 3.1 lists six categories as possible sources of misconceptions.

This classification system also helped teachers anticipate additional misconceptions beyond those provided in the research study. Once teachers started to use the misconception questions and more routinely provided learning opportunities to support student current understanding, they wanted to develop their own questions for topics not covered by the research project.

TABLE 3.1 A classification system for how misconceptions might develop in mathematics

CATEGORY	DESCRIPTION	EXAMPLES
Diagrams, Models, and Conventional Representations	Diagrams and models used in mathematical discourse and materials can be inaccurate, incomplete, or poorly scaled Conventional representations can lead to undergeneralizations of ideas, particularly when teachers use *canonical representations*, for example, always portraying geometrical shapes in the same manner	• parallel lines are always vertical (what students tend so see most often, so they create their own rules based on experiences) • right angles always open to the right (teachers tend not to draw right angles opening to the left) • triangles always have a base down • orientation affects shape/similarity (students not presented with examples of similar shapes that have different orientations)
Abstractions, Generalizations, and Simplifications	Characteristics and descriptions of mathematical procedures, expressions, or concepts can be too abstract, general, or simplified	• addition/multiplication always results in a larger number • fractional pieces do not have to be of equal size • a diagonal line is any line that starts from a corner
Language and Vocabulary	Words, phrases, and descriptors used in everyday communication can convey a constricted, confusing, or completely different meaning in mathematical communication	• average/mean • times • similar • square/diamond • greater/bigger • point/line
"Facts"	"Facts" based solely on intuition or faulty reasoning can be misleading, inaccurate, or incomplete in relation to various mathematical procedures, expressions, or concepts	• there are no fractions between $^1/_3$ and $^1/_2$, for example (students sometimes think this because of the types of fractions they most often experience) • there is a linear relationship among length, area, and volume
Real-World Relevance	Certain mathematical procedures, expressions, or concepts should but do *not* relate to real-world experience	• having remainders or fractional parts of people, vehicles, etc. • previous outcomes influence the probability of an event
Equivalencies	Different mathematical procedures, expressions, or concepts can be seen as being equivalent	• fractions treated as whole numbers • mean and median assumed to be the same • hours and minutes treated as decimals

Results from a study on the use of these misconception questions over the course of a school year showed that more than a third of the participating teachers had not been aware of the breadth of student misconceptions, so using the questions with associated misconceptions explicitly identified served to expand their disciplinary knowledge. Other teachers described how they changed their approach to classroom discussions, taking more time to identify and understand how students were thinking about problems rather than focusing on the correctness of an answer. They valued the formative assessment insights that the questions afforded, and the opportunity to support student learning through the discussions or other next steps that they employed.[21]

This project is just one example of how teachers can be supported to enact the first *HPL* principle, engaging student preconceptions. Other research projects, such as Cognitively Guided Instruction, also place significant emphasis on understanding preconceptions and meeting students where they are in their learning.[22] Understanding students' starting points for learning through formative assessment is a critical first step for teaching.[23] A teacher needs to have a variety of tools to help students articulate and demonstrate their emerging ideas in a classroom environment where those ideas are valued. Ongoing formative assessment will allow both teacher and students to see whether those initial ideas are developing through the learning opportunities provided to more mathematically sophisticated reasoning.

Principle Two: Integrating Factual and Conceptual Understanding

The second principle focuses on the need for students to develop both factual and conceptual frameworks in mathematics, a need that has been recognized in the research literature for some time, although putting it into practice has proven challenging.

> [for example], Schoenfeld (1985) has found that students rely on their knowledge of standard textbook patterns of problem presentation, rather than on their knowledge of problem-solving strategies or intrinsic properties of the problems themselves, for help in solving mathematics problems. Problems that fall outside these patterns do not invoke the appropriate problem-solving methods

> and relevant conceptual knowledge. In other cases, students fail to use resources available to them to improve their skills because they lack models of the processes required for doing so.[24]

Deep understanding of mathematical concepts and the connections among them supports the development of mathematical routines and the use of algorithms that, in turn, can promote more efficient problem-solving. Developing such proficiency requires teachers to engage in instruction that does not focus solely on teaching procedures to students, but also helps them develop conceptual depth. To do this, teachers need to be able to move between "learner-centered and knowledge-centered needs."[25] Being "learner-centered" will focus a teacher on student ideas as a starting point for teaching and learning. A "knowledge-centered" focus will require her to attend to what is to be taught, why it is important, and what successful learning will look like. While it is critical that students express their ideas and thinking, it is also important that the teacher is designing learning activities that help move students to develop both a rich understanding of conceptual ideas and the procedural skills to engage with them efficiently.

Putting* HPL *principle two into action Below we provide a vignette from an eighth-grade mathematics class that illustrates how the teacher engages in formative assessment as he supports students to develop conceptual and procedural fluency.[26] Notice that Mr. Martino designed the lesson with a task that provides an opportunity for students to work with the concept of reflections to create and share their own theories or rules to describe a reflection, rather than giving them a set of rules for the students to test and verify. He collects evidence of student understanding throughout the lesson from observations, written responses, and questions, which he uses to guide discussion, and he supports students in moving from a conceptual understanding toward procedural fluency.

Mr. Martino began a series of lessons focused on reflecting shapes and points across a line based on the following eighth-grade CCSS/Math standard (CCSS.MATH.CONTENT.8.G.A1):

> Verify experimentally the properties of rotations, reflections, and translations:

a. Lines are taken to lines, and line segments to line segments of the same length.
b. Angles are taken to angles of the same measure.
c. Parallel lines are taken to parallel lines.[27]

Additionally, he focused on the fifth practice standard, CCSS/Math PracticeMP5, “Use appropriate tools strategically.”

To address the reflection component of this standard, Mr. Martino introduced the concept of geometric reflections by displaying a picture of a mountain reflected in a pool of water at the base of the mountain. He asked students to respond to two questions: (1) What do you notice? (2) What do you wonder?

Students quietly examined the image and responded to these two questions individually. During this time, Mr. Martino walked around the room reading some of the responses. Next, students were asked to turn and share their responses with their partners. Mr. Martino continued to move around the groups to listen to their discussions. He selected a few students whose responses represented the range of ideas in the class to share their ideas with the whole class, and asked students to raise their hands if they had considered a similar idea. Mr. Martino then explained that the learning goal was to explore reflections. “During today’s lesson, you will begin to make some discoveries about mathematical reflections to generate rules that describe horizontal and vertical reflections.”

After a brief explanation of how to use the reflection tool (a physical tool that is both transparent and reflective so that a student can see how a shape will reflect in a line of symmetry), students individually worked with the tool to reflect points, line segments, and polygons over a line of reflection. Mr. Martino checked to make sure each student was using the tool correctly and provided additional guidance to some students as needed. Mr. Martino’s success criterion at this point was to observe proper use of the tool and reflections that were less than precise were acceptable during this part of the lesson.

Once students showed they were proficient in using the tool, Mr. Martino distributed a paper on which was a right triangle and a line of reflection. He asked students to consider what would happen if they used the tool to reflect the triangle across the line of reflection. Students wrote their predictions: one student wrote, "It will be a triangle," while another predicted, "The triangle will be flipped." Once predictions were completed, students used the reflection tool to reflect the triangle, and then they compared and contrasted the result with their prediction. Mr. Martino directed their activity, "As you compare the original triangle—the pre-image—and the new triangle, make a list of what is the same and what is different."

Working in small groups, some students thought that the angles and side lengths of the two triangles were the same, while others argued that the angles and side lengths were different. Mr. Martino asked the question, "How could we check to see if these are the same or different?" One student suggested, "We would have to measure the side lengths and the angle." The lesson continued with students using rulers and protractors to verify their observations experimentally.

Toward the end of the lesson, Mr. Martino reminded students that the learning goal was to generate rules about horizontal and vertical reflections. He asked students to develop a list of characteristics of shapes reflected across a line, which he documented on chart paper for future reference, noting to the class that they would add to this list over the next couple of lessons as they explored additional shapes and types of reflection.

In a subsequent class period, students were asked to use the reflection tools to reflect a point over the x-axis. Students were able to discover and develop their own procedures to reflect on the coordinate plane. One student claimed, "If I reflect a point over the x-axis, the x value stays the same, and then I have to count the same number of units above or below the axis." Another student stated this more formally as, "You don't need to count, just change the sign of the y value. This is because we know from yesterday that the points need to be the same distance from the line."

Analysis of the classroom example In this lesson, we see evidence of both formative assessment and disciplinary knowledge. From a formative assessment perspective, Mr. Martino collected evidence of students' initial thinking as he read some student responses. When students shared their responses with the entire class, he gained additional insights into their initial ideas. He used the learning goal toward the end of the lesson to bring students back to document their discoveries so that they could develop a set of rules about reflections. With respect to disciplinary knowledge, Mr. Martino started with an example of a reflection that was not mathematical to stimulate their thinking with something familiar so they could develop some informal ideas about reflections. He then provided specific mathematical examples for students to explore so that they could develop rules for reflections that they could initially state in their own words, and then move to a more formal statement of the rule. In this way, Mr. Martino moved between both conceptual and procedural learning opportunities for students, responding to the concern we noted earlier that "students who lack understanding of a topic may rely on procedures too heavily."[28] By the end of the lesson, most students had a conceptual understanding of reflection (that the length of the sides and angles of the reflected shape were the same as the initial shape) and were beginning to develop more procedural rules (change the sign of the y-value) based on that conceptual foundation. The way in which Mr. Martino elicited and responded to students' emerging ideas exemplifies the concept of ambitious teaching introduced in chapter 1.

Principle Three: Supporting Metacognition and Student Self-Monitoring

The final principle focuses on the importance of students developing metacognitive thinking. Metacognitive thinking helps students develop an understanding of themselves as learners, and can be supported by strategies that help them set their own learning goals, monitor their progress toward those goals, recognize the current status of their learning, and develop approaches to support their own learning. Engaging students in metacognitive thinking is a core goal of formative assessment (see chapter 1). Metacognition can be supported with discussions in which students are asked to reflect on the effectiveness of their problem-solving strategy and confer with the teacher about the advisability of using that strategy with similar problems, or by teachers helping students to understand which types of problems they struggle with so that they use their awareness to double-check their solutions before accepting them.[29]

Putting* HPL *principle three into action The second *HPL* principle, the importance of students acquiring both conceptual and procedural fluency, is also relevant in the context of the third principle, students developing metacognitive thinking and self-monitoring skills. One self-monitoring strategy that students can be encouraged to use is estimation to check on the plausibility of a solution. To do that successfully, students need to have sufficient number sense to see relationships across mathematical domains. For instance, consider a mathematics problem in which students are asked to figure out how many 18-seater school buses would be needed to take all 115 fourth-grade students on a trip. A student who struggles with decimal places in division could come up with an answer of 64. A self-monitoring student might then recognize that something was wrong with this answer: since 18 is close to 20 and 114 is close to 120, the likely answer is going to be close to 6. As a result, such a student might reexamine how she did the division to find the error and come up with an answer that was more in line with her estimate.

An example of explicitly supporting students' self-monitoring skills is to provide them with routines that cultivate the kinds of behaviors in which mathematicians engage. One such routine is the Three-Read Protocol to help students approach a word problem or task in a specific way and avoid becoming overwhelmed or incorrectly jumping to a conclusion about what they need to do to solve a problem.[30] In this routine, students read a task three times with a specific purpose each time. The teacher can use choral or echo reading, with the teacher reading aloud, or students can read silently. After the first read, students write a response to the question, "What is this task about?" where they explain the context without using numbers. After the second reading, students answer the question, "What are the quantities or relationships?" After the final reading, students respond to the question, "What questions could be asked?" Students' responses can then be discussed in groups or with partners. This kind of approach to understanding a problem helps students to slow down, consider what the problem is really asking, and better understand what aspects of a problem they do and do not understand. While this self-monitoring strategy applies to more than just mathematics, it may be particularly useful in this area to help students develop a full understanding of a problem before attempting to solve it.

Another example of a teacher who supports student metacognition comes from lesson observations and teacher interviews conducted by the first author. Notice how Ms. Lozano engages students in self-assessment to determine the challenge level of the mathematics problem they will work on during the lesson, and also how she helps a second-grade student develop a metacognitive strategy. In this example, Ms. Lozano uses what she calls a "just-right" task, as shown in figure 3.2.[31]

FIGURE 3.2 A "just-right" task for a second-grade mathematics class

Anju has _____ golden coins. She puts the golden coins into ____ treasure boxes, with the same number of golden coins in each treasure box. How many golden coins are in each treasure box?

(20, 4) (84, 4) (639, 3) (35, 5)

Ms. Lozano's students are familiar with the routine of these problems, understanding that first they have to select the number pair that will provide just the right level of challenge for them. Some students will decide to tackle the problem using the simplest option of tens and units, while others feel that the more challenging number pair with hundreds is better matched to the level of understanding they are aiming for. In an interview with several students who had been using this approach, they described how they thought about the process.

STUDENT A: No, you're asking yourself, "was this a just-right number for me?"

MS. LOZANO: So this whole idea about asking yourself questions about whether "was this a just-right number for me?" So this idea of numbers in math being "just right," can you tell me a little bit more about what "just right" means?

STUDENT A: "Just right" means it's not going be too easy or it's not going be too hard for you. Maybe you get a number that's a little wrong, but you can change it.

STUDENT B: When you do an easy one, you're not going to really learn of the strategies, because when you look at it you can already know the answer, and then you're just doing the strategy because you just like the number or you can already get it easily, and you're just, like, showing how math is easy. But it's actually not, it's just saying that you're just doing something really easy, that you're just not learning things that are challenging.

STUDENT C: I wanted to add on to what [she] said: if you're in math, you have to pick the just-right number for you, not the just-right number for your friend. Because if you pick the just-right number for

> your friend, you're going to struggle and you're going to have to cross it out or erase it.

Ms. Lozano was able to involve all her students in challenging mathematical thinking. She also supported them to think about their own learning and what would push them forward, while communicating an important lesson about learning: learning requires the just-right amount of struggle.

In the next section, we explore the intersection between disciplinary knowledge of mathematics and formative assessment. We examine two approaches that teachers can use to elicit evidence of student learning through the use of rich mathematical tasks, and we offer guidance on how to structure rich classroom questions and discussions to promote deep student learning in mathematics.

THE INTERSECTION BETWEEN THE DISCIPLINE OF MATHEMATICS AND FORMATIVE ASSESSMENT

As we described in chapter 1, formative assessment is a set of practices that involve both students and teachers in a process of eliciting evidence of learning related to specific goals and acting on that evidence to advance learning as it is unfolding. To implement formative assessment effectively in mathematics, it is critical that teachers consider both the CCSS/Math content and practice standards so that they can establish clear and meaningful learning goals that build on each other in a coherent sequence of learning opportunities for students. Teachers also need to be able to recognize and describe the evidence that will indicate that goals have been met, in order to develop clear success criteria that students can apply to their own learning. Additionally, teachers need to be able to select or develop appropriate learning tasks that are accessible to all students, giving each student the right level of challenge and helping each student to develop understanding and meet the learning goals. Finally, teachers need the skills to ask questions and engage students in meaningful discussions that can help move learning forward for both individuals and groups of students. In the section that follows, we consider some resources that can be used specifically to support the development of understanding and the eliciting of evidence of that understanding: classroom tasks and classroom discussions and questions.

Classroom Tasks to Help Students Learn Mathematics

The Mathematics Assessment Project (MAP), a collaboration between the University of California, Berkeley, and the Shell Center team at the University of Nottingham, England, has developed a set of mathematics tasks to exemplify ways to support students in developing the knowledge, skills, and practices embodied in the CCSS/Math. The MAP team created both summative tasks and classroom challenges for the purpose of formative assessment; our focus here is on the latter.

The middle school classroom challenge tasks model an approach to teaching and learning that can be generalized beyond the middle school level.[32] Each model lesson begins with an opportunity for students to work on their own to provide evidence of their current understanding of the concept they are learning about (*HPL* principle one). The teacher notes accompanying the tasks provide details of common difficulties and misconceptions that the designers observed in the early trials of each task. Next in the lesson, students engage in a collaborative activity to develop and deepen their understanding. Guidance is provided for the teacher on how to engage students in a classroom discussion to surface some of their emerging thinking. Finally, the students complete a task on their own, similar to the first one, to provide evidence of changes in their understanding.

In the lesson plan template below, we illustrate one of the MAP tasks that focuses on students' interpretation of multiplication and division when fractions are involved.[33] While the MAP tasks provide much of the information that the teacher will need, we have put this information into the template below (figure 3.3) to illustrate the role of rich assessment tasks in the larger formative assessment context. We will also see this lesson template in chapter 4, and we return to it again in chapter 8, where we propose that the induction period for beginning teachers is a productive time to draw their attention to how to use lesson planning as a way of deliberately attending to particular aspects of formative assessment.

In the first section of the template, the teacher identifies the standards that are addressed, a learning goal for students, and a set of success criteria to help students understand how they will know when they have achieved the learning goal.

The lesson plan template draws teachers' attention to the tasks/activities that they will use during the lesson. For this lesson, students work with sets of cards, some of which have short word problems and others number sentences (e.g., $\frac{1}{3} \times 6$, $\frac{1}{3} \times \frac{1}{6}$, $\frac{1}{3} \div 6$, $\frac{1}{3} \div \frac{1}{6}$), providing a source

FIGURE 3.3 A lesson plan outlined to support the interpreting multiplication and division task from the MAP project

<table>
<tr><td>Standard(s)
Content
6.NS: Apply and extend previous understandings of multiplication and division to divide fractions by fractions.</td><td>Practices
1. Make sense of problems and preservere in solving them.
2. Reason abstractly and quantitatively.
3. Construct viable arguments and critique the reasoning of others.
4. Model with mathematics
5. Use appropriate tools strategically.</td></tr>
<tr><td>Learning Goal
Students will understand the relationships among multiplication and division for problems involving fractions.</td><td>Success Criteria
Students will be able to:
• Develop alternative approaches to describe multiplication and division
• Provide word problem examples for number sentences that involve fractions with either multiplication or division.
• Translate a word problem with fractions into a number sentence.</td></tr>
<tr><td colspan="2">Tasks/activities/strategies to help students meet the learning goal
Pre-assessment set of questions
Card set to match word problems to calculations</td></tr>
<tr><td colspan="2">Formative opportunities in tasks/activities/strategies to gather evidence of student learning
• Review pre-assessment (looking for students who believe division also requires the larger number to be divided by the smaller number, does not recognize that "of" in "one half of one third" signals multiplication, or who struggle to represent the problem in a diagram)
• Observation for the card match activity to identify representations that students find challenging for future discussion
• Selected group presentations of their matches</td></tr>
<tr><td colspan="2">Questions to gather evidence of student learning
How would you represent that diagram as a calculation? Or vice versa, represent the calculation as a diagram?
Can you represent that another way?</td></tr>
</table>

of embedded formative assessment. The lesson plan also highlights potential student misconceptions that might emerge during the task and how to address them. The final section of the lesson plan shows the questions the teacher will use to gather evidence of learning in conjunction with the task.

While the MAP resources do not cover all middle school mathematics standards, they do provide a set of exemplars that demonstrate both the importance of identifying student preconceptions as a first instructional step (*HPL* principle one), and of helping students develop both conceptual and procedural mathematical understanding (*HPL* principle two), two important aspects of ambitious teaching.

Classroom Discussions to Help Students Learn Mathematics

We emphasize classroom discussions because they can be an important formative assessment opportunity to elicit evidence of student learning and because of the direct connections to the three principles from *HPL*. Discussions provide opportunities to elicit student prior understanding and misconceptions, to help students develop fluency, and to involve them in metacognitive thinking. Let us consider the suggestions among the *HPL* principles and strategies for productive mathematical discussions that support formative assessment.

The role of a mathematics teacher is to help students develop rigorous mathematical thinking and reasoning, to facilitate rich mathematical discussions that will help the students make connections among different ways of problem-solving, and to tie those ways to important disciplinary methods or mathematical ideas.[34] As students evaluate multiple methods, teachers can also help them consider which strategies might be most useful in particular circumstances.[35] Discussions are a rich source of formative assessment evidence because a teacher can hear students articulate their emerging mathematical ideas and guide them to deeper understandings through feedback and making connections with other student ideas. Mary Kay Stein and her colleagues, researchers who focus on mathematics teaching and learning in classrooms, have proposed five strategies to support productive mathematical discussions to elicit evidence of student understanding in support of formative assessment.[36] As we explore more fully in chapters 6 and 7, preservice and induction teachers need these kinds of structures to help them develop formative assessment practices. These five strategies help unpack the important planning aspect of questioning and the work that a teacher does during a lesson to support this formative assessment practice.

The first strategy focuses on planning prior to the class discussion, anticipating the kinds of responses that students might make when they respond to a cognitively demanding mathematical task. Planning includes the teacher completing the task, considering the range of strategies that students could use, and thinking about more and less sophisticated responses that students might provide (*HPL* principle one). In many instances, research literature can illuminate possible student approaches (see the earlier section on misconceptions). Anticipating the range of responses that students might make supports formative assessment by readying the teacher to facilitate and steer the discussion in class. Also, the teacher may identify potential follow-up steps to use during the lesson if and when students respond as anticipated. Additionally, considering how students will respond to a task can lead to a revision if the task is not as rich as originally anticipated or is too complex.

The second strategy focuses on how a teacher can observe students' responses to the tasks during the phase of a lesson when they work on a problem individually or in small groups. The purpose of the observations, beyond merely checking to see that students understand the directions or are staying on task, is to identify possible examples that might be particularly productive to share with the class. Noting the kinds of mathematical strategies that students are using, especially ones that are incorrect or partially correct, and deciding what to share with the entire class to support rich sense-making by students provides additional formative assessment insights for the teacher. As noted in chapter 1, ambitious teaching engages students in discourse to support making sense of what they are learning.

The third strategy focuses on being intentional about which students are asked to present their mathematical responses to the class. Of central import is making sure that the key mathematical ideas are visible to the whole class (*HPL* principle two). Sometimes calling on volunteers will work; at other times, a teacher might select a student purposefully to share an incorrect approach or an unusual correct approach to spur discussion. By calling on those students identified during the earlier part of the class, the teacher has greater control of which ideas are presented to support everyone's learning.

The fourth strategy, beyond identifying which students should present their work, is to identify the sequence in which responses should be shared so that the examples appropriately scaffold student learning and discussion. For example, the teacher might start with a common correct approach used by many students in the class, or, alternatively, begin with a common misconception that many students demonstrated. In the process of planning, teachers may have already identified an approach or solution strategy that students could use. If the strategy would be instructive for the class to discuss, it can be shared with them, either under the guise of what someone in another class tried or by directly showing how the teacher approached the problem.

The fifth strategy for productive discussions is for the teacher to help students make mathematical connections, both among different students' responses and between students' responses and the key ideas. Helping students make connections across ideas, strategies, and representations is a critical part of developing mathematical fluency and flexibility (*HPL* principle two). Different kinds of problems may help students think about efficiencies and accuracy, connections to other ideas, or how mathematical patterns can help them when problem-solving (*HPL* principle three). In an earlier example, Mr. Martino charted the list of student-generated characteristics of shapes reflected across a line for future reference as the class continued with the topic over multiple classes.

This set of strategies for productive discussions reminds us that while teachers can engage students with meaningful questions that are developed in the moment of the lesson, planning questions and discussions, and anticipating student responses, can deepen both learning and formative assessment opportunities. Although we have discussed tasks and discussions separately, in reality a teacher and group of students will move back and forth between different ways of eliciting evidence of learning. We see this back-and-forth in a final vignette of practice in an early elementary class of students that is exploring decomposition of numbers. We also pay attention to the ways in which the teacher's disciplinary knowledge is called upon at multiple points. Ms. Cárdenas coteaches two second-grade classes with Ms. Lozano and was part of the lesson observations and teacher interviews conducted by the first author.[37] Notice how she engages her students in sense-making about what they are learning by using a just-right task, which allowed all the students to share their strategies and explain and justify their reasoning. Again, this discourse-based learning is a hallmark of ambitious teaching, as discussed in chapter 1.

Example of Practice

Ms. Cárdenas, a second-grade teacher, had been working with her students on a series of lessons focused on "decomposing" and "composing" two- and three-digit numbers (breaking down and regrouping numbers into units, tens, and hundreds). The specific learning goal that she shared with the students for the lesson was, "As a mathematician today, I will understand how a group of objects can be partitioned into equal shares."

Ms. Cárdenas had created a task for students to work on that aligned to the learning goal. She introduced the task, saying: "You're going be able to show me and yourself that as a mathematician you understand how to group objects and how a group of objects can be partitioned into equal shares." She also provided success criteria in the form of questions to help students understand what will be important for them to be able to do in this task. She presented the success criteria as: "Can you identify what the problem is asking you to do? Can you represent your strategy for solving the problem? Can you explain and justify why your strategy worked?" Ms. Cárdenas made sure that students could distinguish between the terms *explain* and *justify* before presenting the task.

The mathematics problem Ms. Cárdenas wanted the students to solve was:

> Camillo went apple picking. He gathered __ apples and put them in __ baskets.
>
> Each basket had the same number of apples. How many apples were in each basket?
>
> Students were able to select one of three number pairs ([28, 4] or [292, 4] or [568, 4]) to use in their version of the problem so that they could work with numbers that they felt most confident with.

During the independent work time, Ms. Cárdenas moved around the room to see how students were tackling the problem, helping them find manipulatives to use or develop an explanation of the strategy they used. One student who was generally quite confident in her mathematical ability, Lily, had elected to use the numbers 292 and 4. By the time Ms. Cárdenas started to talk to her, Lily had already created a diagram (see figure 3.4) to represent her strategy for how to divide 292 apples among four baskets.

Ms. Cárdenas had to quickly review Lily's work and make a decision, in the moment, about whether this was an appropriate solution strategy to use, and to identify a next step to suggest to Lily.

Ms. Cárdenas did not ask Lily to walk her step-by-step through her approach to the problem, but rather commented on how Lily had decomposed 90 into several sets of 20, and then had to regroup the 10 that was left over with the 2 units to complete the problem. Noting to herself that this was an appropriate strategy, without telling Lily that it was correct (because she wanted Lily to work on her metacognitive skills), Ms. Cárdenas then asked Lily, "What strategy might you be able to use to see if 73 is the right answer?" Lily was hesitant; she indicated that she knew there was another strategy to use, but that she was not sure what it was. Ms. Cárdenas restated her question, "How many apples are in this basket [pointing to the

FIGURE 3.4 Lily's solution to the problem

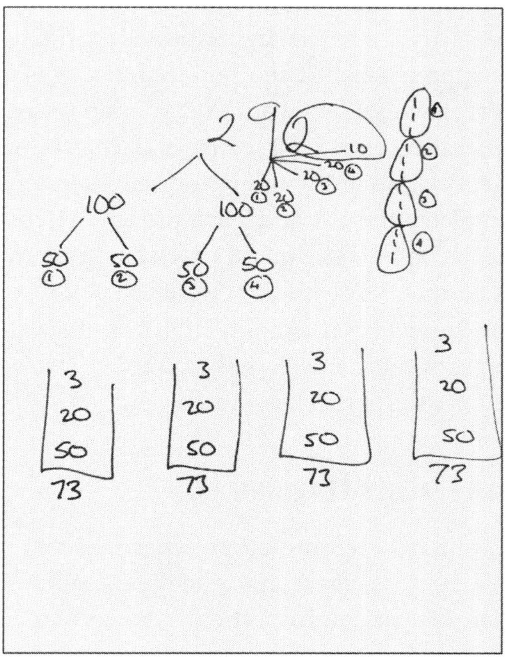

first one] . . . and this one [pointing to the second] . . . and this one [pointing to the third] . . . and this one [pointing to the fourth]?" Lily indicated 73 apples in each basket. Ms. Cárdenas then asked her, "If I joined all the apples together, how many would I have?" Rather than prompting further, Ms. Cárdenas asked Lily to think about what she had said, and let Lily know she would return in a few minutes to see what her plan was. Ms. Cárdenas also asked Lily if she would be willing to share her strategy with the class during the wrap-up discussion.

Analysis of the classroom example In this brief example of practice, we see the application of Ms. Cárdenas' disciplinary and formative assessment knowledge in the design of the task, in her review of the student's work, and in her suggestion for a next step. She created a rich mathematical task that allowed students with varied skill levels to access the task whether they needed to work with tens and units or could work with hundreds, tens, and units. When the students shared with their peers, they drew on a common set of strategies, regardless of the magnitude of the numbers, which provided an occasion for students to hear about strategies other than the ones they used. The independent work time gave Ms. Cárdenas the chance to review student work, listen to their explanations, provide formative feedback, and identify solution approaches that she could ask students to share with the whole group. In reviewing Lily's work, Ms. Cárdenas had to decide if the approach was generalizable and mathematically correct, and, based on her evaluation of the work, identify an appropriate next step. In Lily's case, since she had completed the task and her approach was correct, Ms. Cárdenas decided to focus on how she might check her work, without explicitly telling her it was correct. Most students were still relying on manipulatives rather than using an approach like Lily's diagram for solving their problems. Ms. Cárdenas wanted Lily to talk about her strategy so that other students could compare approaches.

IMPLICATIONS FOR TEACHER LEARNING

In this chapter, we have examined both what students need to learn in mathematics and how teachers can effectively support that learning through formative assessment. In particular, we have focused on the role of high-quality tasks and discussions to help students develop both conceptual and procedural understanding and on the need to balance mathematics content and practice. As noted in chapter 1, we use the idea of teachers' disciplinary knowledge throughout this book to refer to both the knowledge that teachers need to have about the substance and syntax of their particular discipline, and to their understanding of the development of students' understanding of disciplinary ideas. The authors of *HPL* define teachers' disciplinary knowledge as their understanding of mathematics concepts, how these concepts relate to each other in a broader progression of learning, and the development of students' thinking about them.[38] We also examined how an understanding and assessment of student misconceptions can support classroom teaching and learning. Taken together, these tools and resources can support effective formative assessment practices and ambitious teaching.

We have examined vignettes of mathematics teachers in action and noted the importance of their knowledge of mathematics along with their understanding of how students learn mathematics. One way in which formative assessment has been characterized is as a series of three questions: Where are we going? Where are we now? How to close the gap?[39] These questions help us consider the types of knowledge that teachers need to have. Teachers need to understand the CCSS/Math deeply in order to be able to identify important learning experiences for students so that they are going in a mathematically meaningful direction. Selecting tasks and engaging students in discussions, making sense of what students say and do, understanding student misconceptions and naive ways of thinking are all important skills for teachers to gain insight into students' current learning status. In order to close the gap between current and intended learning, mathematics teachers need to be able to respond quickly and flexibly to structure the students' next learning steps.

We began this chapter considering mathematical literacy as an essential twenty-first-century skill. Yet too many students have a fear of mathematics and shy away from it, particularly when the focus is on procedural understanding.[40] Discipline-rich formative assessment practices can help reduce students' fears. As we noted in chapter 1, formative assessment helps teachers keep students at the edge of their learning, continually adapting to students' needs by frequently updating their understanding of what they know and can do. In this way, students have the chance to build their confidence in mathematics by incrementally moving forward from their current learning status to what they can successfully do next.

Mathematics teachers are not born knowing how to engage in formative assessment practices, nor does proficiency in mathematics guarantee understanding of student ways of thinking about mathematics. Rather, these skills can be developed beginning in preservice education and continuing through the induction and in-service phases of professional learning. We pick up the topic of developing teachers' knowledge and skills with formative assessment more fully starting in chapter 7.

SUMMARY: THE BIG IDEAS OF CHAPTER 3

- Mathematical literacy is an essential skill for the twenty-first-century workforce.
- The Common Core State Standards for Mathematics (CCSS/Math) present what K–12 students are expected to achieve in mathematics in terms of both content and practice standards.
- Applying the three principles from *How People Learn* to mathematics teaching and learning emphasizes the importance of: (1) identifying and building off students' initial understanding to help them uncover naive or incomplete understandings or misconceptions, (2) engaging in teaching and assessing that integrates mathematics content and practices, and (3) helping students engage in metacognition through the identification of their own learning goals and self-assessment of progress toward those goals.
- Disciplinary knowledge for mathematics teachers includes understanding mathematics concepts and practices, how these concepts relate to each other in a broader progression of learning, and the development of students' thinking about them. Careful and deliberate planning of classroom tasks and discussions can help teachers anticipate student responses and prepare how they might respond to them, which can enrich the in-class formative assessment process.

CHAPTER 4

Formative Assessment in English Language Arts

The United Nations Educational, Scientific, and Cultural Organization (UNESCO) defines literacy as "the ability to identify, understand, interpret, create, communicate and compute, using printed and written materials associated with varying contexts"[1] This characterization suggests that teachers in the English language arts (ELA) face a broader and more complex set of instructional goals than ever before. A considerable number of people in the late nineteenth and early twentieth centuries could acquire a job with basic literacy skills, such as decoding text and comprehending instructions or short simple texts. However, succeeding in twenty-first-century postsecondary education, whether vocational or academic, being able to earn a decent living in a knowledge-based global economy, and actively participating in a democracy requires advanced literacy skills.[2] As the UNESCO definition elaborates, "literacy involves a continuum of learning in enabling individuals to achieve their goals, to develop their knowledge and potential, and to participate fully in their community and wider society."[3]

Of course, students still need to learn the foundational skills of reading and writing, such as pairing sounds with symbols, decoding words, developing automaticity in word reading, and understanding the main idea of a paragraph, but from the earliest grades, they also need to be learning to think critically, creatively, and metacognitively while using written and oral language in school. Literacy is fundamental to thinking because of the profound connection between language and thought.[4] This is not a new perspective on literacy. The point was underscored over two hundred years ago by the French philosopher, Abbé de Condillac, who argued, "we think only through the medium of words. . . . The art of reasoning is nothing more than a language well arranged."[5] Thinking makes literacy learning possible and, in turn, the development of literacy capabilities become tools or media for learning to think better.[6]

The aim of this chapter is to consider how the development of literacy capabilities, specifically in the context of ELA, are supported through discipline-based formative assessment practices. We begin with a description of the knowledge that students need to acquire to be able to read and write literary and expository texts, followed by an example of classroom practice that illustrates how the teacher uses formative assessment to advance students' skills. Next, we consider the content of the Common Core State Standards in English Language Arts and Literacy in History/Social Studies, Science, and Technical Subjects (CCSS/ELA) which we use as a proxy for state standards that students in each state are required to meet.[7] Following this consideration are two additional examples of classroom practice illustrating the CCSS/ELA integrated with formative assessment. Then we discuss how literacy development is a shared responsibility among ELA and subject-matter teachers so that students acquire literacy in each discipline. We also include consideration of English language learner students and how their literacy development is also a joint responsibility. Finally, we briefly discuss the implications for teacher learning.

KNOWLEDGE FOR ACQUIRING LITERACY COMPETENCIES

In this section, we discuss two main types of knowledge—language and world—that students need to develop to become competent readers and writers of both literary and expository text.

Language

The skills that students need to learn to read and write are grounded in language knowledge. To be able to understand what a speaker is saying or what a writer is writing in increasingly complex texts, and to convey and receive meaning orally, students must progressively develop knowledge of words, sentences, and discourse—any piece of language that extends beyond the sentence.[8] They need to understand both frequently used words and less common words that might be used in literary and expository texts.

To be able to read or write text in English, children need to understand the alphabetic writing system. Early on, they acquire the understanding that marks on the paper represent words which are written from left to right, and they know that twenty-six letters map onto the language's more than forty phonemes. They also need to know that many words do not follow the standard orthographic rules of English and be able to recognize and write them automatically. Their knowledge of sentences encompasses a progressively sophisticated repertoire through the full range of simple to complex grammatical structures that increase in length and in the amount of information contained within a sentence. Students also need to know the significance of morphemes, prefixes, suffixes, and inflections, for example, how to use inflectional morphology (e.g., participial modifiers [verb + ing]) to create more syntactically complex sentences (e.g., The boys running were late for their class).[9]

At the discourse level, genre knowledge is essential. Students need to know that different genres are characterized by different discourse structures, such as choices of clause structures or organizational patterns. For instance, oral or written arguments often include logical (*therefore*) and adversarial connectives (*however*, *nevertheless*), whereas procedures usually incorporate temporal markers (*first*, *then*, *next*) to realize a set of steps or instructions.[10] This knowledge of discourse structures extends to knowledge of text genres, which are identified by recurrent patterns. For example, narrative can be identified by a time sequence structure and by the presence of complicating events; exposition by the author's use of titles, headings, and subheadings; and digital text by the use of hyperlinks. If students understand text structure, they can identify what they are reading and anticipate what they might expect from the text. Also, if students analyze what authors do well (using exemplar texts), they can emulate those qualities in their own writing.

Students' knowledge of how oral and written language works should develop progressively in tandem with their cognitive processing capabilities (analysis, evaluation, reasoning, or synthesis, for example) and the sophistication of the ideas they want to communicate about.[11] A requirement for ELA teachers, then, is to have sufficient understanding of the knowledge and cognitive processes that students need in order to progress.

World Knowledge

This type of knowledge refers to what readers know about a topic or concept, which impacts their capacity to make meaning from text. Individuals who have stronger world knowledge are better able to comprehend or learn from advanced text.[12] For instance, someone with knowledge of anatomy reading the following text would likely have an advantage over someone who didn't.

> The sympathetic trunks are two ganglionated nerve trunks that extend the whole length of the vertebral column. The two trunks end by joining together to form a single ganglion, the ganglion impar. The thoracic part of the sympathetic chain runs downward and leaves the thorax behind the medial arcuate ligament. The preganglionic fibers which are grouped together to form planchnic nerves and supply the abdominal viscera.[13]

When text complexity increases, as in middle and high school, world knowledge is even more important. As reading expert Marilyn Jager Adams notes:

> Texts that are more complex in vocabulary and syntax also tend to be more presumptuous of readers' background knowledge . . . texts that strive to present more precise argument or more specific information on a topic are unavoidably more complex in vocabulary and syntax.[14]

All children have "funds of knowledge," the cultural practices and bodies of knowledge of their lived experiences in their homes and communities. Luis Moll and colleagues advocated drawing on students' funds of knowledge to legitimize students' experience as valid, and to build on familiar knowledge bases that students can manipulate to enhance learning in subject matter content in school.[15] ELA teachers will benefit student learning by leveraging their funds of knowledge in support of literacy learning.

Metacognitive thinking, in which individuals use cognitive functions to operate on their own thinking, is also important for literacy development. For instance, readers engage in metacognition when they monitor understanding while they are reading, and they know what to do when they encounter problems of noncomprehension, using strategies such as rereading, asking questions, or summarizing. Similarly, writers think about whether their writing is conveying their intended meaning and will be accessible to the reader and make revisions when they decide it needs clarifying.

Let us now turn to an example of practice that illustrates how a teacher is promoting her students' knowledge about how written language works at the same time as she is developing their cognitive processes, particularly, reasoning, analysis, and metacognitive thinking. We will also see how her use of formative assessment intersects with her disciplinary knowledge to support her teaching and the students' learning. Recall from chapter 1 that formative assessment is a set of practices that involve establishing clear learning goals and success criteria, eliciting evidence of student thinking, making instructional adjustments, providing feedback, and involving students through self-assessment (for more details on the practices see table 1.1).

EXAMPLE OF PRACTICE

As part of the Advanced Placement (AP) English Language and Composition course, Ms. Eilertsen's eleventh-grade students are required to complete nine timed-writing essays, focused on synthesis, rhetorical analysis, and argument, over a fourteen-week period.[16] In this lesson, which took three class periods of fifty minutes each, the students were focusing on argument. Notice how the teacher uses success criteria, self-assessment, and peer feedback in particular to support students' writing.

Introducing the Learning Goals and Criteria

To begin the lesson, Ms. Eilertsen communicated to students that their goal was to "learn how evidence and claims, along with sophisticated diction and syntax, are used to compose an argument to best support your position." These learning goals focus on language and text structure knowledge, as well as on the reasoning capabilities that students will be required to engage with during the lesson.

Then she reviewed with the entire class several models of effective essays and led a discussion about the qualities that made them successful, which eventually became the success criteria for the learning goal. The success criteria they developed through this process were:

- Structure—short and sweet introduction, (hook, entice the reader) body and conclusion
- Claim = position/argument
- Identify and focus on key issues, impact of issues
- Claims—provide evidence to support the claim and explain (3 sources)
- Address counterargument
- Sentence fluency—varied, keep the reader engaged
- Strong transitions and flow
- Delicious vocabulary, dynamic, professional, accurate

Through their analysis of well-written argument essays, focusing on text structure and language use, and creating success criteria from their analysis, the students had a clear understanding of what they were aiming for in their own work.

Deepening the Students' Understanding of Success Criteria

Next, the class read and discussed the AP prompt that was assigned for the timed writing and brainstormed ideas together. Then they individually completed the timed-writing task. Once they had completed their writing, Ms. Eilertsen invited the students to review specific inadequate, adequate, and effective essays provided with the AP prompts and associated rubrics. From this analysis, the class decided to add more success criteria related to sentence fluency, introducing citations, and weaving in quotes for support as needed.

Preparing for Peer Feedback

At this point in the writing process, Ms. Eilertsen's routine practice is to ask the students to identify specific questions, related to their timed-writing pieces, on which they would like to receive feedback from their peers. However, Ms. Eilertsen had observed that some of the questions students asked tended to be general, and focused only on a narrow subset of skills, for example, "Which words are too vague that I need go back and strengthen to better support the content of my essay?" and "What transitions can I incorporate to strengthen the coherence of my essay?" For this lesson, to help students ask for more substantive feedback, she worked with them to generate a more diverse set of questions specific to argument:

- What other evidence can I utilize to support my claim?
- What other background or context do I need to provide to orient my reader to the text?
- How can I develop my analysis/commentary?
- Where am I best synthesizing and connecting sources to my claims?
- What is my position, and how does my evidence support or not support it?
- What do you see as my main argument, and what are my main claims to support that?
- What clarification do I need in my argument?
- What other ways can I introduce or weave into my evidence to help create flow/coherence?

Through this process Ms. Eilertsen deepened students' understanding of the structure of argument. Notice, too, how the success criteria also relate to thinking skills that the students will use, such as analysis and synthesis.

Implementing Peer Feedback and Self-Assessment

With these questions in mind, the students were invited to reread their essays and write three specific questions to guide their peers' feedback or select three of the ones generated by the class that related to their own work. In groups of three, each student read and provided feedback on one essay, using only the questions that the writer had provided. This feedback process was repeated, so that by the end of the group time each student had feedback from two peers. Writers then reviewed their peers' feedback, along with the success criteria. From that, they identified what feedback they would utilize and why, and what success criteria they would work to improve on in their essays. Ms. Eilertsen also asked each student to make a justification for where their essay fell on the AP rubric (scored from 1 to 9). Here is what one student wrote after she had received peer feedback:

> In my essay, I demonstrated effective word choice by using words such as "primal" and "idolizes." I used a clear thesis to demonstrate the purpose of my essay, and I described the text thoroughly by stating the genre, the name, and the author and her credibility. I clearly stated how the strategies I identified tied to a specific

> appeal, however, I need to explain how each of these appeals tie to the author's purpose and how that is developed. I didn't analyze the time period at all, which is essential to discover the exigence of the writer. Overall, I believe my essay ties closest to 7 because I have significant commentary on each piece of evidence that I provided, and I have a clear and concise thesis.

Through this process of self-assessment, students were engaged in metacognitive thinking. After they had completed their self-assessment, the students rewrote their timed essays.

Ms. Eilertsen undertook her own review of the feedback provided and the students' written self-assessment and decided which students she would confer with individually. Her decisions about conferences were based on which students appeared to be struggling the most, either in content or in confidence of skills.

Ms. Eilertsen uses this same process of peer feedback and self-assessment for each of the nine timed-writing essays. Formative feedback is more effective when it is not tied to a grade, but because these students are working toward a high-stakes examination, Ms. Eilertsen grades every third essay the students write according to the AP rubric so that the students can compare their own assessment of their essay with hers. This process provides an opportunity to further refine their understanding of the criteria on which their ultimate performance will be judged, and once again engages them in metacognitive thinking.

Analysis of Example

Ms. Eilertsen communicated a clear and rigorous learning goal to her students that showed her knowledge of what complex argument writing entails, including that the students would write with sophisticated diction and syntax. She engaged her students in an analysis of argumentative essays so that they could both deepen their understanding of what is involved in high-quality writing in that particular genre and generate success criteria to guide their self-assessment and peer feedback. In this way, she engaged them in building their knowledge of written language communication and applying the cognitive processes of analysis, synthesis, and reasoning to that knowledge. Ms. Eilertsen's genre and language knowledge enabled her to focus the students' attention on the specific aspects of the genre and help them think about specific genre-related, substantive questions to elicit feedback from their peers. By asking the students to reflect on the feedback they received and consider how they would improve their essay, she engaged them in metacognitive thinking, which assisted them in creating mental representations of what they wished to communicate to the reader. Ms. Eilertsen also used her genre and language knowledge as an interpretive framework when she reviewed the students' peer feedback and self-assessment to determine which students she would have conferences with.

Formative assessment was not an adjunct to the lesson; it was embedded in the tasks and interactions the students engaged in, from understanding the success criteria, to providing feedback, to self-assessment. Ms. Eilertsen used her disciplinary knowledge to provide students with rich learning experiences to expand their knowledge and skills, and to provide herself and the students with the evidence to keep their learning moving forward. Additionally, in her own words, Ms. Eilertsen emphasizes that her ability to teach students the skills of critical thinking has improved, and consequently she has increased her expertise in developing advanced literacy skills among her students.

Post-Lesson Interview

The peer feedback process now runs very smoothly in Ms. Eilertsen's classroom, but she comments that she has experienced some "epic failures" along the way. Here, she describes one of them:

> The AP Language & Composition course provides rubrics and models for students and teachers to use. We had just read our first synthesis prompt and students had written the essay the day before. After looking at models and discussing criteria for successful essays, I had students move into groups and "grade" each other's essays using the rubric and models as a guide. This was an epic failure. Instead of focusing on peer feedback, students focused on scores. I had one young man approach me after class in tears because his peers gave him 3s and 4s (inadequate on the AP rubric). With a sinking feeling, I realized students had completely missed the point of this peer feedback session. So, the next

> day, I apologized to students for structuring the opportunity such that the students' peer session was evaluative in nature, which was counterintuitive to building and strengthening each of their writing skills.
>
> Prior to the next peer feedback session, I reminded students of our ultimate goal: to have ownership of their own writing, strengths and weaknesses; to obtain suggestions for improving their own writing; and to have control as writers about what feedback to use.

Ms. Eilertsen's comments reflect what we underscored in chapter 1—when implementing formative assessment, teachers do not go from zero to perfection in one move. Instead, they need to try things out, reflect on their practice, and make improvements. Above all, as in Ms. Eilertsen's case, they should not give up when the going gets hard—they will find success. Ms. Eilertsen reflected on her ultimate success:

> This process puts the students in charge of their own writing . . . the level of critical thinking has improved way beyond what I used to get as a younger teacher and the quality of what they are turning in is so far beyond what I imagined it could be.

Ms. Eilertsen uses the AP course requirements as the roadmap for her teaching, and she uses her disciplinary knowledge and pedagogical skills to plan rigorous learning opportunities for her students. If teachers are not responsible for specific course work such as AP, their guide to the expectations that K–12 students should meet is the ELA standards in each state. In the next section, we discuss the content of ELA standards and what is entailed in meeting them.

ELA STANDARDS

The CCSS/ELA comprise four subdomains: reading, writing, listening and speaking, language and according to the CCSS/ELA document, as students move through the grades, meeting the standards in the subdomains of reading, writing, listening and speaking, and language, they progressively acquire the capacities to be college- and career-ready, and are able to meet the demands of education beyond high school as well as those of the workplace.

The CCSS/ELA do not tell the teachers how to teach, nor do they flesh out the disciplinary knowledge necessary to be able to support students in meeting them. Teachers will need to augment the CCSS/ELA with their own disciplinary knowledge acquired in preservice programs and through continued professional learning and combine this with their knowledge of pedagogy to ensure that their students meet the required expectations.

Subdomains of CCSS/ELA

Although the CCSS/ELA are laid out according to the four subdomains of the discipline in reality they are not separate; each one is dependent on the others. For instance, much of what students do in ELA classes engages them in a constant back-and-forth between tasks that require listening and reading comprehension and responses that require oral and written displays of understanding.[17]

Reading The CCSS/ELA places emphasis on careful, close reading to understand text and to develop knowledge across the curriculum (world knowledge). Specifically, students are required to undertake

> the close, attentive reading that is at the heart of understanding and enjoying complex works of literature . . . seek the wide, deep, and thoughtful engagement with high-quality literary and informational texts that builds knowledge, enlarges experience, and broadens worldviews . . . [and] reflexively demonstrate the cogent reasoning and use of evidence.[18]

The CCSS/ELA also call for students to read both literary and informational texts of increasing complexity as they progress through school. Text complexity involves the grammatical features of the text, vocabulary demands, and other elements such as multiple levels of meanings in a text and the typicality of genre conventions.[19] At the elementary level, half of the texts students read are required to be narrative and half informational in character. At the high school level, the percentage of informational text increases (to 75 percent) to reflect the role of texts in building knowledge across the curriculum and later in college and the workplace.

Beyond developing foundational skills in the elementary grades—such as decoding, word recognition, and reading fluency—the CCSS/ELA emphasize analysis and critique of arguments presented in text, comparisons and contrasts within and across texts with respect to themes, and integration and evaluation of content in multiple media forms. The CCSS/ELA for grades 6–12 reflect the differences across disciplines in the nature of reading and the reasoning process required. For example, the standards relating to craft and structure in history/social science require students to "identify aspects of a text that reveal an author's point of view or purpose (e.g., loaded language, inclusion or avoidance of particular facts)," whereas in science the same standard calls for students to "analyze the author's purpose in providing an explanation, describing a procedure, or discussing an experiment in a text."

Writing By the time students graduate from high school, the expectations of the CCSS/ELA are that they will be able to write skillfully in order to achieve their communicative purpose (for both narrative and informative/explanatory texts), gather information from print and digital sources, convey information accurately and clearly so that their audience can understand a topic or idea, and present arguments logically to defend interpretations or judgments. As students move through the grades, the CCSS/ELA require them to grow in their ability to write well-structured narratives to develop real or imagined experiences, cite specific evidence in defense of the claims in making arguments (both written and oral), and engage in research-based writing that presents complex ideas from an analysis of content. The CCSS/ELA's emphasis on using evidence, analyzing information in writing, and conducting research draws from studies that show these skills are essential for success in an argument-based college culture as well as in today's information-rich work environments.[20]

Speaking and listening Speaking and listening standards are as important as reading and writing standards and need to be intentionally incorporated into lesson planning. The standards call upon students to engage in collaborative discussions and activities, listen carefully and critically to others, pose questions that elicit elaboration, respond to others' questions, build on others' ideas, and clearly express their own. Students are required to develop the capacity to adapt their speech to a variety of contexts and tasks. They are also expected to conduct formal presentations for different audiences and for a range of purposes that integrate information from visual, quantitative, oral, and media sources.

Language Specific language standards outline the linguistic competencies that students need to develop in order to meet the preceding standards. These include: a command of standard English grammar and usage and of the conventions of standard English (e.g., punctuation and spelling), a vocabulary appropriate to each discipline, and the ability to make effective choices in words, syntax, and punctuation to express themselves in order to achieve particular functions and effects.

In sum, when students meet the requirements of the CCSS/ELA, they "develop the skills in reading, writing, speaking, and listening that are the foundation for any creative and purposeful expression in language."[21]

It is important to recognize that standards specify the grade-level outcomes that students need to achieve, but they are not roadmaps for achieving them. The CCSS/ELA do not provide the specifics of what students need to learn, nor do they outline how to get from one year's standard to the next. Standards can guide the development of curricula, but by themselves, they do not constitute a curriculum. While the standards may be signposts along the way, teachers and curriculum developers need to think about what to teach, in what order to teach it, how to teach, what to expect from students, and how those expectations progressively increase across the years of schooling. Teachers need a combination of disciplinary knowledge (including language development), text structure knowledge, knowledge of the cognitive processes that students need to develop, and deep knowledge of the ELA standards, including a roadmap of how students progress across standards, in order to plan learning experiences designed to put students on a trajectory to achieving advanced literacy skills. Knowledge of the discipline and standards is essential for formative assessment, allowing teachers to set clear learning goals that progress toward meeting the standards, to establish success criteria to indicate what meeting those goals entails, to interpret evidence as it arises during the lesson, and to make decisions about next steps in learning for their students.

Next, we turn to an excerpt from a second example of practice that illustrates how a teacher's knowledge of the standards, combined with her disciplinary knowledge, intersects with her knowledge and skills in formative assessment.[22]

EXAMPLE OF PRACTICE

In this example, notice how the teacher elicits evidence from students during her reading conferences, and how she gently nudges them to their next steps in learning. Also notice that while her conferences are focused on one standard, understanding the author's purpose, she incorporates the bigger picture by connecting her responses to other standards that are pertinent to where the students are in their learning.

In recent lessons, Ms. Brennan's second-grade students have been learning about the author's purpose. In one mini lesson, for example, students compared and contrasted a narrative, *The Three Little Pigs*, to an informational text about pigs. They worked together to fill out a graphic organizer and then engaged in a class discussion about the author's purpose for each book. Later, students compared these two texts to Jon Scieszka's *The True Story of the Three Little Pigs*.[23] They have been introduced to the terms *persuade*, *inform*, and *entertain* and discussed the purpose of each. Even though these students are just in second grade, they have been developing analytic skills (compare and contrast) and acquiring genre knowledge alongside their basic reading skills.

In figure 4.1, we can see how Ms. Brennan planned formative assessment opportunities in this particular lesson. She has identified learning goals and success criteria from the standard, planned her mini lesson and then noted how she will obtain evidence through students' learning activities and her one-on-one conferences.

After the planned mini lesson, Ms. Brennan explains to the students their goal for independent reading time:

> Today when you are reading independently, I want you to be thinking about the author's purpose, and I want you thinking about "Why did the author write this?" . . . "What does the author want me to know or explain?" So you are going to find a quiet spot and an informational text that you can read to think about the author's purpose.

FIGURE 4.1 Lesson plan with integrated formative assessment

Standard(s) *CCSS.ELA-LITERACY.RI.2.6* Identify the main purpose of a text, including what the author wants to answer, explain, or describe
Learning Goal: Understand the author's purpose. Why the author wrote the book and what the author wants us to know. **Success Criteria:** Explain what the author's purpose is Explain how you know what the author's purpose it
Tasks/activities/strategies to help students meet the learning goal(s) Mini lesson on the main purpose of an informational text. Students read an informational book specific to one topic (we used "Surprising Sharks" by Nicola Davie"). The topic is sharks, but what does the author want us to know about sharks? Student turn and talk about the author's purpose (most sharks are not scary, humans shouldn't be afraid of them). How do we know? Individual reading of informational text, complete reading notebook response. When I was reading ____________ I think the author wanted me to know ______________ because ______________.
Formative assessment opportunities in tasks/activities/strategies to help students meet the learning goal(s) One-on-one conferences with students during independent reading time (Taruni, Madi, La'Rodney, Ahmed) Review of reading notebook response Class turn-and-talk and discussions
Questions to gather evidence Why did the author write this? What does the author want us to know? Can you show me evidence from the text? Do you have any connections to this idea?

Eliciting and Interpreting Evidence

Students know the routine for independent reading. They quickly select a book to read and find a quiet place in the classroom; some students are sitting on the floor and others are reading at their tables. Once the children are settled, Ms. Brennan moves to sit next to a student who is reading on the rug. She asks, "What are you reading today?" Turning to look at the book cover the student responds, "Snakes." Ms. Brennan writes the title on her clipboard and then she asks, "Any idea about what the main purpose of this book is?" The student responds, "Different kinds of snakes."

Pointing to a page of the book, Ms. Brennan says, "I can see why you are saying that because I'm using the subheading to see that it's about swaying snakes and I'm noticing [pointing to a different page] that the author is naming different kinds of snakes. What does the author want you to know about different kinds of snakes?" The student answers, "Uhm, like these snakes have . . . like some are bigger, some are smaller," and Ms. Brennan responds, "So he's telling you about the size of the snakes on this page?" The student nods.

Pedagogical Response to Evidence

Ms. Brennan presses the student to think about the evidence she is using to justify her conclusion about the author's purpose, "Can you show me a spot where the author talks about the size of the snakes?" The student looks at the text and says, "Right here," then she reads aloud, a little hesitantly "[Snakes] can be big, but they can be small and beautiful."

Ms. Brennan makes notes and then says, "So definitely on this page, the author wants me to know that they can be different sizes. What does the author want me to know about snakes on this page?" The student responds, "Different families that snakes are in . . . so like they can be in a different kind of family." Ms. Brennan again makes notes about what the student is saying. Then she says, "Oh, so interesting. What kind of families are there for snakes?" The student answers, "Um . . . the swaying snake . . . it says the cobra family is a pois . . . poisonous one and contains many kinds of cobras . . . um . . . and yeah."

Giving Feedback

Then Ms. Brennan provides the student with feedback: "Wow! You know what I am impressed with you doing today? Not only are you thinking about the author's purpose and what the author wants you to know, but every time I asked you, 'Can you show me how you know that?' you were able to go back into the text and point to exactly where the author was talking about size of the snake . . . over here [teacher points to the text], and you were able to use this section [teacher points to the section in the book] to tell me exactly where the author was talking about snake families. So you were really using good evidence to support why you think the author wants us know about the size of the snakes and about snake families. Keep doing that while you are reading. That's really great."

Ms. Brennan's next reading conference is with a student who is reading at a table. As she sits by him, she asks, "What are you reading today?"

and he replies, "I'm reading a National Geographic book." Ms. Brennan asks what the title of the book is, and turning to the book cover he replies, "Tiger in Trouble."

Eliciting Evidence

As she writes the title in her notes, the student comments, "It's not just about tigers. It's about animals [they] er . . . lived somewhere but they had to move to a zoo." Ms. Brennan responds, "Interesting because I am noticing that this is a chapter book, and it looks like you're about on the last chapter of the book. So have you noticed something that was similar about the other chapters?" The student takes time to think and then says, "Yeah, all of them like lived somewhere and they were fine, then they were not fine. They just kept getting sick, and then they went to the zoo, and the caretakers at the zoo, then they cared for them very much."

Ms. Brennan continues the conversation, "So if you think about the author, the person who wrote this, what is the author trying to explain about in all these stories [about] animals that were sick, then they went to the zoo to be cared for?" Again, the student takes time to think about her question, then replies, "She's trying to explain about you should care about all animals."

Moving Learning Forward

Ms. Brennan now takes the opportunity to advance this student's learning and asks, "Do you have any connections to that from any other stories we have been reading?" He says he does and adds, "It's about Ivan." She presses his analytical thinking: "How is that book—it's a fictional book—how is it similar to this one?" to which he replies, "Since it wasn't like a true story, it was just made up, it still has animals that were sick and that were took . . . and that were not taking cared well and ended up going to a zoo." Recognizing that he has been able to make connections, Ms. Brennan makes this instructional point: "So what you are doing is making connections, because this is a nonfiction book [points to the book] and you are making a connection to a fiction book called *The One and Only Ivan*, and you're saying that in both books the author wants you to know that it's important to take care of animals. So you're thinking about the theme between two different books. Really excellent job; keep doing that while you're reading."

Analysis of Example

Students do not progress at the same pace, and this example shows how teachers can elicit evidence and move individual student's learning forward from where they are to where they can go next. Ms. Brennan was able to generate evidence using her planned questions and careful listening to the students' responses. Her questions were intended to obtain evidence with respect to the students' understanding of the author's purpose, but rather than focusing her pedagogical responses solely on the target standard, she used her big-picture knowledge of the standards to advance the students' learning in different directions. She assisted the first student to consolidate her understanding related to textual evidence and discussed the idea of theme with the second student, possibly the first time he had been introduced to it. Her disciplinary knowledge supported her interpretations of the evidence she had obtained, and working from the edge of their current learning (see chapter 1), she made instructional responses that nudged students forward in their learning. Ms. Brennan made these responses in situ, but depending on her evidentiary notes, she may decide to form small groups for further instruction. For example, there may be other students in the class who are ready to learn more about the concept of theme across texts.

Next, we turn to a ninth-grade class to illustrate how the teacher, Ms. Johannes, addressed three standards in a project which spanned several class periods.[24]

EXAMPLE OF PRACTICE

The project required students to work in groups to generate and investigate research questions and present their findings to their peers. Specifically, Ms. Johannes focused on the following CCSS/ELA standards:

- Comprehension and Collaboration:
    - Work with peers to set rules for collegial discussions and decision-making (e.g., informal consensus, taking votes on key issues, presentation of alternate views), clear goals and deadlines, and individual roles as needed.

  - Respond thoughtfully to diverse perspectives, summarize points of agreement and disagreement, and, when warranted, justify their own views and understanding and make new connections in light of evidence and reasoning.
- Integration of Knowledge and Ideas:
  - Analyze various accounts of a subject told in different mediums, determining which details are emphasized in each account.
- Research to Build and Present Knowledge
  - Conduct short as well as more sustained research projects to answer a question (including a self-generated question) or solve a problem; narrow or broaden the inquiry when appropriate; synthesize multiple sources on the subject demonstrating understanding of the subject under investigation.
- Presentation of Knowledge and Ideas:
  - Present information, findings, and supporting evidence clearly, concisely, and logically such that listeners can follow the line of reasoning and the organization, development, substance, and style are appropriate to purpose, audience, and task.[25]

Notice how the standards are seamlessly woven together across the project, how Ms. Johannes makes sure there are success criteria for each phase of the project, and how students are engaged in substantive peer feedback opportunities. Prior to beginning the project, Ms. Johannes' class had been studying a painting, a poem, and a novel that focused on the time period of World War I. From their readings and analysis, the students identified significant issues related to warfare, including the traumatic effects of war, the portrayal of war versus the realities of war, and the impact of war experiences on people. To begin the project, Ms. Johannes asked students to consider the issue that was most powerful for them individually from those they had identified, and then form small groups with peers who had selected the same one. Once they had established their groups, Ms. Johannes introduced the four parts of the project: (1) generate their own research questions, based on the issue they had selected; (2) use at least three high-quality sources to investigate their question (they could use the resources they had already read if they wished); (3) represent their research with freeze-frame (a tableau); and (4) write explanations of how the selected issue was present in each of their three sources.

Establishing Success Criteria

Ms. Johannes and her students cocreated success criteria for each part of the project as they prepared to start working on it. The criteria included: generate a research question that is clear and focused and will guide your research; determine what type of information you need to research your topic, in order to select the best resources for locating that type of information; and clearly explain the specific connections between the freeze-frames and the sources. The final product of the research would be a presentation for the entire class.

Over several class periods, students worked in their teams on the different parts of the project. Each team had a team leader, a communicator, a recorder, and a supply manager. Before the students began to work as independent teams, Ms. Johannes discussed with them what each of these roles "looks and sounds like," and the students created success criteria for each one. As the students worked, Ms. Johannes elicited evidence through observation, discussions with students, and listening to students' dialogue. Just as Ms. Brennan did, she made notes and responded to what she saw students do or heard them say, and she made pedagogical interventions to steer them toward meeting the criteria.

Peer Feedback

When the time came for the students to put their presentations together, Ms. Johannes discussed with them what constituted a successful presentation, and together they created success criteria centered on creativity, organization, and choices that enhanced the overall presentation. Teams were paired for their dress rehearsals, and in preparation, each student highlighted two success criteria, related to the parts of the presentation that they were responsible for, about which they would like feedback from the other team.

For the rehearsal, each team performed their full presentation for the partner team—the observer team. Each partner within the observer team took notes that were specific to the criteria their peer had asked for feedback on. Based on their evidence, they provided "warm" (what the student was doing well) and "cool" (suggestions for improvement) feedback. Then the teams switched roles. After all the students had received feedback from their partners, they used it to set personal goals based on what needed to be improved for the final presentation.

Mason shared this feedback with his partner, Holden:

Mason's cool feedback to Holden:

"Could you make sure you are aware of your audience when speaking to help you portray the answer to your research question specifically and fully answer it?"

Evidence: "You talked a little fast, which made it harder to understand what your answer to your research question was."

Mason's warm feedback to Holden:

"You were very precise in giving context for the novel and explaining it."

Evidence: "You very quickly gave context that was understandable to the audience."

Holden thought about the feedback he had received and set the following goals to prepare for the final presentation:

- I will make my speaking clearer, so the audience can understand my key points.
- I will clearly connect our team's subject focus to the novel and provide evidence to do so.

While the teams were rehearsing their presentations and giving each other feedback, Ms. Johannes was also observing and collecting information. From those notes, she, too, provided feedback to the students. Students expressed that incorporating peer and teacher feedback into the dress rehearsal was a positive experience; it enabled them to see their strengths and weaknesses, while allowing them time to make improvements before the final presentation.

Analysis of Example

The CCSS/ELA that Ms. Johannes' project addressed specified the end-of-grade-level expectations, but they did not tell her how to achieve them. She had to use her disciplinary knowledge to understand what constitutes presenting evidence "clearly, concisely, and logically," and similarly, what are the specifics of an enhanced understanding of findings, reasoning, and evidence. This disciplinary knowledge provided the grounding that enabled her to create success criteria with her students and, in turn, enabled them to provide peer feedback. Additionally, this knowledge was foundational to eliciting and interpreting evidence throughout the project, so she knew what she was looking and listening for and could interpret what she saw and heard to make decisions about pedagogical interventions intended to move students toward meeting the criteria. She also used her disciplinary knowledge to select the appropriate materials for her students to read and analyze. Her disciplinary knowledge about the cognitive processes of text analysis was engaged to assist students in comparing and contrasting several genres to determine particular issues about war. Ms. Johannes combined her disciplinary knowledge and pedagogical knowledge to support the development of students' analytic skills.

As in the two previous examples, formative assessment was embedded in the teaching and learning, and because the lesson was grounded in disciplinary knowledge and knowledge of the CCSS/ELA, her students were able to use success criteria, evidence, metacognitive thinking, and feedback to consistently improve learning.

This chapter has focused specifically on ELA teachers. However, the CCSS/ELA emphasize that instruction in reading, writing, speaking, listening, and language must be a shared responsibility within the school. In the next section, we discuss how that responsibility for literacy development can be distributed among a wider range of teachers.

SHARING THE RESPONSIBILITY

The CCSS/ELA emphasize that instruction in reading, writing, speaking, listening, and language must be a shared responsibility within the school. The CCSS/ELA K–5 standards contain foundational expectations for reading, as we identified earlier, including an understanding and working knowledge of concepts of print, the alphabetic principle, and other basic conventions of the English writing system that assist students in developing the capacity to comprehend texts across a range of types and disciplines. The K–5 standards also set expectations for reading, writing, speaking, listening, and language applicable to a range of subjects beyond ELA. The CCSS/ELA 6–12 standards are divided into two sections, one for ELA and the other for history/social studies, science, and technical subjects. This division reflects the unique, time-honored place of ELA teachers in developing students' literacy skills, while at the same time recognizing that teachers in other areas must have a role in this development.[26]

When students enter middle and high school, the expectation is that they will have acquired basic competencies for reading and comprehending text across subject areas and genres so that they are ready to read challenging material within each discipline—science, social studies, and so on. However, the results of the National Assessment of Educational Progress (NAEP) reading assessment, given every two years to a representative sample of US students in grades 4 and 8, and approximately every four years in grade 12, suggest that this might not always the case. The assessment measures reading comprehension by asking students to read selected grade-appropriate materials and answer questions based on what they have read. The NAEP *Proficient* achievement level does not represent grade-level proficiency, but rather competency over challenging subject matter. The results of the 2017 NAEP reading assessment show that only 35 percent of eighth-grade students were at or above the proficiency level.[27] These results are not exactly a ringing endorsement that students in the US are acquiring the advanced literacy skills referred to at the beginning of this chapter. So what to do?

When students in middle and high school encounter more challenging, complex texts, the CCSS/ELA insist that subject-matter teachers will need to share the responsibility with ELA teachers for supporting students' disciplinary literacy development. This does not mean that disciplinary teachers should be reading teachers in the traditional sense. Rather, they need to teach students how to be discipline-specific readers and writers. To do this, middle and high school teachers can identify and integrate relevant literacy practices that promote effective understanding, analysis, and evaluation of texts within their disciplines as implicated in the CCSS/ELA.[28]

Disciplinary Literacy

Each discipline has its own shared way of using language and constructing knowledge. This is reflected in the discipline's unique way of asking questions and solving problems as well as the expectations for the kind of claims that are made and the way those claims are supported. These differences are also manifested in the way that texts are written and in the demands they place both on readers and writers. In acquiring disciplinary literacy, students learn to read, write, and think in ways that are aligned with the experts in a field.[29]

This book's disciplinary chapters give some insight into students' engagement with literacy across disciplines. Chapter 3 highlighted that in mathematics students have to read and make sense of mathematical problems and engage in disciplinary discourse practices. Chapter 5, focused on science, shows students asking questions, constructing arguments, viewing and discussing video content, and expressing their thinking in writing. In chapter 6, we see students viewing and reading source material related to specific questions in social studies and making sense of them through oral and written discourse. In each instance, students were involved in the inquiry practices and ways of reasoning specific to the discipline. They used disciplinary forms of representation and types of texts and participated in the discourse and language structures of the discipline. Subject-matter teachers will need knowledge of the written and oral language competencies that are specific to their subject and be prepared to support their students in achieving proficiency in them so that they can take part successfully in disciplinary literacy practices.

These differences across disciplines in terms of how knowledge is constructed, represented, and communicated also account for why formative assessment needs to be grounded in the disciplines. For example, students write summaries across the curriculum, but what is important to include in a summary of the catalyst of a particular historical event is not the same as a summary of a scientific investigation, nor are the same knowledge and processes used.[30] If teachers are assessing students' summary writing skills, what they count as evidence will be different across subject areas, as will how they make use of evidence to advance thinking, reasoning, and the practices of the discipline.

English Language Learners

Students who are English language learners (ELLs) represent close to 10 percent of the total student population in the United States and make up its most rapidly growing sector.[31] However, the reading achievement of ELLs remains stubbornly low. At the time of writing, the most recent NAEP data for ELLs is not available, but the 2013 reading achievement gap was not measurably different from the gap in either 2011 or 1998, when NAEP first started collecting data on ELL students' status.[32] ELL students must have the opportunity to learn and meet the same high standards as their English proficient peers if they are to access the knowledge and skills necessary in their post–high school lives. Providing these opportunities is a shared responsibility among language specialists teaching English as a second language (ESL) classes, ELA teachers, and teachers within specific disciplines. Shared responsibility means that teachers need to collaborate to identify vocabulary and language structures that ELL students need to acquire and the background knowledge that will help them access text and understand and use oral language to learn. Once each teacher understands what their ELL students need to progress, they will be better able to engage in formative assessment practices to support their students' learning.

ESL teachers and those who teach mathematics, ELA, social studies, and science are not the only teachers who are responsible for ELLs' literacy development. Teachers in every discipline need to engage ELLs in meaningful language use for discipline-specific purposes. For example, in art, students might be asked to justify their use of particular color or line forms, and in physical education, students may have to explain or negotiate the rules of a game.[33] Engaging students in such forms of language use also provide the opportunities for formative assessment.

Reading, writing, listening, and speaking are central to thinking and, therefore, to learning. For this reason, while ELA teachers may do the heavy lifting to support literacy learning, they cannot do it alone.

IMPLICATIONS FOR TEACHER LEARNING

In this chapter, we have seen three vignettes in which teachers engage in formative assessment practices in support of their students' literacy learning. They used their disciplinary knowledge for literacy, their understanding of what meeting the expectations of the CCSS/ELA or AP course requirements entails, and their pedagogical knowledge in combination with their knowledge and skills in formative assessment. The major implication for teacher learning is that teachers will need to develop their expertise in each of these areas, beginning in preservice.

When considering a continuum of learning for ELA teachers, it will be important that in preservice they acquire entry points to disciplinary knowledge and knowledge of the CCSS/ELA sufficient to engage their students in worthwhile discipline-based learning—both of which become progressively subsumed into a deeper, broader knowledge as teachers learn more through their in-service professional learning and through their classroom experience. It is also crucial that, beginning in preservice, subject-matter teachers develop an initial understanding of the reading, writing, speaking, and listening requirements of their disciplines, which continues to deepen as they engage in in-service professional learning.

Beginning in preservice, too, teachers will need to learn the fundamentals of formative assessment and continue to hone their knowledge and skills as they move through induction, in-service, and for some, into teacher leader roles. Teachers' understanding of formative assessment needs to go hand in hand with developing pedagogical content knowledge so they are able to design lessons in which formative assessment opportunities can be productively embedded. With practice and experience, they will become more sophisticated along the professional learning continuum, so that teaching, learning, and formative assessment are almost indivisible in their lessons.

If we are to achieve the literacy goals laid out at the beginning of the chapter for success in the twenty-first century, teachers' disciplinary knowledge will be a significant component. When deep disciplinary knowledge is combined with the knowledge and skills to embed formative assessment into content, we believe that the prospects of students acquiring advanced literacy skills are enhanced.

SUMMARY: THE BIG IDEAS OF CHAPTER 4

- Succeeding in postsecondary education requires advanced literacy competencies, which include the ability to think critically, creatively, and metacognitively.
- Two main kinds of knowledge are necessary for acquiring literacy skills: language and world knowledge.
- The CCSS/ELA provide a guide to the expectations that students need to meet at the end of specific grade levels, but teachers will need to flesh out what meeting the standards entails using their disciplinary knowledge.
- The responsibility for students achieving the CCSS/ELA is shared among teachers to ensure that students are acquiring disciplinary literacy and that ELLs receive the support they need.
- Formative assessment practices are a key driver in students' literacy acquisition.

CHAPTER 5

Formative Assessment in Science

The authors of the important National Academies Press publication, *A Framework for K-12 Science Education: Practices, Crosscutting Concepts, and Core Ideas*, devoted a chapter to issues of equity and diversity in science and engineering education.[1] They note that the term *equity* has been used in different ways by researchers and educators:

> Equity as an expression of socially enlightened self-interest is reflected in calls to *invest* in the science and engineering education of underrepresented groups simply because American labor needs can no longer be met by recruiting among the traditional populations. [Emphasis added.]
>
> Equity as an expression of social justice is manifested in calls to remedy the *injustices* visited on entire groups of American society that in the past have been underserved by their schools and have thereby suffered severely limited prospects of high-prestige careers in science and engineering. [Emphasis added.]

In pursuit of equity goals, the authors make the case that science standards should explicitly acknowledge the significant contributions of women and of people from diverse cultures and ethnicities, and that equity concerns should permeate teaching, learning, and assessment to equalize opportunities for all students to learn scientific concepts and practice. Such opportunities include actively involving students in the practices of science, for example, building on students' cultural funds of knowledge to help them develop their understanding of scientific concepts, engaging students in rich discourse-based learning, harnessing their personal interests, and providing them with multiple ways to demonstrate their understanding. For example, a student who plays sports might more readily be able to understand the parabolic path of a baseball, or recognize that a ball thrown upward will be briefly at rest at the highest point of the throw before falling to the ground. Students from a rural, farming community may have greater awareness of the impact of seasons or genetically modified crops.

The authors of the Framework also want students to develop an appreciation for the natural world and they note in the introduction the following set of interrelated goals:

> The overarching goal of our framework for K–12 science education is to ensure that by the end of twelfth grade, all students have some appreciation of the beauty and wonder of science; possess sufficient knowledge of science and engineering to engage in public discussions on related issues; are careful consumers of scientific and technological information related to their everyday lives; are able to continue to learn about science outside school; and have the skills to enter careers of their choice, including (but not limited to) careers in science, engineering, and technology.[2]

The next generation will inherit a set of environmental problems for which they will have to find solutions. Therefore, it is imperative for our planet that teachers pay attention to how students develop an appreciation for the natural environment and for the sciences. Doing this requires not only assessment of science concepts and practices, but also assessment of student attitudes and feelings toward the content they are learning, and how they see it connecting to their community and their place in the world.

The focus of this chapter is on the nature of the discipline of science and how teachers can use formative assessment to ensure that all students, not just a select few, have access to science learning, opening up the prospects for each one to pursue science and engineering in college and the work place. Formative assessment practices support teachers in identifying where individual students are in their science learning through listening to student discussions, observing their actions, engaging them in dialogue, and examining their work products. From their identification of students' current learning status, teachers will employ a range of next steps to keep students at the edge of their learning (see chapter 1), such as providing feedback, selecting or designing targeted learning experiences, or engaging student peers to explore contradictory views. Any or all of these practices are intended to move learning forward according to student needs.

To understand what is expected for K–12 students in terms of science literacy, we first consider the Next Generation Science Standards (NGSS).[3] The NGSS outline three dimensions of science: the science disciplinary core ideas, crosscutting concepts, and science and engineering practices that students need to understand. The NGSS performance expectations combine these three components to make clear that students are engaged in the practices as they learn about the disciplinary core ideas and crosscutting concepts. We turn then from *what* they need to understand to *how* they can be supported to think and act like scientists through several vignettes of practice that illustrate the pedagogical actions of science teachers that support students in learning to think in this way. Next, we address the intersection between formative assessment and disciplinary knowledge and take a closer look at how the NGSS performance expectations inform learning goals and success criteria, foundational components of formative assessment. Finally, we briefly discuss the implications for teacher learning.

WHAT SCIENCE STUDENTS NEED TO UNDERSTAND

As described in chapter 1, clear learning goals and success criteria form a bedrock for formative assessment practices. To develop these guides for what is to be learned and what indicates successful learning, science teachers need strong disciplinary knowledge, which in turn requires a deep understanding of the standards and what meeting them entails. At the time of writing, nineteen states have adopted the NGSS and another twenty-one states have standards that are based on *A Framework for K-12 Science Education: Practices, Crosscutting Concepts, and Core Ideas* (Framework), which preceded the NGSS.[4] The Framework, which identified the three dimensions of science that all students should learn by high school and is supported by current research on science learning, became the foundation for the development of the NGSS. For these reasons, we use the Framework and NGSS as the main points of reference for science outcomes in K–12 schooling.[5]

The development of the Framework—and subsequently the NGSS—was motivated by the movement across states toward common standards in mathematics and science, the recognition that existing national standards were almost two decades old, and the burgeoning corpus of research on teaching and learning in science. The Framework, published in 2011, presented a set of guiding principles that informed both its structure and content and the ensuing NGSS. The six guiding principles are briefly summarized below:

- *Children are born investigators:* Even before beginning formal education, young children are capable of developing ideas about how the world works. They are able to draw on their direct experiences and observations, along with learning from families, friends, and others with whom they interact to reason in sophisticated ways. Teachers may build on these initial ideas and refine their students' initial reasoning about scientific explanations of phenomena early in their school career.
- *Focus on core ideas and practices:* The Framework proposed a limited set of science and engineering core ideas so that students and teachers could focus more deeply on critical concepts and develop understanding through the use of scientific practices, rather than being forced to rush through topics in the interests of coverage. Students need to develop a structured knowledge base, rather than accumulating pieces of isolated knowledge, and have a solid grasp of core principles and constructs that can be applied later to new problems.
- *Understanding develops over time:* Students need sustained opportunities to work with core ideas to develop their understanding. The Framework supports the use of learning progressions as one mechanism for organizing knowledge about how students' understanding of a topic can extend from early grades to high school and beyond.
- *Science and engineering require both knowledge and practice:* The Framework emphasizes that science and engineering are not just a body of knowledge but also a set of practices that are used to develop, extend, and refine that knowledge. The eight practices for science and engineering are listed in the next section.
- *Connecting to students' interests and experiences:* Science must connect the lived experiences and interests of students and give them an opportunity to pose questions that are relevant and of interest to them. Using students' own questions provides a way to engage students and demonstrate that science is relevant to them.

- *Promoting equity:* Using students' own experiences and cultural capital provides teachers with opportunities to value and make meaningful connections between home and school.

The final version of the NGSS, released in 2013, was produced by a consortium of 26 states, the National Science Teachers Association, the American Association for the Advancement of Science, the National Research Council, and Achieve (a nonprofit education reform organization that has been involved in developing academic standards). The most significant feature of the NGSS are the three dimensions of science, which were first outlined in the Framework: (1) Science and Engineering Practices; (2) Crosscutting Concepts; and (3) Disciplinary Core Ideas. We'll now consider each of these dimensions in turn.

Science and Engineering Practices

The Framework identifies eight practices for both science and engineering:

1. Asking questions (for science) and defining problems (for engineering)
2. Developing and using models
3. Planning and carrying out investigations
4. Analyzing and interpreting data
5. Using mathematics and computational thinking
6. Constructing explanations (for science) and designing solutions (for engineering)
7. Engaging in argument from evidence
8. Obtaining, evaluating, and communicating information

The Framework emphasizes students *doing* science rather than just learning scientific facts and principles. The practices are a core component of that emphasis and provide a mechanism for several of the practices outlined above to be enacted, for instance, supporting students as investigators and providing them with the opportunity to ask their own questions. The practices also help students better understand, through personal experience, how science is done: asking questions that are meaningful to them, proposing models to explain their observations, planning investigations, collecting and analyzing data, developing explanations, and refining models.

For example, an elementary teacher might begin a unit on ecosystems with the overall goal of having students examine the interdependent relationships within an ecosystem by studying the movement of matter between producers, consumers, and decomposers. She could elicit students' prior understanding and funds of knowledge by asking them to predict which fruit and vegetables in an image will rot first and why, then playing a time-lapse video of the fruit and vegetables rotting over a two-month period.[6] From evidence the teacher obtains, she can respond to students' initial thinking to develop their understanding of ecosystems. The prediction activity also provides an opportunity for students to ask questions about what they observe, to develop initial models to explain their observations, and to design some investigations to test out their preliminary theories about the conditions that increase the rate of decomposition.

The practices also support engineering with some minor changes in focus. While explanations and arguments have different goals, purposes, and criteria for quality, in both science and engineering they are iterative and systematic. Scientists and engineers engage in ongoing processes of identifying weaknesses or limitations in their current understanding or design, and they seek additional data following clearly established procedures to refine either explanations or designs. When students participate in these practices, science and engineering can be demystified and made accessible to them. While not every student will enter a STEM career, the opportunities to better understand the processes of science and engineering will provide them with habits of mind that support improved science literacy, important to be an active participant in a democracy, which is surely a critical outcome for K–12 education.

Crosscutting Concepts

The Framework also outlined seven crosscutting concepts, which informed the NGSS. As the name implies, these concepts cut across science and engineering and provide students with an organizational framework to connect ideas across both disciplines. While these concepts are not new, previously they may not have been made as explicit to students or teachers. The crosscutting scientific and engineering concepts are:

- Patterns
- Cause and effect: mechanism and explanation
- Scale, proportion, and quantity
- Systems and system models
- Energy and matter: flows, cycles, and conservation
- Structure and function
- Stability and change[7]

As noted in the Framework, the first two crosscutting concepts are fundamental to the discipline of science: observing patterns can lead to questions about relationships among variables, and investigations to identify cause and effect relationships can discover the mechanisms that underlie them. The third crosscutting concept engages students in applying mathematics to explore relationships. The remaining four concepts occur in almost all science areas and are relevant to engineering contexts too.

Disciplinary Core Ideas

The Framework delineated a set of disciplinary core ideas in physical, life, and earth and space sciences, and for engineering, technology, and applications of science. A core idea meets at least two of the following criteria:

- It has broad importance across multiple sciences or engineering disciplines or is a key organizing principle of a single discipline
- It provides a key tool for understanding or investigating more complex ideas and solving problems
- It relates to the interests and life experiences of students or is connected to societal or personal concerns that require scientific or technological knowledge
- It is teachable and learnable over multiple grades at increasing levels of depth and sophistication[8]

The core ideas are presented as a response to a series of questions (for example, How can one explain the structure, properties, and interactions of matter?), followed by a description of what students should understand by the end of grades 2, 5, 8 and high school. These end-of-grade statements about the core ideas were later integrated into the NGSS performance expectations (described below) along with the relevant practices and crosscutting concepts.

Performance Expectations

The NGSS are written in the form of performance expectations that explicitly integrate the practices, disciplinary core ideas, and crosscutting concepts from the Framework, significantly refocusing teaching, learning, and assessment to center on these three dimensions of science. For example, there are four disciplinary core ideas in the middle school physical science standards, which are broken into sub-ideas, one of which is PS3.C: relationship between energy and forces. The associated performance expectation is MS-PS3-2: Develop a model to describe that when the arrangement of objects interacting at a distance changes, different amounts of potential energy are stored in the system. In this performance expectation, the practice being focused on is developing and using models, and the crosscutting concept is systems and system models.

To summarize, the Framework proposed three dimensions of science. The disciplinary core ideas dimension is likely the most familiar to the majority of teachers. The science and engineering practices describe what scientists and engineers do while developing and applying scientific knowledge, and is similar to what many teachers have previously referred to as "inquiry." The crosscutting concepts can be thought of as principles or habits of mind that guide and constrain scientific practice. All three dimensions are integrated through the performance expectations to explore and explain natural phenomena.

The shift represented in the Framework from teaching students what they need to know about key topics in science to emphasizing phenomena and providing learning activities to help students ask questions about, investigate, and explain those phenomena, as in the rotting fruit and vegetable example, has proved both an opportunity and a challenge. The opportunity is for students to engage in actually doing science. The challenge for many teachers is rethinking how they teach science and assess science learning. For instance, rather than teaching a unit on the topic of photosynthesis, teachers are now called on to engage students in wondering about how plants grow and investigating this phenomenon. Similarly, rather than simply lecturing on the process of cellular respiration, teachers are now required to provide opportunities for students to explore how animals use energy to move. Not only do these changing requirements make new demands on teachers' knowledge and pedagogy, they also make demands on their classroom assessment practices, and in particular their formative assessment practices, which we will explore later in the chapter.[9]

HOW STUDENTS LEARN SCIENCE

In the previous section we have explored the NGSS, derived from the Framework, which represent *what* students should learn throughout their K–12 experience. However, to understand more about *how* students learn science, we turn once more to the landmark publication introduced in chapter 3, *How People Learn* (*HPL*). As we noted previously, the *HPL* authors presented three research-based principles to guide the design of and support for meaningful learning experiences.[10]

1. Students come to the classroom with preconceptions about how the world works. If their initial understanding is not engaged, they may fail to grasp the new concepts and information, or they may learn them for purposes of a test but revert to their preconceptions outside the classroom.
2. To develop competence in an area of inquiry, students must (1) have a deep foundation of factual knowledge, (2) understand facts and ideas in the context of a conceptual framework, and (3) organize knowledge in ways that facilitate retrieval and application.
3. A metacognitive approach to instruction can help students learn to take control of their own learning by defining learning goals and monitoring their progress in achieving them.

These three principles connect to the ideas about formative assessment presented in chapter 1. Principle one focuses on identifying the understanding that students already have when starting a new unit, principle two reminds us that assessment of student learning in science is not merely about factual recall, and principle three focuses on the role of students in formative assessment. Let us now consider how these principles are applied in science teaching and learning.

Principle One: Engaging Student Preconceptions

The first principle requires that teachers engage students' scientific preconceptions and build on the existing knowledge that students bring with them to the new learning. Formative assessment is foundational to this principle, since building on students' existing understandings requires the teacher first to identify what they are. When students begin learning formal science, they have already experienced the world and developed initial explanations for what they have observed. For example, a teacher told the second author about an observation he made of an elementary school student engaged in early exploration of electricity and circuits. The student applied what he already knew about electricity from experience at home: plugging a lamp into the wall socket results in it lighting up. The student was unaware of the circuit within the wall, and that the action of plugging in the lamp completes the circuit and enables the light to shine. Thus, when presented with the materials to create a simple circuit (a bulb, two wires, and a battery) his first attempt at lighting the bulb involved trying to connect the bulb directly to the battery with just a single wire without creating a full circuit—a reasonable application of his prior experiences.

Example of principle one in action Eliciting students' preconceptions can be done by giving students the opportunity at the start of a unit to talk and/or write about what they already know about a new topic. This also provides teachers with the baseline assessment from which to track their understanding over the course of the unit. An experienced ninth-grade biology teacher, Wendy Johnson uses a "driving question board" to elicit students' preconceptions, which then inform her unit planning.[11] The board has three sections: (1) our ideas, (2) our questions, and (3) what we figured out. The first two sections are illustrated in figure 5.1.

During the opening lesson of the unit, Dr. Johnson used the board to document students' initial ideas and questions in response to the driving question, "Why does ethanol burn, but water does not?" After they shared their initial ideas and questions about ethanol burning, the teacher asked a more specific question, "After driving a while, a car's gas tank is empty. Where did the gas go?" to stimulate a discussion. Based on the student ideas suggested during the discussion, Dr. Johnson created a poll to get a sense of which ideas were currently most compelling to students. The response choices included: turns into energy, turns into carbon dioxide, turns into

FIGURE 5.1 A driving question board for a unit on combustion, illustrating the ideas and question generation stages

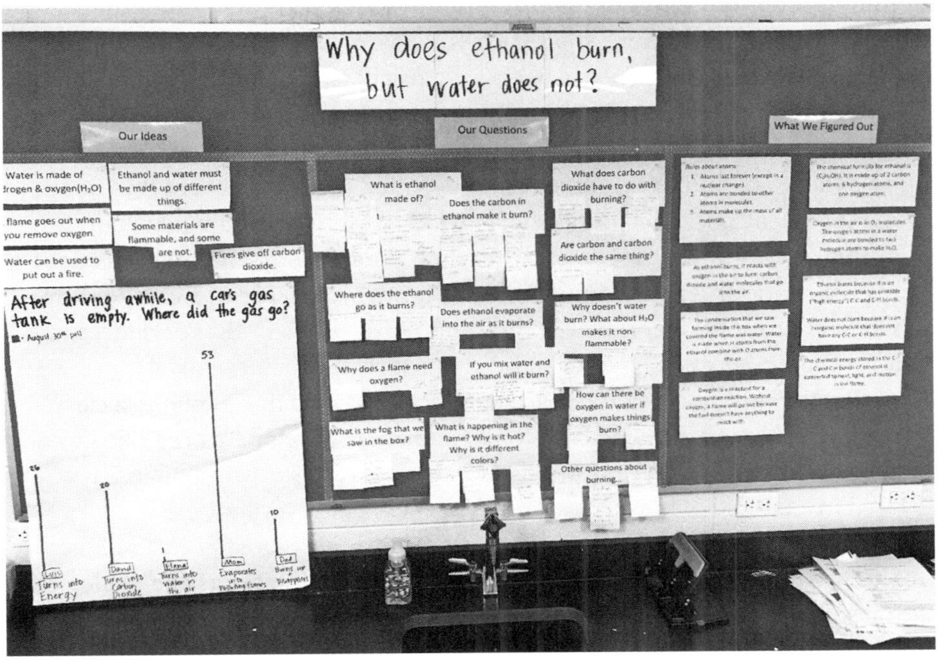

Permission for use granted by Dr. Johnson.

water in the air, evaporates into polluting fumes, and burns up and disappears. The information from the poll gave Dr. Johnson insight into likely student preconceptions, which helped her shape the next learning activities so that the experiences would help advance students' understanding. By posting students' ideas and questions on the driving question board, Dr. Johnson was able to capitalize on the students' curiosity to engage in authentic scientific inquiry, exemplifying the ambitious teaching practices described in chapter 1. Throughout the unit, each learning activity was explicitly related to students' ideas and questions to make learning relevant and meaningful and keep students at the edge of their learning by uncovering preconceptions and building on prior knowledge.

Using misconceptions to put principle one into action Teachers who are experienced in formative assessment anticipate the range of likely student preconceptions and misconceptions that may be present among their students. They intentionally elicit evidence to identify whether students hold those ideas so that they can provide learning opportunities to challenge student thinking and help them develop more sophisticated ways of understanding. However, science teachers, particularly beginning teachers, may not be aware of the range of student misconceptions, as revealed in the research study that we described in chapter 3.[12]

There are online resources and books for science teachers that document student misconceptions that can be useful to consult when planning a unit or lesson.[13] Furthermore, teachers more easily anticipate student misconceptions when they understand how misconceptions can develop, whether through incomplete representations, real-world experiences, or a mismatch between everyday and more formal scientific vocabulary. As part of the misconception research project described in Chapter 3, a classification scheme for science misconceptions was developed, organized into seven categories. Descriptions of the categories are shown in table 5.1.[14]

An example of how the lack of awareness of the limitations of a model can lead to a misconception is a teacher who participated in the study. She was skeptical that students would ever select Jupiter as the center of the solar system (this work predated Pluto's downgrade to a dwarf planet) when other more attractive answers (sun, Earth, moon) were offered in a multiple-choice question. However, to the teacher's surprise quite a few students selected that answer. She asked why, and in response they turned and pointed to the poster of the solar system that showed the edge of the sun on the left-hand side and the other planets arrayed in order to the right, according to their distance from the sun. Jupiter was the center planet on the poster. This experience led to a discussion among the research participants about how they were able to interpret representations of scientific ideas in ways that differed from the students' interpretation. Uncovering these ways of thinking is necessary before a teacher can support students to deepen their understanding.[15]

Another project that focused on student misconceptions is James Minstrell and Pamela Kraus' Diagnoser assessment system. This project emerged as a result of an epiphanic experience during which Minstrell realized that, while his students could recite theorems and formulas in a physics class, they could not apply their knowledge to a novel situation.[16] In the Diagnoser project, Minstrell developed what he termed "benchmark

TABLE 5.1 A classification system for how misconceptions might develop in science

CATEGORY	DESCRIPTION	EXAMPLE MISCONCEPTIONS
Diagrams, Models, and Other Representations	Diagrams, models, and other types of representations used in scientific discourse and materials can be inaccurate, incomplete, or poorly scaled, or the limitations of the model are not articulated	• the solar system (pictured with the sun on the left and planets arrayed to the right, not in scale) • the circulation of blood (images show different colors of blood in veins and arteries) • linear progression from monkeys to apes to humans
Abstractions, Generalizations, and Simplifications	Characteristics and descriptions of scientific groups, objects, or concepts can be too abstract, general, or simplified	• all living things move • magnets attract all metals/silvery objects • all bacteria are harmful • all birds fly • all mutations are harmful
Language and Vocabulary	Words, phrases, and descriptors used in everyday communication can convey a constricted, confusing, or completely different meaning in scientific communication	• speed and velocity are the same • weight and mass are the same • heavy and dense are the same • continents are "drifting" • literal sense of sun "rise/set" • "empty" glass ignores presence of gases
"Facts"	"Facts" based solely on intuition or faulty reasoning can be misleading, inaccurate, or incomplete in relation to various scientific explorations, studies, or concepts	• an object at rest has no forces acting on it • heavier objects fall faster • plants need soil to grow • fish breathe water • gasses have no mass • deserts are hot
Real-World Experiences and Perceptions	Everyday life and perceptual experiences can be misleading, inaccurate, or incomplete in relation to various scientific explorations, studies, or concepts	• heavier objects fall faster • sun and stars "move" across the sky • anthropocentrism/geocentrism • five human senses • "earth's shadow" on the moon causes the lunar phases
Common Sayings, Beliefs, and Myths	Widely heard/communicated sayings, beliefs, or myths can be misleading, inaccurate, or incomplete in relation to various scientific explorations, studies, or concepts	• "lightning never strikes twice in the same place" • humans coexisted with/killed the dinosaurs • a light-year is a unit of time • camels store water in their humps • meteors are "falling stars"

lessons" that he used to start a unit. These lessons often began with a presentation of a puzzling situation and a question to stimulate students' initial ideas, such as "What would happen if . . . ?" Subsequent learning activities tie back to the benchmark activity, and students are constantly asked to think about how the new activity helps them understand the previous problem situation.

As Minstrell notes, "By listening to students' arguments, the teacher can learn what related experiences make sense to them.[17] In this way, formative assessment practice is an integral part of teaching and learning, permitting Minstrell to respond to and build on students' initial ideas right from the start of the unit. Recall from chapter 1 that ambitious teaching involves eliciting student ideas and responding to their emerging ideas as the lesson unfolds, which is exactly what Minstrell was doing.

To assist teachers, there are many resources in science education that document the kinds of preconceptions that students often have.[18] These resources cannot fully capture the breadth of preconceptions and naive understandings that students will bring to the classroom, but can be helpful references and resources for teachers when designing either a driving question or a benchmark lesson to surface whether those ideas, or other related ideas, are present among the class. As teachers gain classroom experience, particularly when teaching the same course for several years in a row, they are able to notice predictable patterns in student thinking, a feature of developing expertise.[19]

An understanding of likely student misconceptions, as well as increasingly sophisticated levels of student understanding, is important for teachers as they listen to student discussions, examine student work, and respond with appropriate learning activities to help students extend their current understanding. Learning progressions are one source that can help teachers' understanding of how students' thinking develops. Two science education researchers, Lei Liu and Teresa Jackson, describe progressions as "a road map that shows how a student's qualitative understanding of particular ideas or practices is likely to change with appropriate instruction."[20] Liu and Jackson also offer some cautions about learning progressions, both in terms of the limited number of validated learning progressions, and the insufficient attention to the three dimensions of science learning in the NGSS. However, existing validated learning progressions can be a useful tool for teachers—for understanding the range of student ideas that might be present in a particular classroom, and for helping them plan next steps to develop student ideas to more sophisticated levels. We will explore the use of learning progressions more fully in chapter 7.

Principle Two: Knowledge of What It Means to "Do Science"

In too many science classrooms, scientific inquiry, as it had been called pre-NGSS, has been treated as something that occurs on a periodic basis, and involves students following prescribed laboratory procedures to demonstrate what they had already been told would happen. As a result, students' experiences did not represent how scientists actually construct knowledge in either science or engineering. There were limited opportunities for students to develop scientific questions, to design inquiries to answer those questions, or to develop and revise models to make and test predictions.

In this regard, the NGSS emphasize the importance of students investigating phenomena and place greater emphasis on the integration of scientific practices with the other dimensions of NGSS. Investigating a phenomenon and developing evidence-based explanations more accurately reflects how knowledge is constructed by scientists, and also requires engagement in all the practices of science. Formative assessment becomes an integral part of an investigative process, helping teachers shape learning opportunities in response to evidence of student thinking. For example, evidence might show which students are struggling to understand how new data provides insight into the phenomenon under investigation, or who is struggling with data collection, and so on. Once teachers have this information, they can make decisions about how to assist students to resolve their struggles.

Example of principle two in action Returning to Dr. Johnson's classroom, we see how students use scientific practices as an integral and essential part of a unit so that the students are learning like scientists. Notice in her unit on genetics how Dr. Johnson structures the initial activity to fully explore initial student thinking about a phenomenon, and then she uses that information to inform her next steps.

In a previous unit, students developed an explanation to answer the question, "How does a baby develop from a single cell?" In doing so, they learned three big ideas: (1) each cell contains DNA which encodes instructions for making proteins; (2) every cell of the human body is a copy of the first cell created by the union of the sperm and egg; (3) cells differentiate into different types by expressing different genes to make the specific proteins necessary to carry out their function. Dr. Johnson's primary goal for the new genetic unit was that students would extend their learning in relation to these three big ideas to understand that alleles, different forms of the same gene that differ in their nucleotide sequence, can alter the structure and function of a protein.

When Dr. Johnson began the genetics unit, she used a video to introduce a set of unusual twins, Lucy and Maria. Lucy has pale skin, red hair, and blue eyes, and Maria has caramel skin, dark brown hair, and brown eyes. This phenomenon was used to stimulate ideas about the driving question, "How can Lucy and Maria look so different if they are twins?"

After the students had viewed the video, they shared their ideas and questions about why the girls looked so different. Dr. Johnson allowed time for individual thinking and writing as well as small- and whole-group sharing. She wanted to ensure that all students had the opportunity to think about the phenomenon and contribute their thinking to the class, regardless of their level of background knowledge or scientific literacy. The mixture of individual and collective responses provided multiple sources of evidence of learning for Dr. Johnson, which helped her refine subsequent learning activities to extend the students' ideas.

Students represented their individual thinking, and the ideas and questions that they had, by writing on sticky notes, which they posted on the driving question board to provide a snapshot of whole-class thinking. Throughout the unit, Dr. Johnson and the students referred to the driving question board to identify and document "what we have figured out" about the phenomenon, and how their thinking had changed. The driving question board represented to the students what it means to "do science" because it mirrored the process that scientists use to figure out natural phenomena.

Reflecting on her practice, Dr. Johnson noted that this initial lesson was perhaps the most important lesson of the unit, because it allowed her to formatively assess students' thinking about a topic to uncover their funds of knowledge from which she could later draw. It also allowed her to elicit students' interests and experiences related to the phenomenon that she could use to motivate their learning throughout the unit. Figure 5.2 shows

FIGURE 5.2 The driving question board for a genetics unit of study

Permission for use granted by Dr. Johnson.

the driving question board toward the end of the unit, on which the teacher had grouped similar student ideas and questions generated in the first lesson and, as learnings emerged, documented those ideas both with headings and summaries of responses provided by the students.

Over the course of the genetics unit, the students first learned about three key genes that influence the amount and type of melanin that a person produces, and therefore control their skin, eye, and hair color. Then they made hypotheses about the particular versions of these alleles that the twins' parents have, and developed a model of the process of meiosis to explain how the girls' mother passed different alleles to her twins (she is biracial and, we assume, heterozygous for all three genes).

Analysis of the example Dr. Johnson's classroom practice illustrates ambitious teaching and many of the Framework guiding principles introduced at the beginning of this chapter. First, she provided students with an opportunity to act as investigators around a core idea in genetics in a way that connected to their own experiences and promoted equity. She helped all students make connections between their lived experiences and school, and to generate questions that were of interest to them. We also saw evidence of both formative assessment and disciplinary knowledge at work. Dr. Johnson drew on her science knowledge to identify a phenomenon that would interest the students and provide a rich entry point into the unit of study. By eliciting students' ideas and questions, she could identify misconceptions which she could then address during the unit. She was also able to gain information about the students' funds of knowledge that she used to support the collective learning of the class over time.

By starting with students' ideas and questions about a phenomenon, she modeled the use of scientific practices, and subsequently tied all of the activities in the unit to the driving question. In some instances, in this unit, students would employ scientific practice skills to learn from text-based resources or other forms of second-hand inquiry (this is not represented in the example, but was reported by Dr. Johnson). In contrast to more traditional science teaching approaches, students were not just presented with the results of Mendel's experiments from crossbreeding plants to memorize. Instead, Dr. Johnson helped her students apply what was learned in those experiments to inform their understanding of the driving question that was the focus of the unit.

Through the three-part structure of the driving question board, Dr. Johnson provided a public record of the questions the students started with, what they learned about each one, and the conceptual understandings that they acquired along the way, thereby also putting *HPL* principle two into action. Dr. Johnson used the board as a structured way to capture and document the ideas that students proposed, as a reference point to contextualize investigations, and as a record of new, updated understandings as they investigated the phenomenon. This visual record reminded students of how they were creating their own understanding of the phenomenon and not just memorizing facts from a textbook.

Principle Three: Supporting Metacognition and Student Self-Monitoring

The final principle focuses on the importance of student metacognition and self-monitoring.[21] A range of strategies can be used to support students over time to develop an understanding of themselves as learners. Strategies can include the teacher setting individual or class learning goals and monitoring the students' understanding as they process a complex text on a science phenomenon, and the students monitoring their own progress toward learning goals, recognizing the current status of their learning, and developing approaches to support their own learning.

Engaging students in metacognitive thinking is a core goal of formative assessment and can be supported through scaffolding activities that help students develop these skills, for example, discussions in which students discuss their thinking and identify conflicting arguments about why a phenomenon occurs. Teachers play an important role in supporting students in these discussions by deciding in the moment how to track competing explanations while also keeping the discussion focused and moving in a productive way and ensuring all students' participation.

The previous example of the driving question board is one approach to helping students monitor their own learning. Similarly, Minstrell's benchmark experiment became a reference point throughout the unit as the students reflected on how each new learning experience helped them better understand the initial experience. The following middle school example illustrates the teacher's use of a variation in backward design as a formative assessment strategy to explore student understanding at the beginning of a unit in order to inform instructional planning and support student self-monitoring.[22]

Example of principle three in action The students in Mr. Spencer's seventh-grade science class came from over a dozen feeder elementary schools and so had a wide variety of previous experiences in science. He aimed to design each unit of study based both on the key learning he wanted them to develop by the end of the unit, and on their previous experiences in elementary school science.

To help him gain awareness of students' prior knowledge, he gave each student the end-of-unit assessment at the start of the new unit. He asked the students to "traffic light" the assessment questions by putting a green dot by those that they knew and could possibly answer already, a yellow dot by questions where they felt they knew something about that part of the topic but were partly unsure of the answer, and a red dot against any question where they had little or no idea about what it meant.

To provide additional insight into student thinking, beyond their self-reported understanding through using the dots, Mr. Spencer also asked students to provide an explanation to any two of the questions that they gave a green dot, or some ideas about two questions if they had only used yellow dots. The teacher then quickly reviewed their self-reports, noting those areas that students indicated needed little or no work (green dots), and those that needed considerable work (red dots). He also skimmed the students' written explanations to gain additional insight about student understanding, emerging ideas, and misconceptions.

Analysis of example Although students came to his class from many different schools, Mr. Spencer found strong commonalities in experience from the evidence he obtained through the dot strategy. He was able to review his existing unit plans and make necessary adjustments so that he could focus on unfamiliar or challenging areas. Mr. Spencer was also able to use insights that he gained about student ideas from their written responses. These explanation samples helped him identify areas that he needed to probe further to really understand student thinking, and they informed the selection and design of learning activities to build on and develop students' emerging understanding ideas.

The teacher used the traffic light student self-assessment strategy to help his students think about their previous learning. However, he did not rely solely on the self-reports, but also collected student responses for some of their green and yellow dot questions to act as a check on whether students were able to accurately assess their own understanding. He also incorporated what he learned from their responses back into the learning activities, particularly the responses that students provided for questions that they marked with a yellow dot. He would be able to refer back to these emerging ideas as the unit got under way, with the advantage that students would recognize that the information they provided had impacted his planning. Mr. Spencer showing that he valued the students' initial ideas strengthened the collaborative culture in the classroom.

A final example of formative assessment that supports student self-monitoring relates to an aspect of the NGSS mentioned in the introduction, the importance of supporting students in developing an appreciation for the "beauty and wonder of science." In this example, the teacher asks questions at the end of the lesson that focus on that aspect of science.[23] Notice that he considered how students would respond to an initial probe and was ready to address their anticipated misconception. Notice, too, that he provided a variety of learning opportunities for students and paid attention to their beliefs about learning science.

Example of principle three in action Mr. Rhodea began a unit on plant growth by asking his class of fifth graders to describe what plants need to grow. Based on previous experience, he anticipated that they would say plants need soil, sun, water, and air. So he prepared a follow-up question, "Why do they need soil?" A student responded that soil provided food for plants. He then asked them, "Why do they need the sun?" Other students answered that plants need sun for the same reason, and that plants use the sun to make their own food. One student knew the term photosynthesis, but could not fully explain it. Mr. Rhodea then asked the question, "Why do plants need to eat the soil if they make their own food in their leaves?" and, after a little discussion, "If plants eat the soil then why don't we find all large trees growing out of holes?"

Shifting from the broad discussion about plant growth, Mr. Rhodea wanted to narrow the focus to oxygen and carbon transfer and the production of oxygen as a by-product of photosynthesis. To help students develop a mental model of this process, Mr. Rhodea used small plastic cubes to represent atoms and molecules: two blue cubes for a carbon dioxide molecule, two blue cubes for the oxygen atom, and one green cube for the carbon atom. He wanted students to understand that as they breathe in oxygen (two blue cubes) their lungs attach a carbon to it (one green cube) and then they breathe it out, losing mass in the process. By contrast, when a plant breathes in carbon dioxide, it removes the carbon (the one green cube) gains mass, and oxygen is the by-product.

The teacher used a student volunteer to stand at the front of the class to act as a plant. The other students handed the "plant" student carbon dioxide cubes, one after the other, and the "plant" broke off the green carbon cubes, kept hold of them, and passed along the blue oxygen cubes, modeling how plants grow. Eventually, the "plant" had a difficult time holding on to all the green cubes in his hands, illustrating that the plant is gaining mass by keeping a carbon atom from each carbon dioxide molecule.

Mr. Rhodea continued with questions for students to consider: "What then does the soil provide for the plant? Where are the mouths and nose of the plant?" He wanted the students to challenge their earlier thinking as they recognized that the plant was able to grow without drawing "food" from the soil. These questions launched a lesson from the California Academy of Sciences in which students use a microscope to examine the surface of plants' leaves and determine how carbon dioxide enters a leaf.[24] The students investigated leaves from different plants around the school yard at the microscopic level. They discovered stomata as well as many other plant structures and features. The students had an opportunity to share their discoveries with one another, which was very motivating for them because they were *their* discoveries.

Finally, the lesson concluded with a review of the learning goal outlined by the NGSS performance expectation, and with Mr. Rhodea's questions, "How did it feel to do science today? How do you feel about your school environment now? Is this environment worth taking care of?" Mr. Rhodea also made a point to comment to his students, "I am so proud of you all, it is a privilege to work with such fine scientists." The final metacognitive questions (*HPL* principle three) connected the students to the natural environment they find themselves in each day while they are at school, and also gave Mr. Rhodea insights into whether and how they were beginning to develop an appreciation for the environment.

Analysis of example In this example, Mr. Rhodea's learning goals related to the students' ability to develop a scientific argument that plants get the materials they need for growth chiefly from air and water, based on the modeling activity and their observations. From his previous experience and understanding of fifth-grade students' thinking, Mr. Rhodea anticipated how his students would respond to his initial question and designed a set of learning experiences to guide them to a deeper understanding of plant growth. At the same time, he was also attending to students' beliefs about science, to their feelings about the learning process, and to what they learned about the environment. Surfacing students' feelings about science supports the important goal he has for students: to develop an appreciation of the beauty and wonder of science.

In the next section, we explore the intersection between teaching and learning science and formative assessment by focusing on a specific aspect of formative assessment: learning goals and success criteria. We provide two examples of how teachers can use the NGSS to develop lesson-sized learning goals and criteria for success.

THE INTERSECTION BETWEEN THE DISCIPLINE OF SCIENCE AND FORMATIVE ASSESSMENT

In chapter 1, we introduced the FAST SCASS definition of formative assessment and the practices that support the formative assessment process. The first practice is "clarifying learning goals and success criteria within a broader progression of learning." We also noted Shulman's advice to consider how effective formative assessment involves the interaction of the generalizations and particularizations and their engagement with each other.[25] While establishing learning goals is an essential formative assessment practice that generalizes across grade levels and disciplines, the content and use of learning goals will reflect disciplinary differences. For instance, an ELA teacher is working toward a different set of disciplinary outcomes (see chapter 4) compared to a science teacher, and as a result will think differently about learning goals.

Creating learning goals and success criteria is a foundational formative assessment skill for science teachers in order to narrow the focus for specific lessons that build toward broader performance expectations for a unit of study. Below, we provide two examples of creating learning goals and success criteria from life science progressions, excerpted from the NGSS's Appendix E, which extend from kindergarten through high school (table 5.2).

Learning Goals and Success Criteria: Elementary School

The NGSS performance expectation for grades 3 through 5 states that students should be able to "support an argument that plants get the materials they need for growth chiefly from air and water." As is the case for all NGSS performance expectations, it is constructed from three dimensions:

- Disciplinary Core Idea (LS1.C, 3–5): Organization for Matter and Energy Flow in Organisms—Plants acquire their material for growth chiefly from air and water

TABLE 5.2 The progression of learning for two life science core ideas

	K–2	3–5	6–8	9–12
LS1.A Structure and function	All organisms have external parts that they use to perform daily functions.	Organisms have both internal and external macroscopic structures that allow for growth, survival, behavior, and reproduction.	All living things are made up of cells. In organisms, cells work together to form tissues and organs that are specialized for particular body functions.	Systems of specialized cells within organisms help perform essential functions of life. Any one system in an organism is made up of numerous parts. Feedback mechanisms maintain an organism's internal conditions within certain limits and mediate behaviors.
LS1.C Organization for matter and energy flow in organisms	Animals obtain food they need from plants or other animals. Plants need water and light.	Food provides animals with the materials and energy they need for body repair, growth, warmth, and motion. Plants acquire material for growth chiefly from air and water, and process matter and obtain energy from sunlight, which is used to maintain conditions necessary for survival.	Plants use the energy from light to make sugars through photosynthesis. Within individual organisms, food is broken down through a series of chemical reactions that rearrange molecules and release energy.	The hydrocarbon backbones of sugars produced through photosynthesis are used to make amino acids and other molecules that can be assembled into proteins or DNA. Through cellular respiration, matter and energy flow through different organizational levels of an organism as elements are recombined to form different products and transfer energy.

- Science and Engineering Practices: Engaging in Argument from Evidence—Support an argument with evidence, data, or a model
- Crosscutting Concept: Energy and Matter—Matter is transported into, out of, and within systems

The progression of the core idea gives an upper elementary teacher a sense of what students should have been exposed to in the earlier grades, and how it will connect to their middle school science learning. In this specific instance, the performance expectation is not so broad that it cannot directly function as a learning goal for a sequence of lessons in which students explore the factors that impact plants' growth. A phenomenon such as finding plants growing out of a rock or on a rooftop can be an engaging way to start students thinking about this topic. Using a driving question board similar to the one shown earlier, a teacher might pose a question such as "How is a plant able to grow out of a rock?" or "What does a plant need to survive?" Developing a set of success criteria is an important next step for a teacher as he or she considers learning activities that will provide insights to students to answer the driving question. One possible set of three success criteria for this performance expectation is:

- Describe the structure of the plant
- Explain how the structure of plants enables them to acquire material to grow from air and water
- Construct a model to convince someone that plants grow mainly because of the air and water they get

These success criteria will serve multiple roles for the teacher. They will support the alignment of learning activities and formative assessment opportunities with the learning goal or performance expectation, communicate to students how they will know if they have achieved the learning goal, support student self-assessment and/or peer feedback, and guide teacher reflection on whether the activities planned for the lesson are likely to result in the learning expressed by the success criteria.

Sometimes, success criteria might reveal what a teacher wants students to discover for themselves through a sequence of learning activities (such as, plants grow from the material they acquire from air and water). Depending on the structure of the lesson, a teacher may choose to reveal the success criteria after students have been engaging with the driving question and learning activities for a little while.

Learning Goals and Success Criteria: High School

An NGSS performance expectation for high school states that students should be able to "Construct an explanation based on evidence for how the structure of DNA determines the structure of proteins, which carry out the essential functions of life through systems of specialized cells." It is built from three dimensions, listed below:

- Disciplinary Core Idea (LS1.A, 9–12): Structure and function—DNA is a warehouse of the genetic code that provides information that controls cellular structure and activities
- Science and Engineering Practices: Developing and using models—model how DNA is transcribed into RNA and how RNA is translated into polypeptide protein; make models to describe the function of DNA
- Crosscutting Concept: Structure and function—the way in which an object or living thing is shaped and its substructure determines its properties and functions

Unlike the previous performance expectation, this example is too large to be a learning goal in a sequence of lessons, and so a teacher will need to develop a smaller learning goal that students will need to meet as they work toward the larger performance expectation. For example, a learning goal might be, "Understand how the *structure* of DNA relates to its *function*." A teacher could then use this learning goal to develop a series of success criteria such as:

- Define the terms *structure* and *function*
- Describe the structure of DNA
- Explain why the base pair rule means DNA forms complementary strands and a double helix
- Use a DNA sequence (structure) to construct a polypeptide/protein (function)
- Explain how a mutation (change in DNA base sequence) may, or may not, alter the function of a protein[26]

The combination of the learning goal and success criteria provide a strong foundation from which the teacher can then build a series of learning activities with embedded formative assessment opportunities to help develop and deepen the students' understanding across the three dimensions of NGSS. The learning goal and success criteria also provide a foundation for formative assessment, helping teachers focus on what they want students to understand and be able to do, rather than focusing on students completing the activities as a goal. The learning progression for LS1.A in table 5.2 is also a useful formative assessment tool, since it provides the teacher with information about what the students ought to understand already from previous grade levels as a starting point for thinking about prior learning.

IMPLICATIONS FOR TEACHER LEARNING

In this chapter, we have examined what students need to learn in science, and how teachers can help students approach learning in science in a way that more closely follows how scientists work. We have looked at the opportunities and challenges posed by NGSS, and how teachers can effectively support learning that attends to the three dimensions of science through formative assessment. As noted in chapter 1, we use the idea of teachers' disciplinary knowledge throughout this book to refer to both the knowledge that a teacher needs to have about the substance and syntax of their particular discipline, and to their understanding of the development of students' understanding of disciplinary ideas. The NGSS require teachers to integrate the core disciplinary ideas with scientific practices and crosscutting concepts in order to help students understand scientific phenomena. In parallel with chapter 3, focused on mathematics, we observed how an understanding of student misconceptions and the use of learning progressions can support classroom teaching and learning and formative assessment practices.

We have seen examples of science teachers in action and noted the importance of their knowledge of science and their understanding of how students learn science. One way in which formative assessment has been characterized is as a series of three questions: Where are we going? Where are we now? How to close the gap?[27] These questions help us consider the types of knowledge that teachers need to have.

First, teachers need to understand the NGSS deeply to be able to translate them into appropriate learning goals and success criteria as a foundation from which to identify important, scientifically meaningful learning experiences for students. Likewise, coconstructing learning goals or success criteria with students also requires disciplinary knowledge, so that students can explore ideas within certain boundaries that make sure the student goals are feasible.

Second, selecting tasks and involving students in discussions, making sense of what students say and do, and understanding student misconceptions and initial ways of thinking are all important skills that allow teachers to gain insight into students' current learning status. Each method for eliciting evidence of student understanding also requires strong disciplinary knowledge to understand what constitutes evidence, create the opportunity for evidence to be obtained, and to appropriately interpret what might be only partial explanations from students.[28] The final step of closing the gap between current and intended learning requires science teachers to respond quickly and flexibly to structure next learning opportunities for students based on evidence. Again, disciplinary knowledge is needed to create new learning experiences, often in the moment, that allow students to develop understanding rather than simply being told what they ought to understand.

Science teachers are not born knowing how to engage in formative assessment practices, nor does proficiency in science guarantee their understanding of student ways of thinking about science. Rather, these skills can be developed beginning in preservice education through induction and in-service. We pick up the topic of developing teachers' knowledge and skills with formative assessment more fully starting in chapter 7.

SUMMARY: THE BIG IDEAS OF CHAPTER 5

- An equity focus in science includes actively involving students in the practices of science, building on students' cultural funds of knowledge to help them develop their understanding of scientific concepts, providing rich discourse opportunities for students to learn with and from others, harnessing their personal interests, and providing students with multiple ways to demonstrate their understanding. Formative assessment is an integral part of these various steps.

- The Next Generation of Science Standards (NGSS) present performance expectations that combine the three dimensions of science (disciplinary core ideas, crosscutting concepts, and science and engineering practices) to emphasize the importance of students engaging in the practices as they learn about the disciplinary core ideas and crosscutting concepts.
- Applying the three principles from *How People Learn* to science teaching and learning emphasizes the importance of identifying and building off students' initial understanding to help them develop deeper conceptual understandings, engaging in teaching and assessing that honors the relationships among the three dimensions of science, and helping students engage in metacognition through the identification of their own learning goals and self-assessment of progress toward those goals.
- Teachers need to understand the NGSS deeply to be able to translate them into appropriate learning goals and success criteria as a foundation for formative assessment.
- Teachers can gain insight into students' current learning status through purposeful selection of tasks and through engaging students in discussions that reveal misconceptions and initial ways of thinking.
- Teachers can help close the gap between current and intended learning through quickly and flexibly structuring next learning opportunities for students.

CHAPTER 6

Formative Assessment in Social Studies

Recently, the Organisation for Economic Co-operation and Development (OECD) published a position statement on the future of education and skills, which called for some wide-ranging education reforms in member countries to prepare students to meet the "unprecedented" social, economic, and environmental challenges the world is facing. A clear message in the paper is that "education needs to aim to do more than prepare young people for the world of work; it needs to equip students with the skills they need to become active, responsible and engaged citizens."[1]

The OECD message has echoes of a statement from the National Council for the Social Studies (NCSS) which was published several years earlier: "The primary purpose of social studies is to help young people make informed and reasoned decisions for the public good as citizens of a culturally diverse, democratic society in an interdependent world."[2]

From these two sources, we can infer that today's students will be confronting complex and pressing issues as adults and, as a result, will need to have some depth of historical, political, and cultural understanding to make good decisions for the benefit of their world.

The NCSS elaborates this inference: "students need the intellectual power to recognize societal problems; ask good questions and develop robust investigations into them; consider possible solutions and consequences; separate evidence-based claims from parochial opinions; and communicate and act upon what they learn."[3]

In this chapter, we focus on how students can be supported through engaging with the disciplinary content and practices of social studies to acquire knowledge and skills in preparation for the complex world they face in and beyond school. Specifically, we consider the epistemic knowledge—knowledge about the discipline of social studies, ways of thinking in the discipline, and their associated analytic practices—and how teachers can use discipline-based formative assessment to support their students in acquiring social studies knowledge and practices. We structure our review using the *College, Career, and Civic Life (C3) Framework for Social Studies: Guidance for Enhancing the Rigor of K–12 Civics, Economics, Geography, and History* (C3 Framework) and related commentary and analysis as our sources for examining the epistemology of social studies.[4] We anchor our consideration of formative assessment rooted in social studies disciplinary knowledge in two examples of actual classroom practice. We conclude the chapter with a brief discussion of the implications for teacher professional learning.

THE C3 FRAMEWORK AND THE INQUIRY ARC

The C3 Framework, similar to the vision for the science Framework discussed in chapter 5, is intended to be used for enhancing social studies state standards, so its implementation does not necessarily depend on its formal adoption by states.[5] However, the influence of the C3 Framework on social studies learning in US schools has been considerable. For example, as of June 2018, twenty-three states had used the C3 Framework in developing their learning standards and/or frameworks, and it should follow that some districts have aligned their curriculum with it.[6] For these reasons, we use the C3 Framework as the reference point for considering the disciplinary content and analytic practices that K–12 students need to learn in social studies.

The impetus for creating the C3 Framework arose in 2010 when the Common Core State Standards were being released and the Next Generation Science Standards were in development. At the same time, alarmed by the erosion of social studies instruction in many schools, in part because of the emphasis on English language arts (ELA) and mathematics for accountability purposes, the NCSS, along with the Campaign for the Civic Mission of Schools, convened a meeting of organizations representing different aspects of social studies.[7] A decision was made at this meeting to move forward with a framework for informing state standards based on a shared agreement:

> Social studies is an interdisciplinary exploration of the social sciences and humanities, including civics, history, economics, and

> geography, in order to develop responsible, informed, and engaged citizens and to foster civic, global, historical, geographic, and economic literacy.[8]

The C3 Framework resulted from the efforts of many state representatives. With resonances of the OECD position paper cited earlier, it calls for "students to become more prepared for the challenges of college and career," united with preparation for civic life, which entails an awareness of "changing cultural and physical environments," knowledge of the past, the ability to "read, write, and think deeply," and a willingness to "act in ways that promote the common good."[9]

INQUIRY ARC: A MODEL FOR TEACHING AND LEARNING

The C3 Framework uses an Inquiry Arc, a set of interlocking and mutually reinforcing dimensions, to frame the way students learn social studies:

- Developing questions and planning inquiries
- Applying disciplinary concepts and tools
- Evaluating sources and using evidence
- Communicating conclusions and taking informed action

The Inquiry Arc represents a model of teaching and learning that is consistent with the research on ambitious social studies teaching, defined as teachers knowing:

- their subject matter well and seeing in it the potential to enrich students' lives;
- their students well, including knowledge of the students' lived experiences; and
- how to frame instruction using big idea questions that reflect intellectual rigor and relevance to students.[10]

An example of ambitious teaching is a history lesson (available online) titled Lunchroom Fight, from the Stanford History Education Group, in which students are honing their ability to reconcile conflicting claims, consider multiple perspectives, and evaluate the reliability of sources.[11] The teacher introduces the students to the lesson in this way:

> Imagine that you are the principal of a school and you just found out that there was a fight in the lunchroom during lunch. You've asked many students and teachers who witnessed the fight to write down what they saw and who they think started the fight. Unfortunately, you have received many conflicting accounts that disagree not only as to who started the fight, but also as to who was involved and when the fight even started. It's important to remember that NO ONE is just plain lying.

In pairs, the students consider the following questions:

- Why would there be different stories of the event if no one is just plain lying?
- What are the different types of people who might have seen this fight? (e.g., friends of those involved versus people who don't know the kids who were fighting; those who were fighting versus those who were witnesses; adults versus kids)
- What might make one person's story more believable or plausible than another person's?

After the paired discussion, the teacher leads a discussion guided by these questions and issues:

- Why might people see or remember things differently?
- Who has an interest in one kid getting in trouble instead of another kid? Who was standing where? Could they see the whole event?
- How do you determine the plausibility of the stories themselves (considering issues of exaggeration and how the stories fit into what is known about the students' prior histories, for example)? Is the story believable, trustworthy?
- *Time:* Do stories change over time? How might what we remember right after the event differ from what we remember a week later? Does time make the way someone remembers something more or less trustworthy?
- *Physical Evidence:* What kinds of evidence might have an effect on what you believe (bruises, missing objects, et cetera)?

In this lesson, students apply inquiry to a scenario that is relevant to their own lives. They are engaged in intellectual rigor in the discipline through considering a series of substantive questions related to how events are interpreted, remembered, and judged to be trustworthy, and through taking into account people's perspectives and biases. In addition, the students are applying social studies disciplinary skills. They analyze the context in which the events happened to gain a better understanding of people's testimonies, motivations, and perspectives. Students also learn that history is actually written from someone's perspective and, as a consequence, the value of corroboration in assessing the trustworthiness of information presented. This activity represents a touchstone experience for students' future reference when considering the roles of time, memory, bias, or conflicting accounts in other primary source material.

Let us now consider in detail the four dimensions that comprise the Inquiry Arc.

Developing Questions and Planning Inquiries

In social studies, two forms of questions are essential to framing and advancing an inquiry: compelling questions and supporting questions. Compelling questions focus on enduring concerns, including how things work, interpretation and applications of disciplinary concepts, and constructing arguments in response to unresolved issues. The focus on enduring concerns is also intended to drive student curiosity and engagement by creating relevance to students, which is often a struggle when teaching about events far in the past.

Supporting questions focus on descriptions, definitions, and processes on which there is general agreement in the discipline, and entail constructing explanations that advance understanding in response. For instance, a compelling question might be, "Why do we need rules?" because it reflects a social concern relevant to students and an enduring issue in civics. Supporting questions could include, "What are some rules families follow? What classroom rules are important for learning?" Supporting questions are also the guideposts for students in their journey toward answering the compelling question, and they provide natural points for teachers to formatively assess students during an inquiry.

Applying Disciplinary Concepts and Tools

There are four core interrelated disciplines within social studies: civics, economics, geography, and history, each of which "offers a unique way of thinking and organizing knowledge as well as systems for verifying knowledge."[12] Learning concepts and ways of thinking from these disciplines play out across the Inquiry Arc and form the base from which students can begin to answer their compelling and supporting questions. For instance, concepts in civics include participation by others and oneself in a democracy; central to economics is how individuals, governments, and societies choose to use resources; a key concept in geography is that each place on earth has a unique set of local conditions and connections to other places; and history explores how perspectives of people in the present shape their interpretations of the past. An example of a concept in economics, the impact of scarcity of resources and the corresponding trade-offs in terms of resource allocation, could be investigated through the compelling question: "What is the impact of scarcity of resources on people's economic conditions?" along with supporting questions such as, "How is people's financial decision-making affected? What is the difference between producers and consumers in a market economy? What disparities exist across the nation in terms of economic assets and choices?"

Evaluating Sources and Using Evidence

From compelling and supporting questions and relevant concepts and ideas, the Inquiry Arc moves to sources and evidence. Social studies, just like science, is an evidence-based field, and a core feature of the discipline is developing a capacity for gathering, evaluating, and using evidence in responsible ways. Evidence comes in many forms, including historical and contemporary documents, direct observation, graphics, statistics, digital media, legislative actions, and legal rulings.[13] The use of evidence in social studies involves evaluating the relevance of the source, followed by rigorous analysis and the application of the information gained from the analysis to make evidence-based claims to form the basis of conclusions. For example, in a series of lessons from the Stanford History Education Group students investigate the compelling question "Were African Americans free during Reconstruction?" and the supporting questions "What does it mean to be free?" and "In what ways were African Americans free during

Reconstruction?"[14] Students have access to a Reconstruction timeline and a number of evidence sources: Amendments Thirteen to Fifteen of the US Constitution; a Black Code from Opelousas, Louisiana, dated July 3, 1865; a modified statement by a former slave, Henry Adams, made before the US Senate in 1880; portraits of elected African American officials during Reconstruction; and a quote from Sidney Andrews in the *Joint Report on Reconstruction*, 1866. Students work in groups of four, subdivided into team A and team B. Team A argues "African Americans were free during Reconstruction," and Team B argues "African Americans were not free during this period." Students collect data from the sources to support their side of the argument. Each team in the group presents an evidence-based argument, and through discussion, the group aims to reach consensus. Once the students have concluded their discussions, they share their consensus, leading to a whole-class discussion guided by the teacher around the compelling and supporting questions. Their final discussion is to consider whether they think Reconstruction was a success or a failure, based on the evidence sources the groups had analyzed.[15]

Communicating Conclusions and Taking Informed Action

After students have applied disciplinary concepts and have used evidence to investigate their questions, the final dimension of the Inquiry Arc involves them in formalizing their arguments and explanations and in taking action. Students are given opportunities to represent their ideas in a variety of forms and communicate their conclusions to a range of audiences. For example, students who had been conducting an inquiry into the geography of their community through investigating the question, "How do the types of businesses change as we move along this street?" might culminate their study by presenting their conclusions in a report to the local Chamber of Commerce. Whereas, students investigating the question, "Why do these trees near the school show signs of stress?" could decide that the audiences for their conclusions would be the environmental protection service of their local government and the principal of their school.[16] Such communications help connect the work of the students to larger concerns and help them appreciate that informed action can be the result of investigating important societal questions.

Throughout the C3 Framework, strong connections are made to the English Language Arts/Literacy Common Core State Standards (CCSS/

ELA), which we discussed in chapter 4. Questioning skills are specified in the CCSS/ELA and are a driver of social studies inquiry. The CCSS/ELA emphasize analysis, argumentation, and the use of evidence, which as we have seen through the previous examples are central to the discipline of social studies. When students engage in social studies learning, they are developing the skills of reading, analyzing, thinking critically, and working collaboratively, which are also integrated throughout the CCSS/ELA. Students in social studies need to develop CCSS/ELA skills such as identifying the type of source and how that informs purpose to assist in evaluating the usefulness of a source. For example, today, a diary would be regarded as a private piece of writing, and therefore likely to be truthful (why lie when you have no public audience?), but three hundred years ago it was often an official record when written by a government official or military officer.[17]

The C3 Framework promotes engagement with the discipline of social studies and is not focused on acquiring rote knowledge of dates and events, which is likely to be "shallow knowledge."[18] Knowledge in social studies is important, but if students are going to develop capabilities through this discipline that prepare them for college, careers, and civic engagement, they will need to be involved in critical and creative thinking to make meaning of the phenomena that are the focus of their learning.[19]

In the next section, we turn to two examples of practice, characterized by the Inquiry Arc, in which the teacher has embedded opportunities for formative assessment.

LESSON EXAMPLES REFLECTING THE INQUIRY ARC

Example One

The first example is from Ms. Closs's ninth-grade US history course. Notice how Ms. Closs embeds formative assessment into her lesson. As sources of evidence about students' thinking, she uses students' responses on whiteboards along with her probing questions about them, she listens to students' discussions, and she makes use of the students' homework task as well. Based on the evidence, she makes instructional decisions, for example, redirecting students to choose one option, referring students to the Chinese Exclusion Act and anti-immigration political cartoons, and advancing the lesson from one part to the next. Ms. Closs also provides the students with opportunities for peer feedback to improve their work.

Introduction to the lesson In this lesson, Ms. Closs's students were learning about the 1941 attack on Pearl Harbor, and the complexity of the decisions Franklin D. Roosevelt made as the nation's leader in the wake of that national tragedy. In this lesson over four class periods, students specifically focused on the decision to place Japanese Americans in internment camps shortly after the attacks on Pearl Harbor. This lesson was guided by the compelling question "Can we be both free and safe?"

Lesson goal and success criteria The goal for the lesson was that students would develop an understanding of the complexities in decision-making as a leader.

There were two success criteria for this goal: to understand the decision President Roosevelt made about Japanese Americans' internment in the US and why he might have made it, and to gain some understanding of what it is like to be the leader of the nation and the pressures that come with having to make hard decisions that could impact a large number of people.

Students were seated in four groups, each with a whiteboard so that the students could respond collaboratively to the prompts throughout the lesson and log their responses, which Ms. Closs could use as a source of evidence throughout the lesson.

Ms. Closs shared the goal and success criteria with the students and made sure they understood what meeting the goal entailed.

Student discussion Ms. Closs began by stimulating an activity with an imagined scenario to give the students a firsthand experience in decision-making. She used the scenario of dealing with a deadly virus with only two available courses of action to help students understand the moral dilemma and difficulties involved in making a decision when the circumstances are very challenging. She began the activity by saying, "Attention students! There is a virus in this room. You can keep the virus in our room and it will kill us all. Or, you can release the virus from our room, save yourselves but wipe out the entire population of the school. Which do you choose? You have five minutes to deliberate on which decision your group will make."

Once the clock started, students began to debate the best course of action. Many students jumped to quick decisions in either direction. However, as the dialogue continued, students considered the fear of doing harm, the possibility of guilt, and even a desire to protect siblings and loved ones who are in the building as well. Once the five minutes were up, Ms. Closs asked the groups to focus on the rationale behind their choice by responding to the following questions:

- What did you decide?
- What led you to that decision (what was your rationale)?
- What did your group value in making your decision?
- How strongly, on a scale of one to ten, do you feel that you made the right decision?
- You open the newspaper tomorrow; how do you think your decision will be seen by the rest of the world?

Using sources of evidence and adjusting teaching As the students engaged in group discussion about these questions, Ms. Closs circulated, looking at what they had written on their whiteboards and asking probing questions, for example, "Could you explain that more? I am interested in how you came to that decision. What do you mean by that?" The student responses to her questions provided insights into their emerging thinking about the complexities involved in decision-making.

Interestingly, during the group discussion and decision-making process, many students attempted to find loopholes and workarounds to avoid making a decision, such as throwing the virus out of the window. Ms. Closs redirected them to choose one option or the other.

Three groups decided to sacrifice themselves and one group decided to place the virus in the hallway and sacrifice the rest of the school's population. Following the group work, the students shared what they had discussed with the class. One of the groups that had decided on self-sacrifice expressed their rationale: "We made the decision we made because we figured it was only twenty-four of us in the class and there are 260 other people out in the school. If we died that would mean less people would be affected."

Another group added to this response: "We felt similar, but I also had a fear of how I would feel waking up tomorrow knowing that all of those people were dead because of me. Living like that for the rest of my life would eventually eat away at me. I would not want to live that way. It is kind of like I made the right choice but for selfish reasons in a way."

As each group shared their ideas with the entire class, Ms. Closs guided their discussion so that the students came to the realization that there really is no "correct" answer to a scenario such as the one they had considered. Legitimizing the challenges experienced in some of the groups, Ms. Closs referred back to what she had heard during the small group discussions, noting that if everyone was trying to find a way around making the decision at all, the decision was clearly a hard one.

Next steps and eliciting further evidence Based on the student responses to the questions and her probes and the discussion that ensued, Ms. Closs determined that they were beginning to grasp the complexities of decision-making using this particular scenario. She decided that in the next class period they would move on to thinking about the complexity of the decision President Roosevelt faced in 1941.

At the beginning of the next class, the students watched a short summary video about Executive Order 9066 and the three-year-long internment of Japanese Americans. Ms. Closs provided a supporting question for this viewing: "What rationale was given by the government when the executive order was issued?" As they watched the video, the students took individual notes, which they used as a basis for group discussions to explore the rationale. Ms. Closs used the notes and discussion as a formative assessment opportunity to gain insights into how student thinking was developing.

Next, the students read a firsthand account by an internee, Aiko Herzig-Yoshinaga, using the supporting question "How did Japanese Americans experience internment?" Ms. Closs observed that their discussions centered on the harsh living conditions, her separation from her family, the challenges of being newly married in a communal setting, and how gradually the internees made their living conditions a little more comfortable. From her observations, Ms. Closs noted that the students were using social studies disciplinary practices, evaluating sources' strengths and limitations based on their origin, purpose, audience, and perspective. Her evidence for this conclusion was that the students were comparing the video content to the personal account, discussing whether the two sources were corroborative and what information one source had that the other didn't, underscoring the importance of having several sources of information to understand an event.

Group discussions Students were asked to synthesize the information from the text and the video through small-group discussion, which was followed by a whole class share-out.

During that class discussion, the students raised the issue of preexisting racism in the US toward Asian Americans, which they had uncovered in the source material. Based on this discussion, Ms. Closs decided that in the next class period she would refer them back to the Chinese Exclusion Act, as well as to the anti-immigration political cartoons they had examined earlier in the year. This time, the supporting question they used to analyze these resources was: "How had the US viewed and treated Asian Americans prior to internment?"

As she was listening to the discussions, she heard a student making a connection among the events:

"If we were racist towards that group, it would make putting them in internment camps easier. People already did not like them, so it made it acceptable."

Another student added, "It is different but also similar to the Holocaust. I know we did not kill millions of people, but the Nazis were racist and did what they did based on that belief. It is not that much different than the internment camps."

When Ms. Closs brought the students back together as a whole group, she asked these two students to share their ideas, which propelled a class discussion about the role of racism in the internment decision.

After this discussion, students analyzed the decision that President Roosevelt made based on the same questions they had used to think about their own decisions in the starter activity during the first class period. Students responded to the following questions:

- What did he decide?
- What led him to that decision (what was his rationale)?
- What did he value based on the decision?
- How strongly do you feel on a scale of one to ten that he made the right decision?
- How did the news and, subsequently, history look upon his decision?

In their group discussions, students made statements like, "He valued their safety," or "He valued Americans." To encourage the students to think more deeply, Ms. Closs asked probing questions such as, "What do you mean by safety?" and "When you say Americans, remember that two-thirds of the people in the internment camps were American citizens, can you explain more clearly?"

Probing thinking and next steps Several students said they thought Roosevelt's actions were illegal, but when Ms. Closs probed their thinking, they were unable to explain why. In response, Ms. Closs asked them to think about the documents or legislation they had considered previously that they thought Roosevelt had violated. Students recalled the Fourth Amendment: search and seizure, the Fifth Amendment: rights of the accused, due process of the law, and eminent domain. Another student even quoted the Constitution, stating, "All men are created equal." As students discussed these laws, they began to list all the ways in which the internment camps violated the rights of Japanese Americans. Hearing the connections that students were making, Ms. Closs determined that the class was ready to move on in the next class period.

Ms. Closs began the next class by asking the students to consider why President Roosevelt was allowed to violate the basic rights of American citizens; even the Supreme Court supported his ruling, in the case *Korematsu v. United States*. She asked them, in their groups, to refer back to what they thought Roosevelt's rationale was for his decision. Many students mentioned his rationale was fear: fear of an invasion, fear of spies, fear of another attack. Hearing their comments, Ms. Closs invited them to think about how Roosevelt's fear and the fear the American people felt would give him the license to act swiftly. She asked students to think back to when they learned about the Sedition Act of 1918 in World War I, and the expanse of power Roosevelt used as president during the early years of the Great Depression, and consider what all these periods of time had in common. When the students came together as a whole-class group, they all agreed that the commonality was fear; when Americans are fearful and feel unsafe, they are more willing to give up freedoms or the freedoms of others to ensure their own safety.

Concluding the lesson Ms. Closs concluded the lesson by asking the students how this decision is viewed today as opposed to in 1941. One student referred to the decision as a "boo-boo." Another student said it was "a bad choice and sort of a bad mark on his presidency." She then asked students to put themselves in Roosevelt's shoes and decide whether or not they would have signed Executive Order 9066. Students were not willing to respond and seemed uncomfortable. Ms. Closs asked them why they were all so uncomfortable with the decision, and a student said, "It is hard because we know how it is viewed today. We know it is wrong." The student also stated, "I know why he made the decision, but there was probably a better way to solve the problem."

For homework that evening, Ms. Closs asked students to reflect on all the events in the class that day, summarize the history of the internment camps, and reflect on the decision made by Roosevelt. While she thought that generally the class had met the success criteria, she would use their homework task as evidence of their individual level of understanding of the goal.

Peer feedback In the fourth class period, she followed up with a few specific students whom she felt needed more support to consolidate their understanding while the class was involved in creating an argument to answer the compelling question. The students were required to offer an opinion supported by a synthesis of the source evidence to support a claim. Once the students had created their drafts, Ms. Closs asked them to review a peer's argument and provide feedback against these criteria:

- Does the argument answer the compelling question?
- Does the argument make sense?
- Is each claim supported by relevant evidence?

When the students had received their peers' feedback, they were given time to revise their work before turning it in to Ms. Closs.

Post-lesson interview In a post-lesson interview, Ms. Closs reflected that, based on the evidence from their responses and discussion in class, the students were clearly able to grasp the complexity of this period in history. They could see valid reasoning for the president's choices, but also could look at history through a present-day perspective and see the inherent flaws in his decision. Students were able to understand the complexity of making tough decisions as a leader. They felt those pressures firsthand, and they could see how such decisions can impact many people in both a positive and negative way. Along the way, they also gained knowledge of the history of the Japanese American internment camps.

Disciplinary knowledge What disciplinary knowledge did Ms. Closs use in this example? First, she presented the topic of Japanese Americans' internment after the attacks on Pearl Harbor as an enduring concept which has relevance today. Second, she knew how to structure collaborative inquiry-based learning about an important period in US history, which involved her students in critically considering the complexity of a decision and teasing out societal issues of fear, equity, and injustice.[20] Third, she had command of the facts and the concepts that she engaged her students in learning about, and she was knowledgeable about rich resources to motivate the students' investigation. Fourth, because of her disciplinary knowledge, Ms. Closs was able to help make connections between other periods in history and the one they were focusing on. Fifth, she integrated literacy into her students' inquiry by asking them to read and synthesize text and to write an argument focused on discipline-specific content. Sixth, Ms. Closs used embedded formative assessment, which, in combination with her disciplinary knowledge, enabled her to be responsive pedagogically, consistently guiding students to make meaning through discourse and through her questioning. Finally, a goal of social studies is to prepare learners to be informed advocates for an inclusive and equitable society.[21] We would venture to say that Ms. Closs clearly accomplished this goal with her students.

Example Two

In the second example centered on the Inquiry Arc (drawn from direct observations and interviews by the first author), we see a lesson with first- and second-grade students that is part of unit on the study of the local community. The students in this class come from diverse economic backgrounds and many of them speak Spanish in their homes. In Ms. Closs's lesson, she selected the topic of inquiry, whereas in this lesson the students generate their own line of investigation. In this example, we see various ways in which the teacher, Ms. Cárdenas, uses formative assessment opportunities, listening to students' discussion to assess how well they were analyzing their source material, probing their thinking to lead them deeper into their analysis, and making notes about what she heard the students say to guide her next steps in developing their inquiry.

Initiating students' questions Ms. Cárdenas initiated her students' study of how a community is structured and how it functions with a walking field trip around the school's local community. During their walk, the class witnessed a large group of people who were on strike. They were carrying banners with messages about the strike such as "On Strike, Fighting for Equality" and "Equality Fairness Respect." Although the focus of the field trip was not specifically the strike, the students began to ask questions about what was happening: "Why are they on strike?" "Why would people need to go on strike?" "Why do people carry signs that say 'fighting for fairness and equality'?" "Is that what they want?"

The students continued to raise questions about strikes in class discussions after the field trip:

- Why do people go on strike? (Ashley)
- I wonder why those people are on strike? (Esther)
- Well, I did see a sign that says equality and I think that's what they want because equality means that not one person is more valuable or important than another. We are all valuable and should be treated the same. (Chloe)
- I think they need to strike, it's not that they want to. (Esther)
- I agree with Esther. I think people protest to get treated fairly. They should have the right to get what they need, like to be treated equally. (Lindsey)
- Yes, people shouldn't have to strike, they should be treated fairly from the beginning. (Finn)
- I wonder why not everyone is treated fairly? People shouldn't have to wish to be treated better, they should just be treated better. (Kati)
- Why do people protest in front of one building when it's happening in many places? (Isa)

Responding to students' questions Ms. Cárdenas decided to capitalize on the students' curiosity, and to help them understand more about strikes and why people participate, she read and discussed two books with the students:

¡Si, se puede! Yes, We Can! Janitor Strike in L.A., by Diana Cohn, and *The Youngest Marcher: The Story of Audrey Faye Hendricks*, by Cynthia Levinson.[22] Both books helped answer several questions about why some groups of people have gone on strike or participated in marches. The students' interest in strikes and marches persisted, and through continued discussion they generated compelling questions for further inquiry: "Why would people need to ask to be treated fairly?" and "Isn't everyone treated fairly?"

Continuing the inquiry To investigate these questions and understand the history of how people marching, boycotting, and going on strike has changed and continued over time, Ms. Cárdenas involved her students over several days in closely analyzing historical sources of many different types that she had carefully selected to stimulate their thinking and inquiry. The students were placed into four groups, and each group had a set of sources to analyze. Table 6.1 below shows the sources that each group investigated.

TABLE 6.1 Source material for strikes and labor inquiry

GROUP 1	GROUP 2	GROUP 3	GROUP 4
Image: Suffrage envoys from San Francisco greeted in New Jersey on their way to Washington to present a petition to Congress, 1915	Image: Janitors for Justice protest, Los Angeles, May, 1992	Image: Demonstrators protesting the lack of counseling services and educational opportunities for Latino students, 1966	Image #1: Civil Rights March, Washington, DC, August 28, 1963
Image: Suffragists protest Woodrow Wilson's opposition to woman suffrage, 1916	Flyer: "We're sorry we weren't able to clean your offices last night . . ." November, 1989	Image: Children and their parents demonstrate against English-only proposition, Oakland, CA, 1998	Image # 2: Civil Rights March, Washington, DC, August 28, 1963
Image: Women's Strike for Peace and Equality in New York City on August 26, 1970	Flyer: Protesting International Service Systems in Century City, CA, 1990	Image #1: Elementary School Students for Equality March, Los Angeles, 2017	Flyer: Event honoring Rosa Parks, September 23, 1956
Image: Baltimore Women's March, 2018	Image: Housing and commute costs squeeze low-wage workers, Oakland, CA, 2008	Image #2: Elementary School Students for Equality March, Los Angeles, 2017	Image: Montgomery Bus Boycott, November 13, 1956

The students examined their sources guided by these questions provided by Ms. Cárdenas:

- What is happening?
- Why do you think this is happening?
- Why do you think what is happening is important?
- What can you learn from this source?
- What questions do you have?

Eliciting and using evidence of students' thinking As the students were working in their groups, Ms. Cárdenas listened to their conversations to make sure they were evaluating and analyzing their sources, and to probe their thinking so that she could press them to deeper levels of analysis. She made notes about her discussions with each group, and when she reviewed these after the lesson she noticed that the issue of rights had arisen in several groups. For instance, in one group she had heard a student say, "Why do people continue to protest after so many years?" to which another responded, "They have to for their rights." And in another group, a student stated, "I think they should be on strike because they need to show others what they need. They have the right to be on strike."

In response to the evidence about rights that emerged in the lesson, Ms. Cárdenas began the next day's social studies class period by letting the students know what she had heard in groups' discussions the previous day about people's rights. She stimulated further discussion on this topic with the question, "What is a right?" One student answered, "A right is something you are allowed to do that no one can take from you." Ms. Cárdenas continued to propel the discussion, inviting students' ideas about rights with questions such as, "Who has rights?" and "Do we all have the same rights?" Toward the end of the discussion, a student returned to the strike, saying "Why do people do things that are not fair? That has to change and perhaps marches and strikes for human rights would not be necessary!"

Ms. Cárdenas asked the students to return to the groups they had worked with the previous day and to brainstorm what they felt the most important rights to hold on to were. When they convened again as a whole class and used their brainstorming to consider rights in relation to the community, the students concluded that what was of primary importance to them was a community where "We all have the right to feel and be safe."

Making connections to students' own lives To bring the idea of rights back to the individual student's experience, Ms. Cárdenas invited the students to use clay to represent what was an important right for them personally, and to write a caption accompanying it. Here are some examples of what they wrote:

- I have the right to have a family because if I did not have a family I would be very, very sad because I was not going to have someone to love.
- I have the right to play soccer.
- I have the right not to be perfect because we all make mistakes and I do not like to be perfect.
- I want to always have the right to live with my brother because in some places today, families are separated.
- I want to have the right to believe in God because he takes care of me and my family.
- I have the right to be bilingual because if I'm not bilingual I cannot do things like talk to my grandma and read in more than one language.

With evidence from their clay representations and captions, Ms. Cárdenas concluded that her young students had an emerging idea about rights in a democratic society and determined that she would build on it by spiraling back to the issue in social studies lessons later in the year.

Ms. Cárdenas laid out the clay representations and captions in an exhibit, along with the primary sources they had analyzed, the brainstorm they had conducted, and many of the questions and comments they had generated along the way. Other first- and second-grade classes were invited to visit the exhibit with Ms. Cárdenas's students available to guide them and answer questions. The students' parents were also invited to visit. For the parent visit, the students stood by their own clay representations so they could express why they had chosen that particular right and answer any questions asked by the adults.

Analysis of the example A standout feature of this example is how attentively Ms. Cárdenas listens to her students, and how she plans an interdisciplinary inquiry guided by their curiosity from their lived community experience and their ensuing questions. Her strong disciplinary knowledge about concepts, analytic practices, social movements, and disciplinary forms of representation gave her both the security and freedom to engage students' inquiry in response to their questions and interests, rather than being constrained within the parameters of a textbook. Ms. Cárdenas integrated two disciplines of social studies, history and civics; the students investigated the history of different types of protests, and as their study advanced, they were engaged in "developing the skills and dispositions necessary for an active civic life."[23] Ms. Cárdenas used the evidence she obtained from watching and listening to the students to advance the students' inquiry and deepen their learning. The students expressed a claim in their clay representations and captions stemming from their inquiry. Through the parent visits to the exhibit, they were also able to voice their message to a wider audience and gain beginning experience in advocating for something they felt was important to the broader community.[24]

In both lessons, the students' inquiry clearly reflected the four dimensions of the Inquiry Arc and unfolded in response to student ideas as a result of the teachers' formative assessment. In this regard, Ms. Cárdenas' practice is reminiscent of the Swiss sociologist Philippe Perrenoud's distinction between lessons which follow a sequence of prescribed activities, and those in which tasks are not "imposed on learning but [adjusted] once they have been initiated."[25] In the former lesson design, opportunities for formative assessment are restricted and generally become occasions for determining if students got it, or didn't get it, with remediation as the primary pedagogical response—their understanding, or lack thereof, has to be fixed.[26] In the case of Ms. Cárdenas, and also Ms. Closs, formative assessment was a tool to take pedagogical action in support of students' ongoing learning as they engage with important social studies concepts and practices. The lesson progresses in response to learning rather than a more prescribed approach determined solely by a textbook.

In the two examples of practice, we have seen skilled social studies teachers engage in ambitious teaching and use formative assessment to support students' evolving ideas. It is evident from these teachers' practice that their teaching and learning in social studies aligns with the C3 Framework, which goes beyond past approaches where students were passive receivers of knowledge and facts. Contemporary ideas about teaching and learning in social studies situate inquiry at the heart of the discipline, through which students critically question and investigate the world, communicate their conclusions, and take informed action.[27] From this perspective on social studies, which we have seen in action in the classroom examples, what are the implications for teacher professional learning? We begin to answer this question in the section that follows.

IMPLICATIONS FOR TEACHER PROFESSIONAL LEARNING

When considering the implications for teacher learning from our discussion of the C3 Framework and the examples of practice, it is instructive to refer to the NCSS *National Standards for the Preparation of Social Studies Teachers* (Teacher Standards).[28] The Teacher Standards outline the disciplinary knowledge that social studies teachers need to acquire, and the pedagogical practices necessary to be effective in their instruction. In terms of disciplinary knowledge, teachers need to be knowledgeable about the concepts, facts, tools, disciplinary inquiry, and disciplinary forms of representation in each area of social studies they are responsible for teaching (history, geography, economics, and civics). Teachers also need to know about students' own cultures and communities, so that they can leverage these familiar knowledge bases to enhance the students' learning in social studies.[29]

Social studies teachers must be able to plan ambitious learning sequences that integrate content and analytic practices, involve students in disciplinary discourse practices, and respond to their thinking as it emerges. Students need to learn concepts, facts, and tools through a process of disciplinary inquiry, including questioning, gathering and evaluating sources, developing claims and using evidence, communicating conclusions, and taking informed action. The learning sequence should also involve students in creating disciplinary forms of representation—the practices and norms of sharing information tied to each area of social studies—to convey the results of their inquiry.

The Teacher Standards emphasize that enactment of ambitious teaching is contingent on instructional planning that aligns curriculum, instructional strategies, and resources, and that takes into account the intersection of disciplinary knowledge, learners' needs, and diverse contexts. Accomplishing this contingency will be dependent in very large part on teachers' knowledge of and skills in formative assessment. The Teacher Standards also call for learner-centered approaches in classrooms, which are well supported through formative assessment practices. Teachers will need to understand these practices and develop the skills in implementing them so that their teaching can be contingent upon a student's current learning status. As teachers obtain evidence of learning from formative opportunities in their lessons, their disciplinary knowledge provides the interpretive framework through which they can draw inferences about their students' learning and take pedagogical action to move them forward.[30] The Teacher Standards also call out a specific practice of formative assessment—student self-assessment—stressing that it is linked to self-regulation, which is associated with greater learning and achievement success.

We will return to developing teachers' skills with formative assessment more fully in subsequent chapters. However, for now, let us return to where we began this chapter.

ENDING WITH THE BEGINNING

We started this chapter with reference to the OECD position paper about education for the future, which stressed the need for students to become active, responsible, and engaged citizens in preparation for the challenges they will undoubtedly face during their lives. From our discussion of the C3 Framework, the examples of practice, and the disciplinary knowledge and skills teachers need, it is evident that social studies teachers are charged with the development of an engaged and participatory citizenry, as called for in the OECD paper.[31] Social studies teachers need support to develop what Lee Shulman referred to as "the special amalgam between content and pedagogy," beginning in preservice and continuing through their professional careers, so that they are prepared to take on the challenge of "educating students for their future, not our past."[32] We take up this topic in the remaining chapters of the book, beginning with a focus on preservice preparation.

SUMMARY: THE BIG IDEAS OF CHAPTER 6

- The primary purpose of social studies is to help young people make informed and reasoned decisions for the public good as citizens of a culturally diverse, democratic society in an interdependent world.

- The C3 Framework uses an Inquiry Arc, a set of interlocking and mutually reinforcing dimensions, to frame the way students learn social studies.
- Learning in social studies is inquiry-based, and two forms of questions are essential to framing and advancing an inquiry: compelling questions and supporting questions, which provide natural points for teachers to formatively assess students during an inquiry.
- The use of evidence in social studies involves evaluating the relevance of the source, rigorous analysis, and application of the information gained from the analysis to make evidence-based claims to form the basis of conclusions.
- Throughout the C3 Framework, strong connections are made to the English Language Arts/Literacy Common Core State Standards (CCSS/ELA) that emphasize skills central to social studies, for example analysis, argumentation, and the use of evidence.
- Social studies teachers need to be knowledgeable about concepts, facts, tools, disciplinary inquiry, and disciplinary forms of representation, and they also need to know about students' own cultures and communities.

CHAPTER 7

Supporting Teacher Learning During Preservice

Students entering a preservice program have already had more than a decade of experiences in school, across a wide range of subjects and teachers, in what has been termed an "apprenticeship-of-observation."[1] Often those experiences are what motivated individuals to enter the teaching profession and have shaped what they think it means to be a teacher. It is possible that as students they had some experiences with formative assessment and likely that they have a background in the content that they want to teach, although they have probably not thought about that content from the perspective of how students learn. They may also have had some experience reflecting on their own learning. No doubt, they have already formed beliefs about the roles of a teacher and students, which may or may not align with the idea of ambitious teaching presented in chapter 1 and illustrated in chapters 3 through 6.

Teachers' beliefs and attitudes tend not to change much from the time they enter their preservice programs until the time they leave.[2] Their beliefs serve as filters through which new information is processed, which probably accounts for their persistence.[3] The time spent in preservice preparation is an opportunity to introduce new ways of thinking, to reframe or reexamine previous school experiences, and to establish the concept and practice of teachers as reflective practitioners.

This chapter focuses on the initial experiences of preservice teachers that introduce them to the profession of teaching and that provide the foundational knowledge, skills, and habits of mind that they will build on throughout their careers. The chapter is organized into three main sections. First, we outline contemporary scholarship on preservice education, with a focus on three ideas: representations, decompositions, and approximations of practice.[4] In the second section, we apply those ideas to how

FIGURE 7.1 Components that support the development of formative assessment expertise

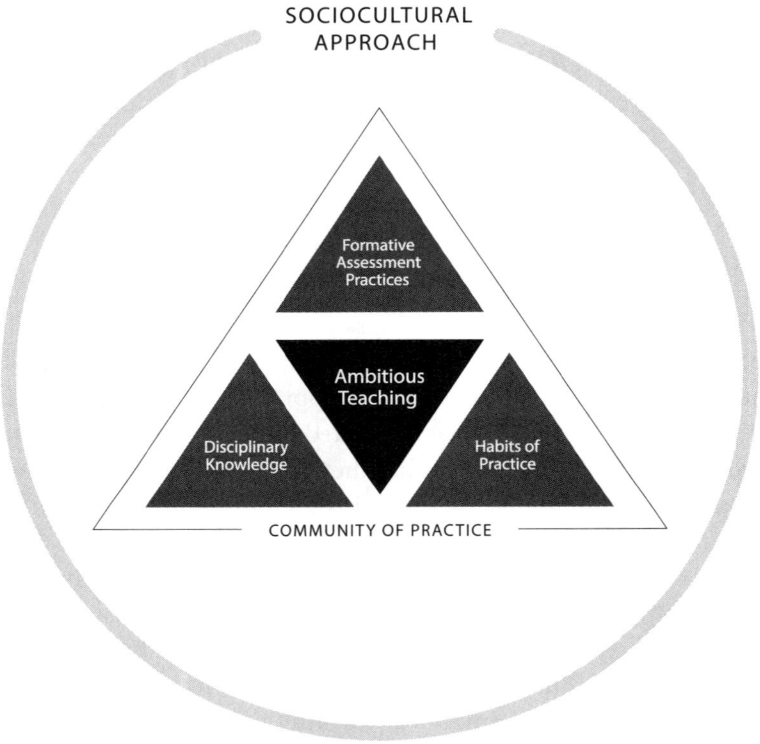

preservice teachers might develop formative assessment expertise across the three interrelated domains (formative assessment knowledge and skills, disciplinary knowledge, and habits of practice) proposed in chapter 2 and represented in figure 7.1. In the final section, we reflect on the importance of linking preservice teachers' coursework and field experiences to support a coherent learning experience.

PERSPECTIVES ON PRESERVICE EDUCATION

The process of preparing potential teachers for classroom work has been a long-term focus of research, and some common threads across fifty years of investigation are evident. Nathanial Gage, described as the "father of modern research on teaching," spent the majority of his distinguished career at the Stanford Center for Research and Development in Teaching.[5] Based on his research, he articulated a set of "technical skills" for teachers, which he described as:

> the attempt to analyze teaching into limited, well-defined, components that can be taught, practiced, evaluated, predicted, controlled, and understood in a way that has proven to be altogether impossible for teaching viewed in the larger chunks that occur over a period of an hour, a day, a week, or a year.[6]

Although this writing is just over half a century old, many of these technical skills still sound familiar today: using an "establishing set" such as an analogy to hook students at the start of a lesson and "achieving closure" to connect old and new understandings at the end of lesson are both recognizable to current teachers. What Gage referred to as "technical skills," contemporary scholars might call core teaching practices or high-leverage practices. It is important to note, however, that while recognizable, some of Gage's technical skills would today be considered dated, as they are very teacher-centric, with a focus on the transmission of knowledge to students and the determination of whether students had learned the presented material. Some will also be less relevant, given changing expectations for what students should know and be able to do and the societal demand that students be prepared for a rapidly changing work environment (see introduction to chapter 1).

While Gage was at Stanford, preservice teachers had opportunities to engage in "microteaching," so called because it was a scaled-down teaching exercise that took place over a shorter time, with fewer students, and would give the teacher an opportunity to practice one or more of the technical skills. The microteaching was captured on videotape, and the preservice teacher was able to review it, receive feedback, and then repeat the lesson with a new group of students to improve performance on the specific technical skill.

The process of microteaching is similar to what has been more recently called by Pamela Grossman (previously at Stanford and now dean of the Graduate School of Education at the University of Pennsylvania) and colleagues an "approximation of practice."[7] Based on a study of how people are prepared for professional practice across several disciplines, these researchers proposed three critical concepts for engaging novices in learning about the important practices of their profession: representations, decompositions, and approximations. These concepts are somewhat overlapping and mutually supporting. First, representations of practice illustrate critical aspects of practice, and as Grossman and her colleagues noted, "comprise the different ways that practice is represented in professional education and what these various representations make visible to novices."[8] Second, decompositions of practice break down professional practices into discrete components that can be approximated "for the purposes of teaching and learning."[9] Third, approximations of practice provide preservice teachers with "opportunities to rehearse and enact discrete components of complex practice in settings of reduced complexity."[10]

The role of the preservice teacher often determines the kind of activity. For example, if the preservice teacher is an observer of a video, which is then discussed in the light of a rubric or other tool to identify key pedagogical moves, then the video likely serves as a representation of practice. Alternatively, if the preservice teacher is being recorded providing feedback to peers who are acting the role of students, then the recorded engagement is an approximation of practice.

A researcher who has focused much of her studies on the work that reform-minded teachers do in the classroom, Magdalene Lampert, noted, "A synonym for the verb form of practice is rehearse."[11] Gage was an early pioneer in the use of technology to support preservice teachers in rehearsing specific pedagogical moves through cycles of practice, feedback, and more practice, and his approach, broadly speaking, continues to still be relevant.

As we shall explore in more detail in the next section, some activities that promote preservice teachers' learning can be either approximations or decompositions of practice. For example, preservice teachers could be given one or more key ideas from a set of standards and asked to develop an engaging, relevant, and accurate introduction to a key idea in a lesson with their peers acting as students. Rehearsing individual components can build confidence for when preservice teachers apply this knowledge in classroom practice.[12] Planning an introduction in this way both decomposes the task of leading a class discussion into smaller pieces, focusing only on the introduction initially, and gives the preservice teachers an approximate experience of presenting that introduction.

BEGINNING THE APPRENTICESHIP JOURNEY

As we described in chapter 2, preservice teachers are beginning their apprenticeship into the teaching profession. Unlike guilds of old, the apprentice is not learning from a single master teacher but has opportunities both within the preservice institution and during field placements to observe and work alongside multiple experts. As we will explore more in the final section of this chapter, when there is coherence in what is being emphasized by the various people with whom the preservice teacher comes in contact, there are opportunities for reinforcement and amplification of critical learning about formative assessment.

As noted earlier, what Gage called technical skills might more currently be called core practices or high-leverage practices. While there are some variations across researchers, a common set of characteristics of core practices have been identified:

- "Practices that occur with high frequency in teaching;
- Practices that novices can enact in classrooms across different curricula or instructional approaches;
- Practices that novices can actually begin to master;
- Practices that allow novices to learn more about students and about teaching;
- Practices that preserve the integrity and complexity of teaching; and
- Practices that are research-based and have the potential to improve student achievement."[13]

Formative assessment is a high-frequency, research-based practice that positively impacts student learning and can be enacted with any curriculum or instructional approach. However, while we believe that preservice teachers are not ready for the complexity of all aspects of formative assessment practice, there is evidence that they can begin to master aspects of the practice, and in so doing learn more about their students and how to teach them.[14]

At the start of this chapter we reprised the framework (figure 7.1) first introduced in chapter 2 for developing teachers' formative assessment expertise that comprises three interrelated domains: formative assessment knowledge and skills, disciplinary knowledge (both knowledge of the content and knowledge of how students learn the content), and habits of practice. In chapters 3 through 6, we explored key features of mathematics, English language arts (ELA), science, and social studies, and the ways in which formative assessment can support students in learning both the content and practices of these different disciplines. In this section of the chapter, we expand on the ways in which knowledge can be represented to preservice teachers and describe experiences to support the development of their skills in each domain of figure 7.1. We use the idea of representations, decompositions, and approximations of practice to distinguish among the various learning opportunities. Table 7.1 presents

TABLE 7.1 Summary of knowledge representations, decompositions, and approximations in three domains of expertise

	KNOWLEDGE REPRESENTATIONS	EXPERIENCES: DECOMPOSITIONS AND APPROXIMATIONS OF PRACTICE
Formative Assessment	• A shared definition of formative assessment • Rubrics that describe a continuum of expertise	• Observe and analyze expert formative assessment practice (decomposition) • Learn and practice specific formative assessment skills (approximation) • Use technology-based simulations
Disciplinary Knowledge	• Disciplinary content standards • Representations of how students learn (e.g., learning progressions)	• Analyze disciplinary standards (approximation) • Use standards and learning progressions to develop learning goals and success criteria (approximation) • Develop hinge-point questions (approximation) • Use learning progressions to examine student work (approximation) • Use learning progressions to plan next instructional steps, including feedback (approximation) • Examine model curriculum materials (decomposition)
Habits of practice		• Examine beliefs that influence formative assessment • Reflect on one's own formative assessment implementation • Observe and analyze preservice teachers' formative assessment implementation (decomposition)

a summary of the key ideas presented in the sections that follow, distinguishing between resources that support the developing knowledge base for preservice teachers (representations), and experiences that allow them to put that knowledge into practice in scaffolded ways (decompositions and approximations).[15]

USING REPRESENTATIONS TO CONVEY IMPORTANT IDEAS ABOUT FORMATIVE ASSESSMENT

Drawing on figure 7.1, we note the importance of preservice teachers having opportunities to develop both an understanding of formative assessment practices and disciplinary knowledge to support those practices. Recall that we consider disciplinary knowledge to comprise both subject matter knowledge and knowledge of how students think about and learn in particular disciplines. In this section, we propose four representations of knowledge for preservice teachers, two that focus on formative assessment, and two focused on disciplinary knowledge.

To support preservice teachers' conceptualization of formative assessment, we suggest that they have access to a definition of formative assessment that provides clarity about what it is, as distinct from other types of assessment, and also rubrics of expertise describing what more or less sophisticated formative assessment practice looks like by discrete dimensions. These two representations of formative assessment should be consistent with each other, with use of one reciprocally supporting deeper understanding of the other. To support the development of disciplinary knowledge, we propose opportunities for preservice teachers to use both a definition of formative assessment and rubrics of expertise, while also acquiring skills in relevant content standards and learning progressions or in other representations of how students develop understanding of the disciplinary content and practices.

Definition of Formative Assessment

The FAST SCASS definition introduced in chapter 1 is one example of a definition that aims to provide clarity about formative assessment.[16] Deconstructing the definition, discussing its elements, reading associated literature, and seeing examples of the definition in action, for example through video exemplars of lessons, are ways in which a developing understanding of formative assessment can be supported.[17]

Preservice teachers' understanding gained from analyses of definitions can be augmented by considering existing instructional frameworks that embed formative assessment. For instance, in a recent book edited by Valerie Mills and Edward Silver, chapter authors connect formative assessment in mathematics with specific instructional perspectives, including Cognitively Guided Instruction, the mathematical tasks framework, and the NCTM mathematical practices.[18] Other chapters in the book connect formative assessment to approaches that are not specific to mathematics, such as culturally responsive teaching and response to intervention.[19] Across the book, it is clear how formative assessment is central to the work of teaching, whether focusing on classroom discourse, the tasks that students complete, or analyzing student work. Similarly, having access to vignettes of formative assessment practice, such as those presented in chapters 3 through 6, help preservice teachers recognize that formative assessment is relevant across subjects, grade levels, and school contexts.

A way to further expand preservice teachers' understanding of a formative assessment definition is to provide opportunities for them to develop a broader understanding of assessment literacy that helps them distinguish formative assessment from other assessment types that they will experience in K–12 teaching contexts.[20] Examination of comprehensive, coherent, and continuous assessment systems to understand the purpose of various assessments will be an important component of developing assessment literacy and understanding the specific role that formative assessment plays in student learning.[21]

While a clear understanding of a definition of formative assessment is likely to be helpful for preservice teachers, we do not anticipate its being specific enough for them to apply it to their own emerging ideas about what is and is not formative assessment. The next section describes a set of rubrics that preservice teachers can use to better understand what the novice-to-expert range of practices can look like.

Rubrics That Describe a Continuum of Expertise

An example of rubrics that describes a continuum of formative assessment expertise comes from the Formative Assessment for Teachers and Students

(FAST) State Collaborative on Assessment and Student Standards (SCASS) of the Council of Chief State School Officers. The FAST SCASS members commissioned the development of a set of rubrics to support teachers' engagement in structured self-reflection and peer observation of their formative assessment practices.[22] The resulting resource was the *Formative Assessment Rubrics, Reflection, and Observation Protocol* (FARROP). The FARROP breaks the domain of formative assessment into discrete dimensions that provide a level of specificity that enables teachers to focus on particular aspects and provide targeted feedback.[23]

The FARROP comprises ten dimensions of formative assessment, all of which are grounded in the FAST SCASS definition. These dimensions direct attention to specific aspects of formative assessment, including learning goals and success criteria, approaches to eliciting evidence of student understanding, student self- and peer assessment, feedback, and a collaborative culture for learning. The rubric for each FARROP dimension has four levels (beginning, developing, progressing, and extending) and a "not observed" category, which allow for reasonable discrimination among practices while not requiring teachers (the ultimate users) to make such fine distinctions that training and use would be burdensome. By way of illustration, the rubric for the *Learning Goals* dimension is provided in the appendix. Preliminary evidence suggests that the FARROP is an effective tool for supporting formative assessment implementation among classroom teachers, and for this reason we recommend its use in preservice programs.[24]

K–12 students benefit from using rubrics that have clear descriptions of what constitutes quality work to evaluate their own work and that of peers.[25] Paralleling that approach in relation to teachers, the theory of action for the use of the FARROP posits that high-quality descriptions of the domain of formative assessment (codified by a set of rubrics) will help teachers better understand the characteristics of effective formative assessment in action. Reading only the highest levels of practice described in each dimension of the rubric can also help a preservice teacher begin to conceptualize what characterizes effective formative assessment implementation. Reading all the rubric levels for a specific dimension gives preservice teachers a picture of what increasingly skilled practice might look like on that dimension.

Disciplinary Content Standards

In chapters 3 through 6, we provided an overview of key features of current standards in mathematics, science, ELA, and social studies. We noted, for example, the intertwining of science and engineering practices, crosscutting concepts, and disciplinary core ideas in the new science standards. Beginning teachers and their more experienced peers are equally held responsible for their students' achievement of the standards adopted by the US state in which they receive teacher certification. Thus, one starting point for developing disciplinary knowledge is becoming familiar with the student-level expectations detailed in the state's standards.

Acquiring knowledge of the standards includes tracing the development of concepts across grade-level standards to understand how they progressively increase in sophistication, as well as examining, where appropriate, how practice standards interact with content standards.

Important as deep knowledge of the standards is, the standards have limitations for the purpose of formative assessment. This is because, by their nature, standards describe the learning expectations for the end of a grade level rather than identifying the intra-grade development of concepts, skills, and analytical practices. Consequently, standards lack the specificity needed to understand the incremental development of student learning, which is necessary for both teaching and formative assessment. In contrast, learning progressions describe in more detail how student learning develops over time and can add to preservice teachers' knowledge in important ways to support formative assessment.[26]

Representations of How Students Learn

In their landmark review of studies of formative assessment, Black and Wiliam called for "sound models of students' progression in the learning of the subject matter" so that teachers could interpret and respond to assessment evidence in a formative way.[27] Along these lines, the idea of learning progressions—descriptions of how student thinking about a concept typically evolves over time—has recently gained ground as a way to provide more detailed and nuanced descriptions of learning in support of instruction and assessment, particularly in mathematics and science.[28] Including an analysis of learning progressions, in conjunction with examining related standards, offers preservice teachers a deeper perspective on how students' learning develops. To make preservice teachers' experience with learning progressions productive, particularly as they are being prepared to teach a range of grade levels, we propose that they examine only a few progressions in depth, rather than superficially addressing many. Once they understand the nature of learning progressions and how they can be used for teaching, learning, and formative assessment, they can take advantage of them for continued professional learning as teachers.[29]

The Progressions for the Common Core State Standards in Mathematics are one example of a resource that preservice teachers could profitably examine to understand how progressions can both undergird and augment standards.[30] The Common Core State Standards for Mathematics (CCSS/Math) were created from the logical structure of mathematics and research on how students' mathematical understanding develops. The progressions provide a level of detail that can support the development of deeper disciplinary knowledge about the standards as they "explain why standards are sequenced the way they are, point out cognitive difficulties and pedagogical solutions, and give more detail on particularly knotty areas of the mathematics."[31] Understanding cognitive difficulties and "knotty areas" is likely to benefit formative assessment—teachers can pay attention to the possibility of their presence during learning and make appropriate pedagogical responses when necessary.[32] The Next Generation Science Standards (NGSS) documents similarly trace how student thinking deepens and evolves over the grade levels.[33]

An ELA example comes from New Hampshire's Performance Assessment for Competency Education (PACE) program.[34] The PACE program identified a set of eight ELA competencies with descriptors of each competency in grade bands. Even for teachers not operating in a competency-based system, these progressions provide a helpful tool to understand how grade-level expectations for a group of standards change as students develop. For example, table 7.2 describes the expectations for grades 3 through 8 for opinion/argument writing.

Examining what changes across the different levels of this progression can help preservice teachers better understand students' skill development, allowing the teachers to plan appropriate learning goals.

Another example is an empirically grounded science progression that describes student understanding of properties and structure of matter, shown in abbreviated form in table 7.3.[35]

TABLE 7.2 Excerpt from New Hampshire ELA competency statements

	3–4	5–6	7–8
Competency Statements for Opinion/ Argument Writing	Students will analyze a topic or text(s) using a variety of sources and apply organizational strategies and evidence to support an opinion for varied audiences.	Students will produce clear, coherent, and effective opinion/argument writing for a range of text types, purposes, and audiences.	Students will produce clear, coherent, and effective argumentative writing for a range of text types, purposes, and audiences.
	• I can state an opinion that answers a question about a topic or text. • I can use sources (pictures, primary and secondary sources, discussion) to expand my understanding of the topic/text and locate information to support my point of view. • I can organize my ideas by stating reasons that support my opinion, and use facts and details to say more about each reason. • I can add visuals to help elaborate on my reasons. • I can connect reasons and facts with linking words and provide a conclusion that restates my opinion and considers why others might not agree with me. • With support, I can edit and revise my text for clarity, focus, and coherence (e.g., using grade-appropriate mechanics, grammar, language, sentence types, description/elaboration, and relevant visuals).	• I can employ organizational structures and persuasive techniques (rhetorical devices, elaboration) to establish and support a claim about a topic, text, or issue. • I can use relevant sources (video, primary/ secondary sources, interviews, discussion) to expand my understanding of the topic/text/issue and locate information to support different points of view, including mine. • I can maintain a focus and develop my point of view by analyzing hard evidence (data, text evidence, quotes) in support of each stated reason or criterion for my claim/thesis. • I can logically connect reasons, facts, analyses, and sources and provide a conclusion that addresses why others might not agree with me. • With guidance, I can edit and revise my text for clarity and coherence (e.g., conventions, grammar, focus, transitions, and chain of logic).	• I can employ argumentative structures and persuasive techniques (rhetorical devices, elaboration, call to action) to convey claims and counterclaims related to a topic/text/issue. • I can use reliable and credible sources (print/ nonprint primary and secondary sources, interviews) to expand my understanding of the topic/text/issue and locate information to support diverse points of view. • I can maintain an authoritative stance for my claim/thesis by analyzing hard evidence used (data, text evidence, quotes) in support of each stated criterion for my position. • I can logically connect reasons, facts, analyses, and sources and provide a conclusion that addresses possible counterclaims. • I can edit and revise my text for clarity, coherence, and intent (e.g., conventions, grammar, focus, and chain of logic), with guidance as needed.

TABLE 7.3 Abbreviated learning progression for the properties and structure of matter

LEVEL 1: Macroscopic Compositional Model
• Students hold a macroscopic compositional model of matter, in which matter is viewed as something that can be touched or felt, and objects can be broken down or divided into smaller parts and the parts still maintain their material identity (e.g., tiny chunks of a plastic object are still plastic). • Samples of materials can be imagined as being composed of smaller equal-sized units. • At this level only liquids and solids and physical reshaping or cutting are considered and reasonably explained.
LEVEL 2: Microscopic Continuous Model
• Students hold a microscopic compositional model of matter, in which matter is still seen as something that can be touched or felt, but students can begin to conceive of objects or materials as being composed of very tiny pieces that one needs sensitive instruments to detect. • Liquids and solids and grinding (into powders or other fine particulates) and melting are more adequately explained and investigated at this level than other physical transformation or remodeling events.
LEVEL 3: Developing Particle Model of Matter
• Students have a developing nanoscopic notion of a particle model of matter and sometimes recognize that different materials are made of different particles (e.g., wax is made of wax particles and water is made of water particles). • May associate macroscopic properties (e.g., hardness or temperature) with individual particles. • Do not recognize that properties of materials are determined by the collection of the particles' moving and interacting with each other.
LEVEL 4: Particle Model of Matter
• Students hold a particle model of matter, in which all matter (be it in a solid, liquid, or gas form) is comprised of tiny particles that are in constant motion. • Students now have a description of, and explanation for, gases, and a basis for investigating them, and phase changes involving them.
LEVEL 5: Atom/Molecular model
• Students have a refined nanoscopic notion of material identity: they recognize that different materials are made of specific atoms or combinations of atoms forming molecules, and that the arrangement of the atoms and molecules determines the properties of the material. • Conceives of matter as made of atoms, or molecules composed of atoms, and that the atoms have mass and volume.

A learning progression such as the one in table 7.3 describes the development of understanding that takes place over multiple grade levels, and the nature of naive understandings that students may have. Preservice teachers can begin to develop a repertoire of commonly held misconceptions or preconceptions so that they can anticipate, recognize, and respond to them when they arise during teaching and learning.

In addition to examining the details of progressions to enhance their disciplinary knowledge, preservice teachers need to leave their programs with several core understandings about progressions:

- Progressions are pathways that students typically follow, although they may not hold true for each student.
- While progressions trace the development of concepts and skills, progressions are not developmentally inevitable, but rather are dependent on effective instruction.
- The nature of progressions takes into account the axiom that learning does not proceed in lock step. Students will likely not all reach the same point in learning at the same time, but all students can progress from where they are. This idea goes to the heart of formative assessment—teachers find the status of student learning and match their instructional response to where the learning currently stands.
- Learning is not best characterized in a binary "got it/didn't get it" manner, but rather evolves from partial and naive understandings that can be productively built on through their pedagogical actions, including feedback that students can use to move their own learning forward.[36]

We believe that knowledge representations such as a clear and elaborated definition of formative assessment, a representation of practice in action like the FARROP, and content standards and representations of student understanding in the form of learning progressions can help preservice teachers develop a disciplinary schema for formative assessment. This initial schema will progressively increase in sophistication as they implement formative assessment in their classrooms. We recognize that schema development is unlikely to occur without experiences in applying the kinds of knowledge representations we have described, and we next consider experiences (decompositions and approximations) for this purpose that can be included in preservice programs.

USING DECOMPOSITIONS AND APPROXIMATIONS TO SUPPORT LEARNING ABOUT FORMATIVE ASSESSMENT

In this section, we propose supporting preservice teachers to deepen and apply their understanding of formative assessment by decomposing and approximating formative assessment practices in three ways. We also propose five approaches that support the development of their disciplinary knowledge.

Observe and Analyze Expert Formative Assessment Practice

Researchers have noted the importance of expert models to support learning during the apprentice stage in a community of practice.[37] However, research also suggests that preservice teachers struggle to identify critical features of classroom interaction.[38] Recognizing interactions between teacher and student and among students as sources of evidence for formative assessment will necessitate structured observation and analysis of carefully selected exemplars and models of ambitious teaching and formative assessment that explicitly draw the attention of preservice teachers to the critical features.

The FARROP or other similar observational protocols may help preservice teachers more readily identify features of formative assessment to which they should attend, by breaking it apart into more discrete dimensions. After developing their observational skills more generally, preservice teachers can observe video recordings of expert practice on specific aspects as a stimulus for rich discussions. These discussions help them connect the aspects of practices named in an observational protocol to their representation in actual classroom practice.[39]

Discussions of expert formative assessment practice need to be grounded in the content of the lesson and must encompass the relevance and importance of the learning goals and how they relate to the standards, the ways in which the teacher elicited evidence of those goals, how the teacher analyzes students' understanding, and the type of feedback that the teacher provides to support productive struggle and deeper learning.[40]

Learn and Practice Specific Formative Assessment Skills

Brent Duckor and Carrie Holmberg from San José State University support preservice teachers in their program as they begin their formative assessment work by helping them acquire specific skills that focus primarily on eliciting evidence of student understanding through class discussion.[41] They propose that preservice teachers acquire a series of seven moves: priming, posing, pausing, probing, bouncing, tagging, and binning. These moves specifically help a preservice teacher to appropriately set up a discussion (priming), engage all students in a meaningful discussion (posing, pausing, probing, bouncing), and make sense of the evidence of student thinking that arises in the discussion (tagging, binning) to inform next instructional steps. In this approach to apprenticing new teachers in formative assessment, Duckor and Holmberg focus less on some aspects of formative assessment practice, such as student self-assessment or peer feedback, leaving those for in-service development. These moves appear to have payoff for preservice teachers and provide them with early success in their implementation of formative assessment.[42]

Learning to implement these seven moves can be considered both decompositions and approximations practice.[43] Examining the process of supporting students engaged in a discussion and naming these distinct aspects of it is a decomposition. Preservice teachers can then put into practice some of these moves in more or less realistic situations as approximations. For example, tagging student comments during a discussion by writing a word association web for a new concept is a way for a teacher to help make the range of student ideas and questions visible to the whole class. Similarly, asking students to think-pair-share initial ideas or questions on a topic on sticky notes and grouping like ideas together is another way to generate initial thinking from the whole class. The driving question board (figure 5.2) in chapter 5 was an example of tagging that not only documented initial ideas during the introductory lesson, but also tracked the class's learning as the unit progressed. Preservice teachers could practice tagging student comments by recording student ideas generated (by their preservice peers) in a discussion on a key disciplinary idea or concept. This approximation both provides opportunities to rehearse different ways of recording student ideas, and helps the preservice teachers learn to anticipate ways that students might approach important disciplinary concepts. Rehearsing individual components can build confidence for when preservice teachers apply this knowledge in classroom practice. More recently, Duckor and Holmberg have incorporated the use of construct maps and scoring guides to model how each of these moves develops from novice to expert to support the provision of more targeted feedback to preservice teachers.[44]

Use Technology-Based Simulations

A third example of approximation of practice comes from the use of a digital simulated classroom environment.[45] This technology tool allows teachers to interact with simulated students, controlled by a behind-the-scenes trained human who provides the voice and movement for all of the student avatars, permitting them to interact with the teacher and each other. The emerging research associated with the use of this tool has focused on tasks that require preservice teachers to lead argumentation-focused discussions in both mathematics and science.

This research project built off previous work, both in the context of preservice education and as an approach to licensure assessment.[46] One clear value of this use of technology is that preservice teachers can engage repeatedly with a set of simulated students on the same task. As the teachers improve in their ability to coordinate a discussion that requires them to attend to multiple goals (both disciplinary content and practices), help students interact with each other, and respond to emerging student ideas, they can observe how their actions lead to different kinds of outcomes with students. In a real-life classroom there are not the same opportunities to repeatedly practice in this way with a class of students.

It is not an insignificant design challenge to develop tasks, associated rubrics, and resources such as student work samples to contextualize the task. In addition, the simulation specialists (who control the student avatars) must be trained to respond to the teacher differently depending on how he or she engages students in the discussion. However, preliminary research suggests that providing preservice teachers with opportunities to participate in simulations offers a positive and authentic learning experience as the basis for rich discussions among preservice teachers and teacher educators. Because the students are avatars, the simulation specialist can be trained to start a discussion with assumptions about what has transpired before the start of the simulation, or trained to only focus on a narrow aspect of practice. Working in a simulation allows for the decomposition of key features of the formative assessment practice (e.g., eliciting evidence of student understanding and responding to it), making that the singular focus of the interaction.[47]

Analyze Disciplinary Standards

In an earlier section, we identified content standards as a representation of knowledge. Developing an understanding of content standards underpins much of the work of teaching, from creating learning goals to designing appropriate learning opportunities that are grounded in the standards. A series of reviews of the standards, increasing in depth on each successive occasion, builds familiarity and can help preservice teachers learn about the standards and identify areas where they need additional learning opportunities. One approach is outlined as a series of seven steps:

1. Browse the standards and form general impressions about the nature of the standards, noting points of interest for discussions among the group.
2. Identify the standards that are least familiar for further examination.
3. Think about the relationship between content and practices as represented by the standards.
4. Analyze standards (depending on elementary, middle, high school preferences) domain by domain, categorizing them into facts, procedure, concept, and/or combination.
5. Identify standards from the grades below and above that connect to the set being analyzed.
6. Discuss the categories in terms of the different teaching and learning they require.
7. Consider what evidence would be required to indicate students had met the standards.[48]

A standards review exercise like this is likely not just something that is done once, but could be repeated across multiple subsets of standards over the course of a year. Preservice teachers will strengthen their disciplinary knowledge as they analyze what meeting the standard entails. Conversely, examining the discipline from the perspective of the standards provides an opportunity to consider how understanding of critical disciplinary ideas develops over time.

Use Standards and Learning Progressions to Develop Learning Goals and Success Criteria

One particularly valuable follow-up activity, after preservice teachers have closely examined the standards, is to then deconstruct standards into lesson-sized component goals or subgoals. While learning progressions are not usually at a grain-size to inform learning goals directly, they can be used in conjunction with the standards to provide support in two ways. First, the learning progressions often articulate naive ways of thinking that teachers ought to be alert for as students make progress toward the goals.[49] Second, they support the development of horizon knowledge, which can help preservice teachers envision how an individual lesson goal fits into a larger view of learning within and across grades.[50]

In the process of creating goals, preservice teachers need to learn that goals are specific and should reflect the language and values of the discipline. For example, a goal of "80 percent correct by each student on the quiz at the end of the lesson" is not useful because it does not specify the mathematics that students will learn. However, the goal: "students should construct relationships between the value of a decimal fraction, the sum of the values of each of its digits, and increasing (and decreasing) powers of ten" makes clear the intended mathematical learning.[51] When learning goals are specific, preservice teachers can then be supported to think about what counts as evidence for achieving the goal—what are the learning performances that will indicate that students are meeting the goal?

Spending time on learning goals should help preservice students develop the habit of creating learning goals that are both meaningful and at an appropriate grain-size for formative assessment to guide decisions both within and between lessons.[52]

Develop Hinge-Point Questions

Another tool for preservice teachers that is grounded in the discipline, and that they can begin practicing during their preservice training, is the development of hinge-point questions. Dylan Wiliam coined this term for a diagnostic question asked at a critical point in a lesson when the teacher wants to understand whether students are ready to move on and in which direction.[53] Hinge-point questions can be in any form but are intended to be quick to answer and quick to analyze. The misconception questions in chapters 3 and 5 could be used as hinge-point questions in science and mathematics lessons. In the ELA example of a hinge-point question below, a teacher who has just taught a lesson introducing students to a number of rhetorical devices wants to check on this understanding. She uses the question in figure 7.2.[54]

Dylan Wiliam recommends students writing answers on mini whiteboards or holding up fingers to signal answers. The most essential learning for preservice teachers is to understand the importance of checking on

FIGURE 7.2 ELA hinge-point question

Which of these is alliteration?

1. The golden disc of the sun burned.
2. The sizzling summer sun smiled sweetly.
3. I felt the red hot sun on my back.
4. The trees swayed gently in the wind.

where students are in their learning at least once during a lesson and making this check a routine part of their planning. They should also have a plan for what action to take, depending on the students' responses. Teachers will become more sophisticated in their formative assessment planning as they gain experience, looking for more than a single formative assessment opportunity during a lesson. However, starting with a single hinge-point question is a good entry point for beginning teachers.

Use Learning Progressions to Examine Student Work

Student work that illustrates critical aspects of a learning progression can be examined to help preservice teachers understand the qualitative distinctions in the levels of a specific progression. It is also helpful for preservice teachers to examine student work against a progression and gain insights into the students' reasoning and understanding, then think about how they can build on the students' current learning status. This approach is similar to how others have used learning progressions with teachers. For example, the *Ongoing Assessment Project* (OGAP) used research-based mathematics learning trajectories to support the development of teacher knowledge and their capacity to elicit, interpret, and respond to student thinking.[55] This use of progressions led to more differentiated teaching that better met the learning needs of individual students. Cognitively Guided Instruction uses a similar approach.[56]

Use Learning Progressions to Plan Next Instructional Steps, Including Feedback

Learning progressions can help preservice teachers identify and categorize student thinking (Duckor and Holmberg call this process "binning"), but this is only a first stage in planning next instructional next steps. An essential, and often challenging, second step is to identify how to productively build on the current status of student understanding. While learning progressions can help preservice teachers understand what learning a particular concept entails and what the next level of understanding might be, they do not generally define specific ways to advance learning. One exception is the Enhanced Learning Maps, materials for mathematics teaching that include progressions illustrating the connections among concepts and skills that students need to construct, instructional activities that suggest ideas for teaching, and solution guides to provide insights for diagnosing misconceptions and informing next steps in learning.[57] In the absence of such materials, once preservice teachers understand the current status of student thinking, working collaboratively with peers, mentor teachers, and program faculty can help them identify possible instructional responses, including feedback to students to assist their next steps. This same peer group can also provide opportunities for post-lesson reflection on the success of their actions.

Examine Model Curriculum Materials

In most districts, teachers are expected to follow a specific curriculum. It is unlikely that preservice programs can familiarize participants with all the curricula they may encounter as teachers. However, preservice teachers can engage as learners with model curricular activities that teachers employ with their students.[58] Such firsthand experiences may provide insights into the design of curricular materials and how they describe the development of learning. When combined with analysis of their own experience, preservice teachers can think about student learning, how it develops as a result of the activities, and what student misconceptions or partial understandings students might have as they engage in the activities. They can also become familiar with how to find and use resources to obtain insights into student thinking.[59]

In the next section, we focus on our third area of expertise for formative assessment, habits of practice.

EXPERTISE IN HABITS OF PRACTICE

In chapter 2, we identified three critical habits of practice that we believe are essential for teachers, both beginning and more experienced, as they develop and deepen their disciplinary knowledge in conjunction with their formative assessment expertise: a commitment to participate in continued inquiry about, and reflection on, their practice; a willingness to deprivatize practice and engage in collaboration with colleagues; and a willingness to engage in deliberate practice. Orienting preservice teachers to the acquisition of these habits of practice lays a foundation on which they can continue to build over the course of their careers.[60]

Preservice teachers need to begin to develop these habits of practice and understand their significance to their continuing professional lives and, in particular, to the development of formative assessment expertise. One of us (Wylie), reflecting on her own experience in preservice education, recognized with hindsight the ways in which she had not yet developed views of herself as a continual learner.

> At twenty-one years old, with my newly minted undergraduate degree in hand, I began a one-year teaching certification course to become a secondary-level mathematics teacher. Near the start of the year, one of my professors mentioned that this course might not be our last engagement with the school of education, and that we might return for a master's or doctorate in education. This casual statement opened my eyes to new possibilities and directly lead to me applying for and completing my doctorate, entering a world of educational research. Reflecting back on my preservice training I realize however that not only had I not yet considered additional *formal* learning opportunities, I had not yet truly developed an approach to my own *informal* learning and reflection. At that time, a reflection was simply the final section of a lesson plan that our professors expected to see completed after the lesson was taught, but it had no intrinsic value to me. The habits of mind introduced in chapter 2 had not yet become part of my explicit practice.

Among the experiences that inculcate habits of practice are enabling preservice teachers to collaborate in assisting each other's learning, for example, by sharing problems of practice related to formative assessment implementation from their field experiences and collaboratively finding solutions guided by program faculty, or by creating opportunities for reflection and revision through a cyclical process of learn, practice, revise.[61] Below we highlight two experiences that we deem important to be woven throughout preservice: opportunities to examine beliefs about learning that can impact formative assessment and opportunities to engage in meaningful reflections on practice.

Examine Beliefs that Influence Formative Assessment

As we noted in the introduction of this chapter, preservice teachers carry a set of beliefs about teachers and teaching that were formed during their own K–12 experiences. To help ensure that their beliefs do not become obstacles to effective teaching and assessment, program faculty need to help preservice teachers resolve any conflicts between their previously established beliefs and the knowledge representations and experiences they are exposed to in their program. For instance, teachers can examine the beliefs held by individuals that might negatively impact student learning and formative assessment, with a view to internally examining their own beliefs. Such examinations can encompass any or all of the following:

- the stereotypes or other beliefs that impede the empowerment of particular groups of students
- how beliefs are conveyed in the classroom and the social environment
- beliefs about learning that may be instilled as a result of their own school experience, for example, learning mathematics is about memorization and speed, students learn best when they work independently, and classrooms are quiet places with very little student talk
- beliefs about assessment, such as that weekly quizzes are the best type of assessment, that assessment always requires a score, that assessment occurs to figure out if students "got it" or "didn't get it," and that grades are the best forms of feedback.[62]

Clearly, any examination of beliefs needs to be undertaken with sensitivity and care. A community of practice, in which preservice teachers have created mutual trust and collaborative relationships, is a context in which the participants can engage in this examination without feeling undermined or threatened.[63]

Reflect on One's Own Formative Assessment Implementation

During their teaching practice, preservice teachers should all be provided with structured time to support reflection on their own developing formative assessment practice as an essential component of deliberate practice. Structured time means that reflection time is not an afterthought but rather allocated as an explicit and rigorous part of their teaching experience, indicating that it is valued by the preservice teacher, mentor teacher, and program faculty.

When lessons are thought of as "experiments" preservice teachers' reflection can be supported through the use of tools such as the FARROP, or, in the case of the "moves" discussed earlier by reflecting on the lesson in terms of which moves worked well and why, and which were less effective and why, followed by revisions to strengthen their practice.[64] Program faculty or mentor teachers can also provide protocols to guide preservice teachers' reflection incorporating guiding questions such as:

- Did you think that your learning goals and success criteria guided your lesson and helped you obtain evidence of students' understanding of the concept?
- Did students have opportunities to engage in productive struggle?
- What evidence do you have that your students learned or did not learn what you intended? How did you interpret the evidence?
- Did any student responses surprise you? Why?
- What contingent action did you take to a student or a group of students based on the analysis? Was your response effective? How do you know?
- How might you modify your response in the event of similar evidence in the future?
- How does your analysis of this lesson impact your planning for the next lesson?[65]

Protocols for reflection often require members of a community of practice to share teaching artifacts, including samples of student work, with their colleagues. Sharing student work makes both the tasks used and the student responses readily accessible for analysis. Examples of protocols for this purpose include the Guided Reflection Protocol which provides a series of steps for teachers to reflect alone on classroom episodes; a Critical Incidents Protocol which offers similar steps for reflection, but this time with colleagues; a tuning protocol which outlines a series of steps for teachers to present student work to colleagues in a structured, reflective discourse aimed at tuning the work to a higher standard; and a questioning protocol, designed to engage teachers in examining their teaching experiences from different perspectives to generate new thinking.[66] Each of these protocols could be used to focus on one or more dimensions of formative assessment, using tasks or activities that help preservice teachers reflect on their effectiveness of implementation and what they could do to make improvements.

Preservice teachers are not only learning about teaching and formative assessment; they are also beginning to develop their identities as teachers. The habits of practice promoted in their preservice programs will go a long way to influencing and shaping their identities as professionals who are committed to progress along the continuum of expertise that they have just begun.

COHERENCE ACROSS COURSEWORK AND FIELD EXPERIENCES

The focus in this chapter has been on the use of representations, decompositions, and approximations to support preservice teachers in beginning their apprenticeship into the teaching guild. We anticipate that many of these experiences would happen within a methods class. However, it is essential that there is coherence across coursework experiences in methods classes and field experiences, whether observing site-based teachers or completing student teaching in a classroom. One project that has recognized the challenge of preservice teachers hearing one message within the educational institution but a very different message from their cooperating teachers in the field is a Tennessee-based program, Strengthening Instruction in Tennessee Elementary Schools–Focus on Mathematics (SITES-M). The program provides learning opportunities for college and university mathematics and mathematics education professors, preservice teachers, and in-service teachers in partner schools. Learning opportunities for participants include summer professional development institutes, weekend mathematics workshops during the school year, access to rich and engaging classroom tasks, and the use of observation protocols. By involving learners at all levels in the system, faculty were able to deepen their experiences of K–12 classrooms, teachers were exposed to formative assessment and supported to improve their own assessment practices, and preservice teachers benefited from having supervising teachers who had been involved in formative assessment focused learning opportunities. One of the project goals was to increase consistency of message for the preservice teachers.[67]

Observe and Analyze Preservice Teachers' Formative Assessment Implementation

Preservice teachers are observed while completing their field experiences. Some of the observations will be formative and others more consequential, depending on program requirements. Using rubrics such as the FARROP for observing and discussing an observation of a preservice teacher's lesson and providing feedback can build on work done during methods classes to make the dimensions of formative assessment more explicit and concrete for the preservice teacher. Ensuring that the observers involved in the field experience observations are using the same language about formative assessment can help support coherence across the system. To the degree possible, supporting the field placement teachers to engage with the definition of formative assessment and the FARROP can also help ensure more consistent messages across system components.

In this chapter, we have advanced proposals for how preservice teachers can develop a baseline competency for formative assessment. While preservice teachers will need to wait for their own classrooms to establish a culture for learning and formative assessment, including expectations and routines for student interaction and collaboration, and to develop skills in fostering student self-regulation, the baseline competency we have proposed will equip them to engage in formative assessment immediately. The next two chapters propose how to support teachers as they take on sole responsibility for their classrooms and students.

In chapter 2, we introduced the concept of a community of practice, and in this context, adopted a sociocultural perspective to describe our approach to teacher learning. In this chapter we have focused on preservice teachers as apprentices into the teaching guild and have considered how they can engage in collective learning experiences in preservice programs. This perspective supports the mentoring of preservice teachers in the practices of formative assessment through inquiry, active engagement, collaboration, feedback, reflection, and the development of their own agency in learning, all of which we suggest can lead them to develop critical habits for ongoing professional growth.

SUMMARY: THE BIG IDEAS OF CHAPTER 7

- An important component of preservice education is to provide teachers entering the profession with an opportunity to examine their prior experiences as students, and, if necessary, to challenge their "apprenticeship-of-observation."
- Learning opportunities for preservice teachers should intertwine formative assessment practices, disciplinary knowledge, and habits of mind.
- Representations of practice illustrate critical aspects of practice. Decompositions of practice break down professional practices into discrete components that can be approximated. Approximations of practice engage preservice teachers in opportunities to rehearse discrete components of practice in settings of reduced complexity.
- Knowledge representations include: (1) a shared definition of formative assessment; (2) rubrics that describe a continuum of expertise; (3) disciplinary content standards; and (4) representations of how students learn (e.g., learning progressions).
- Decompositions and approximations of practice include: (1) observe and analyze expert formative assessment practice; (2) learn and practice specific formative assessment skills; (3) use technology-based simulations; (4) analyze disciplinary standards; (5) use standards and learning progressions to develop learning goals and success criteria; (6) develop hinge-point questions; (7) use learning progressions to examine student work; (8) use learning progressions to plan next instructional steps, including feedback; (9) examine model curriculum materials.
- Support preservice teachers to develop appropriate habits of mind by helping them examine beliefs that influence formative assessment and learn to meaningfully reflect on their own formative assessment implementation.
- It is essential that there is coherence across coursework experiences in methods classes and field experiences, whether observing site-based teachers or completing student teaching in a classroom.

CHAPTER 8

Supporting Teacher Learning During Induction

Imagine this scenario:

> The last time this newly minted third-grade teacher had been in a classroom was when she completed her final eight-week student teaching in the spring with her cooperating teacher. The walls of that classroom were covered in posters, brightly decorated bulletin boards displaying examples of student work, and various records of studies-in-progress for mathematics and science projects. The mat at the front of the room for class meetings was strategically placed near a flipchart and markers for recording student ideas. Nearby, the reading corner had books organized by topic in clearly labeled bins. One side of the room was lined with low shelves with folder organizers for student work alongside more bins filled with rulers, calculators, pencils, and mathematics manipulatives. By the window there were small pots of seedlings growing as part of a science experiment.
>
> In stark contrast, this early August classroom was near empty with blank walls, bare bulletin boards, and all the tables and chairs stacked up on one side of the room to allow the school custodians to do their summer deep clean. Suddenly, the reality of setting up a classroom rather than just stepping into one that was already established and smoothly running hit her; she had no idea how to get started. Her preservice teacher training had not prepared for her this.

What this teacher experienced is repeated a myriad of times as teachers begin their careers and reminds us that the transition from preservice to the first year of teaching can often be a jarring and incongruous one.[1] The experience of working midyear alongside a cooperating teacher who has, by that time, established classroom routines and organizational structures is very different from having sole responsibility for a classroom that begins with the setting up of an empty room in late summer.[2] The challenge for new teachers is only just beginning with the classroom setup. Creating units, planning lessons that build on each other so that students develop deep understanding of key ideas within a discipline, embedding formative assessment into ongoing teaching and learning, managing the entire class in terms of learning and behavior, and communicating with other teachers, administrators, and parents is a vastly different experience from teachers' preservice experience of working closely with cooperating teachers. The leap from preservice to being entirely responsible for a class is broad and often lonely.[3] For this reason, induction programs are offered to new teachers to provide the support they need, bridging the transitional phase between the "externally supported" phase in preservice programs and the "self-regulatory" phase when teachers strive to deepen their expertise through in-service learning.[4]

In this chapter, we explore some of the challenges identified by beginning teachers that must be addressed so that they can build fruitfully on their preservice formative assessment experiences. We consider the link between the classroom culture and formative assessment, emphasizing that as beginning teachers create rich learning cultures, they concurrently create classroom environments that are collaborative and respectful, rather than focusing on establishing control through rules and management that constrict students' classroom experience. We explore the characteristics of effective induction programs and how they can support beginning teachers to integrate classroom management skills and instructional routines with formative assessment to continue on a trajectory toward ambitious teaching practices as described in chapter 1.[5] One thread that runs through all the examples of practice presented in this chapter is the expectation that beginning teachers have purposeful opportunities to work with other more experienced teachers in their school. Learning to teach is a social enterprise and beginning teachers will develop their practice as they observe, practice, and reflect both with their assigned mentor and with other teachers in their new school community.[6] To do so will draw on the beginning teacher's habits of practice: an inquiry stance to help the apprentice teacher ask questions about what might be most successful with a particular class of students; deliberate practice to try out new approaches and to modify them as needed to make them work in a particular context; and critical reflection (including operating on feedback from others) to think about what is working well and what needs further refining. Let us first consider the challenges beginning teachers routinely face.

CHALLENGES FOR BEGINNING TEACHERS

The move from short preservice student teaching placements to sole responsibility as the classroom teacher of record can be abrupt and bring many challenges and concerns for those starting their teaching careers. Beginning teachers' concerns mostly center on relationship building, classroom management, and pedagogical issues.[7] New teachers also worry about developing relationships with students, parents, colleagues, and administrators. They may be reluctant to ask for help from other teachers or school administrators for fear that request will be reflected later in a poor evaluation. Classroom management concerns run the gamut from dealing with latecomers to class, to students coming unprepared, to disruptive students. Pedagogical issues include understanding what is most important to teach and assess; how to engage students in critical ideas; planning to address the range of student understanding, misconceptions, and skills in the same class; and how to answer unanticipated student questions when they arise. In addition, beginning teachers are also struggling with workload and time management challenges as they develop and select resources and lessons plans for the first time (we assume that beginning teachers are less likely to be involved in curriculum development). Beginning and more experienced teachers differ most in terms of concerns about classroom management and dealing with parents, suggesting these are two important areas of focus for induction programs to address.[8]

There is no shortage of advice for new teachers, and an internet search will quickly bring up many teacher blogs, articles, and books on classroom routines and management.[9] Establishing a set of expectations for how students will function together harmoniously in a class is an important part of the work to be done in the first weeks of a new school year for any teacher. Early career teachers are developing their own ideas about what to include and not include in this process, how much input to solicit from the students themselves, and how to balance providing rules versus developing routines that provide structure for students without constraining learning or the capacity for self-management. Establishing routines that support instructional engagement and ensure that all students can share their own learning focuses beginning teachers on productive practices rather than on a compliance culture of rules. Furthermore, without such clear routines, opportunities for formative assessment are reduced. For example, if students do not have the routine of listening carefully to each other during a class discussion or in dialogue with their peers and fail to understand that their job is to build on each other's ideas, then teachers will not have access to an important source of evidence of students' thinking. In this vein, one aspect of formative assessment practice that can be particularly anxiety producing for beginning teachers as they elicit evidence during a class discussion is not knowing how to respond to a student idea or not being able to recognize an underlying misconception that students might reveal. Similarly, a beginning teacher will benefit from explicitly establishing a classroom culture in which incorrect or partially correct ideas are viewed as productive ways to explore student thinking and help develop and deepen understanding for all students. Without this culture, students may be reluctant to share their thinking, which will reduce both the opportunities for teachers to collect and act on evidence of learning, and for students to learn from each other.

Given these concerns and the often unfiltered avalanche of well-intentioned advice, it is no wonder that beginning teachers are stressed and exhausted during their first year. They need carefully designed mentoring and support. Approximately 20 to 50 percent of new teachers leave within the first five years of entering the teaching profession.[10] This is clearly a concern, not only because of the potential impact on student learning, but because their teachers may not have the capacity to be fully effective if they have not received mentoring and other support. Students benefit from more experienced teachers, so it is incumbent on schools to make use of comprehensive induction programs to accelerate improvement for beginning teachers and to reduce teacher turnover, ensuring that students experience the lowest number of beginning teachers as possible.[11] In addition, replacing early career teachers includes both financial costs for recruitment, hiring, and onboarding of new staff, and less tangible costs in terms of the disruption to relationships among teachers and students, and the loss of institutional knowledge that occurs when teachers leave.

WHAT IS COMPREHENSIVE INDUCTION?

While estimates vary and are trending upward, approximately 80 percent or more of new teachers participate in some form of an induction program.[12] However, only a very small proportion of beginning teachers experience what would be considered a "comprehensive induction program," as defined by the National Association of State Boards of Education (NASBE).[13] NASBE considers a comprehensive induction program to be one that includes "support for new teachers for at least two years; high-quality mentoring utilizing carefully selected and well-prepared mentors; regularly scheduled common planning time with other teachers; ongoing professional development; and standards-based evaluation of new teachers throughout the process."[14] One study indicated that approximately two-thirds of teachers reported having a mentor, with 48 percent reporting a mentor from the same field, and 18 percent reporting one from a different field. Just over two-thirds of beginning teachers had collaboration or common planning time with other teachers who taught the same subject.[15] Much less common were reports of a reduced teaching load or additional classroom support.

Evidence from several longitudinal surveys helps us understand which kinds of mentoring and induction activities are likely to be most effective.[16] The most critical activities include having access to a mentor from the same field, common planning time, and being part of an external network of teachers. In chapter 2, we noted that teachers make greater gains in their effectiveness when they teach in a supportive and collegial working environment. In this context, more experienced teachers are able to confer benefits to their colleagues and to the school as a whole, as well as to their own students.[17] Therefore, bringing beginning teachers into the community of practice (see chapter 2) at the start of their first full-time, professional placement is going to be of benefit to them, and likely also to the teachers mentoring them.

High-quality induction is more than just having an in-school buddy system for new teachers; a mentor alone has little impact on teacher retention.

Successful induction programs include regularly scheduled common planning time with other teachers within their school. This common planning time can be particularly beneficial when it is used to support meaningful sharing of instructional and formative assessment practices and to review student work to help new teachers appropriately match tasks to learning goals. Common planning time can also help beginning teachers create lesson plans and make sense of evidence of student learning to inform future learning plans.[18] Furthermore, these meetings are opportunities to bring new teachers into the larger community of practice and to provide scaffolded learning opportunities from the more experienced community members in their school. Beginning teachers need ongoing professional development that helps them strengthen their disciplinary knowledge and formative assessment practices, focuses on practical classroom challenges, supports collaboration, and allows beginning teachers to bring their own problems of practice for consideration with more seasoned teachers.[19]

Taking account of NASBE's recommendations and research discussed above, we propose that a comprehensive induction program should comprise four main components: (1) high-quality mentors; (2) common planning time with other teachers; (3) ongoing professional development; and (4) observation and feedback opportunities. In the remainder of the chapter, we will address each component in turn and show how each one supports teachers' emerging formative assessment skills.

COMPONENTS OF A HIGH-QUALITY INDUCTION PROGRAM

In chapter 2, we introduced the concept of apprenticeship to describe how a community of teachers supports those who are new to the profession through social participation and interaction, observation, and imitation.[20] During their induction program, teachers continue this mode of learning as they aim to become fully fledged professionals. Each component of the induction program enables this apprenticeship status and is designed to provide the necessary support new teachers need as they continue learning in the workplace context.

High-Quality Mentors

Induction programs should support beginning teachers for at least two years after they complete preservice in order to see the anticipated impact on teacher practice.[21] Selecting high-quality mentors who have been carefully prepared is important to ensure that mentors model reflective practices, have strong disciplinary understanding, engage in ambitious teaching and rich formative assessment practices, are committed to their own professional learning, and are empathetic to the needs of new teachers. High-quality formative assessment mentors regard formative assessment as a critical classroom process that they are continually seeking to refine and improve through reflection and analysis, both as an individual and with peers.

Mentors also need the skills to coach and guide the beginning teachers. Not all experienced teachers are good at explaining their tacit knowledge, such as how they established the systems and procedures in their classrooms that seem effortless to an outsider and that they may do without a second thought.[22] Those who take on mentor roles may need help turning their tacit knowledge into explicit knowledge that can be shared with the teacher apprentices.[23]

A fifty-state review of policies around teacher induction by the New Teacher Center highlighted both the importance of a rigorous mentor selection process, and the need for professional learning for mentors and a manageable caseload of mentees.[24] Mentors need assistance to ensure that the support they provide for beginning teachers is truly useful.[25] Ideally, mentors will have reduced teaching loads or be full-time coaches so that they are available to offer in-class support and feedback based on observations to the apprentice teachers.[26] Beginning teachers should know who their mentors are from the start of the new school year so they may establish productive collaborative relationships and feel secure about receiving ongoing support.

Mentors should provide beginning teachers with wide-ranging support, not all of which will be directly related to formative assessment but will help them to acclimatize to their new environment: insights about the local community and school, school and district policies and procedures, advice related to first-time employees, how and where to find teaching resources, how to organize their classroom, how to interact with parents, and so forth.[27] Mentors can also act as "connectors," providing suggestions to beginning teachers about whom they might benefit from observing to see a particular aspect of formative assessment practice in action. Many of the activities suggested in the section on common planning time that follows could also be activities for the mentor and beginning teacher, if common planning time is not available for the entire grade-level team or department.

Common Planning Time

Our second recommendation for a high-quality induction program is that beginning teachers share common planning time with other teachers. Being able to meet regularly with teachers from the same grade level or content area can provide beginning teachers with a range of rich experiences if the time is used productively. Common planning time is a chance for beginning teachers to deepen their disciplinary knowledge as they interact with more experienced peers who will inform their lesson planning and formative assessment practices. For example, while they may not yet be able to anticipate the range of student responses or misconceptions in all the content they are likely to teach, especially if they are elementary teachers, they can draw on the knowledge of the larger school-based community. For example, they might discuss how to connect a new mathematics unit to students' out-of-school experiences and how to pose purposeful questions to support students' science understanding and reveal their thinking during the lesson, all of which will be beneficial to new teachers' formative assessment practices.[28] There are a number of shared experiences for beginning teachers to help them develop their formative assessment knowledge and skills. Below, we elaborate on them.

Sharing approaches to lesson planning Teachers use a wide range of approaches for lesson planning.[29] Some write out detailed plans for each lesson, some make briefer notes in a day planner, some use extensive binders in which they compile resources to be used in conjunction with the lesson plan, while others use electronic software to develop and store plans. In some schools or districts, teachers are required to show their lesson plans to the principal, in others only beginning teachers are required to do so, and for yet other teachers, their lesson plans are entirely within their own purview with no oversight from anyone. Apprentice teachers can use a planning template to keep critical aspects of lesson design front and center in their thinking. While their more experienced colleagues may not always use it as formally, a shared understanding of the lesson plan can support professional conversations and inquiry about lesson design.

In chapters 3 and 4, we presented a lesson plan outline which prompted the teachers to consider critical components of a lesson with integrated formative assessment: clear learning goals and success criteria, tasks that are aligned to the goals, formative opportunities to collect evidence of learning, and additional questions to probe student thinking, anticipating how students might approach the content of the lesson. A grade-level team or department group can have a powerful conversation about the critical components of a lesson plan, creating modifications as needed, depending on the content area. For example, while teachers in a mathematics department might want to focus explicitly on both content and practices standards for lesson planning, science teachers may want to begin from the phenomenon to be explored.

Using common planning time to share and analyze lesson plans that follow a common structure can help beginning teachers internalize these critical components and see them put into practice if they are given the chance to observe other teachers. Then they can begin to adapt them for their own use. Furthermore, the use of shared lesson plan templates can reinforce best practices, which can also have a positive impact on the practice of the entire grade-level team. Adopting a common lesson plan structure is a powerful way for a beginning teacher to engage in social participation with and imitation of his or her peers around a critical aspect of practice.

Shared lesson structures In addition to using lesson plan templates as an aide-mémoire, some teachers also routinely use consistent lesson structures. For example, the second-grade teacher introduced in chapter 3, Ms. Cárdenas, frequently follows a specific lesson structure: she begins with a warm-up activity related to the lesson topic; she presents learning goals and success criteria to the students, making sure that they understand the vocabulary and expectations; and she engages students in a discussion about the mathematics they are working on, which may also include opportunities for students to talk in small groups to develop their ideas. Furthermore, students have independent work time to work alone or in small groups, during which time Ms. Cárdenas can talk with each of them about what they are learning; and finally, she wraps the lesson up with a brief discussion with students focused on the learning goals.

By using the same structure lesson to lesson, Ms. Cárdenas can be more efficient when planning a specific lesson, since she knows how it will flow. Students also benefit by having a consistent routine: they know that Ms. Cárdenas will be asking them about their work and wanting them to explain their thinking, for example, during the group work time. Sharing these structures as well as lesson plan templates with beginning teachers can be very beneficial in helping them more quickly develop instructional routines, particularly routines with which most students have developed familiarity from other teachers in previous grade levels, and routines that support formative assessment practice.

Beginning teachers will also benefit from observing a lesson that follows a predictable routine or structure as one way of learning how to use those structures. However, it is equally important to hear the teacher articulate the rationale for the structure. For example, Ms. Cárdenas would likely draw attention to the relationship between various formative assessment practices and segments of her lesson structure. Beginning teachers might not necessarily make those connections on their own as they are still developing their professional vision and do not necessarily attend to or observe the same things as an expert teacher.[30]

The common planning time can also be used for communicating ideas across a team about different kinds of routines to end a lesson, for instance exit tickets or other forms of self-assessment than can be incorporated into a lesson plan. Sharing ideas can help a beginning teacher build on strategies that are already habitual for students and so will require less scaffolding and encourage coherence of experiences across classrooms.

Analyzing student work Common planning time can also be productively used for the analysis of student work samples by groups of teachers to support inquiry about ambitious teaching and formative assessment.[31] When teachers examine work together, beginning teachers come to understand a broader range of what is possible for students to achieve. Additionally, access to a discussion with more experienced teachers can help apprentice teachers think about their expectations and deepen their understanding of what their students can learn, as well as help them advance their own learning from its current status. Making sense of what students understand and where they are still struggling, and deciding on next steps are essential formative assessment skills. Analyzing student work can support beginning teachers to develop these skills. The analysis process can also deepen beginning teachers' content knowledge for teaching as student misconceptions or partial understandings are identified and discussed.

Examining student work can range from a quick review of evidence of learning collected near the end of a lesson to a more formalized analysis of selected pieces of student work. Beginning teachers will benefit from observing how more experienced teachers review and make sense of formative assessment evidence so that it actually informs decision-making about future lessons. For example, they might observe experienced teachers sort responses into categories such as "got it," "almost there," and "not yet," and how the categories inform planning for the next lesson.

There are a variety of protocols available to structure conversations about student work, which often focus teachers on first describing the work without judgment before they make any interpretations of what the work shows.[32] Other protocols focus on the intellectual demand of a task and the depth of student thinking required.[33] Using these rubrics with apprentice teachers can be helpful to distinguish between task demands (Is it a cognitively demanding task?) and student responses to the task (Were students able to respond to the task in a sophisticated way?). These analyses can inform discussions about how to focus on learning opportunities that might be needed to scaffold student learning toward deeper levels of thinking. Such conversations can help beginning teachers continue to refine their understanding of applicable content standards and how to engage student in learning that is aligned with those standards, which in turn can support their formative assessment practice.

A set of rubrics for analyzing learning tasks and student work was created by the Chicago Annenberg Research Project (CARP). The rubrics for mathematics tasks focus on whether the task presents opportunities for: knowledge construction, written mathematical communication, and connections to students' lives. The rubrics for student work focus on whether students engaged in mathematical analysis, mathematical concepts, and written mathematical communication. The writing task rubrics for ELA similarly focus on: construction of knowledge, elaboration of written communication, and connections to students' lives. The rubrics for student work focus on whether students were engaged in construction of knowledge, elaborated written communication, and made connections to their lives.[34] Tables 8.1 and 8.2 show the mathematics Knowledge Construction rubric and the writing Elaborated Written Communication rubric respectively.

While a team of teachers would not use these rubrics on a regular basis to score student work, they can be used occasionally to support rich discussions about the nature of tasks and what they are demanding of students. Listening to and engaging in discussions grounded in these rubrics can support deepening of disciplinary knowledge for beginning teachers. For instance, they can use the rubrics, tasks, and student responses to examine how the nature of tasks influences the kind of work that students can produce, and the kinds of insights about student thinking that can be gained from a close examination. The use of concrete information and evidence in this way can help beginning teachers better design tasks that assess their learning goals and assist them in analyzing student work.

Observing more experienced teachers bringing problems of practice to common planning time models the process of deliberate practice and the value of collective inquiry. As beginning teachers move through the induction period, they can bring their own problems of practice to the group to be discussed, supporting the development of their inquiry skills.

TABLE 8.1 Rubric for examining a mathematical task for evidence of knowledge construction

Possible indicators of requiring mathematical organization are tasks that ask students to decide among algorithms, to chart and graph data, or to solve multi-step problems. Possible indicators of requiring mathematical interpretation are tasks that ask students to consider alternative solutions or strategies, to create their own mathematical problems, to create a mathematical generalization or abstraction, or to invent their own solution method. These indicators can be inferred either through explicit instructions from the teacher or through a task that cannot be successfully completed without mathematical organization and/or mathematical interpretation.	
3	The task calls for mathematical interpretation of information. Tasks that require mathematical interpretation are assumed to require mathematical organization.
2	The task calls for mathematical organization of information, but minimal or no mathematical interpretation.
1	The task calls for very little or no mathematical organization and mathematical interpretation of information. Its dominant expectation is for students to retrieve or reproduce fragments of knowledge or to repeatedly apply previously learned algorithms and procedures.

Source: Stacy Wenzel et al., "Documentation of the 1996–2002 Chicago Annenberg Research Project Strand on Authentic Intellectual Demand Exhibited in Assignments and Student Work: A Technical Process Manual," (Chicago: Consortium on Chicago School Research, 2002), 21.

TABLE 8.2 Rubric for examining student responses to a task for evidence of elaborated written communication

Elaboration consists of two parts: a conclusion, generalization, or argument AND support for it, in the form of at least one example, illustration, detail, or reason. Elaboration is coherent when the examples, illustrations, details, or reasons do indeed provide appropriate, consistent support for the conclusions, generalizations, or arguments. To use the criteria, the scorer should identify specific points in the student work that are elaborated and should make a judgment about their coherence.	
4	Substantial evidence of elaboration. Almost all the student's work comprises an elaborated, coherent account.
3	Moderate evidence of elaboration. A moderate portion of the student's work comprises an elaborated, coherent account.
2	Some evidence of elaboration. A small portion of the student's work comprises an elaborated, coherent account.
1	No evidence of elaboration. No portion of the student's work comprises an elaborated, coherent account.

Source: Stacy Wenzel et al., "Documentation of the 1996–2002 Chicago Annenberg Research Project Strand on Authentic Intellectual Demand Exhibited in Assignments and Student Work: A Technical Process Manual," (Chicago: Consortium on Chicago School Research, 2002), 36.

Ongoing Professional Development

In this chapter so far, we have explored the role of a mentor and ways in which common planning time can be productively used with a grade-level or department team. The third NASBE suggestion focuses on the need for ongoing professional development for beginning teachers that goes beyond support from a mentor and common planning time. The NASBE suggestions include a focus on deepening beginning teachers' content knowledge and addressing the challenges of day-to-day teaching practices.[35] The suggestions also include scheduling regular professional development sessions to address these topics with beginning teachers, allowing them to ask questions, present their own problems of practice, and engage in collaborative work to develop solutions.[36]

One of the challenges of day-to-day practice faced by beginning teachers is establishing classroom routines that set expectations for student behavior that support a learning orientation and culture; these routines, in turn, set the foundational structure that enables formative assessment practices. Induction programs need to focus on developing and reinforcing beginning teachers' ability to establish routines to support effective formative assessment practices.

In chapters 3 through 6, we saw multiple examples of students engaging in teacher-facilitated formative assessment practices in ways that were clearly understood and internalized, given how smoothly routines were implemented. The mathematics examples in chapter 3 included an initial idea generation routine from Mr. Martino in which students responded to the questions, "What do you notice? What do you wonder?" Ms. Cárdenas asked her students to use the "just-right problem" approach to use self-reflection in selecting the difficulty of the mathematics problem they were ready to tackle. Both strategies require explanation, modeling, and practice so that students take them seriously and can seamlessly engage in them without interrupting the flow of the lesson. In one of the ELA examples from chapter 4, we examined how Ms. Eilertsen's AP class participated in goal setting and peer feedback processes. This example illustrated the scaffolding that students needed to be successful participants in this practice, and the refinements that may be needed along the way. In chapter 5, one of the science teachers used a "traffic-light" strategy that engaged students in self-assessment. Clearly, this was not the first time students had been asked to use this approach. The teacher had a careful check in place that required students to respond to a subset of questions to provide additional evidence of learning or confusion, which helped ensure that the students did not just identify every concept as "green," an indication that they believed they understood what they were learning about. In the two examples of social studies practice from chapter 6, both teachers used small-group work to involve students in discussions and analysis before sharing their ideas with the whole group.

In the next section, we address the importance of classroom norms for formative assessment, followed by four routines around learning goals and success criteria, classroom discussions, self-assessment and peer feedback, and collecting evidence of student thinking.

ESTABLISHING CLASSROOM NORMS OF COLLABORATION

Successful engagement in the routines just described requires that norms of collaboration are part of the classroom DNA. Beginning teachers can learn from members of a grade-level or content team about how different teachers go about establishing norms of collaboration, and they should be offered support from their mentor to think about how they will approach establishing their own classroom norms in the first weeks of school. In addition, specific professional development sessions early in the year should focus on how to create and uphold classroom norms. These sessions can be followed by informal classroom observations by the mentor, who can provide specific targeted feedback if refinements are needed. For example, one elementary school teacher recognized that for students to be able to give and receive peer feedback, she needed to first help them understand what feedback was, so they could grasp the norm, "We provide feedback, not criticism to our fellow students." Below is her description of how she worked with her grade-level team for this purpose.

> We do emphasize a huge distinction between feedback and criticism. We even model and role play what criticism sounds like versus what feedback sounds like. Once students understand the difference then they're able to accept the feedback that we give them. Once they can accept the feedback from the teacher, then we move on to peer feedback, again modeling. We even allow students to come and observe us giving feedback to other students in our one-on-one teacher conferences, so that they can hear and understand what the process is like. Then we allow them to practice as peers with one another, giving and receiving feedback and what that is like.

This teacher believed strongly in the value in peer feedback, so she invested time in helping students understand what it was and was not. She reported that the time invested paid off later in the year as students were able to support each other's learning. Teachers like this one, who can articulate what they value in the classroom and how they establish conditions under which those behaviors will flourish, are invaluable resources to beginning teachers as they continue to develop their skills in formative assessment practices.

Beginning teachers can benefit from support and examples of practice for developing guidelines for students to help them listen supportively to other students' ideas, and for establishing classroom norms to support students sharing their thinking, even when they express ideas that are incorrect or not yet quite right. Beginning teachers may need help to show that they value all student thinking, and that sometimes incorrect explanations can be the most useful for moving everyone's understanding forward, while still supporting individual student learning. Help may be provided in the form of observing a teacher in the school, talking with colleagues about how they respond to incorrect answers, and preparing in advance some responses to students should incorrect explanations arise in the lesson. Some beginning teachers annotate their lesson plans with reminders about how they want to respond to students.

Routines to Support Use of Learning Goals and Success Criteria

A foundational formative assessment skill for beginning teachers is the use of learning goals and success criteria, so that students understand where learning is going and how they will know when they have reached the goals. Given the foundational but challenging nature of learning goals and success criteria for effective formative assessment practice, this topic is one that should be included early in induction programs. To develop strong learning goals and success criteria requires deep disciplinary knowledge. While we hope beginning teachers had some opportunities in preservice education to deepen their understanding of how student learning develops over time, it likely was only in a limited number of areas. This is an important topic for a yearlong focus as beginning teachers tackle each unit of study for the first time.

Beginning teachers will benefit from developing routines around lesson preparation, sharing goals, and revising them as the lesson has taken place. Identifying a place on a whiteboard to write goals, or some other strategy to keep them visible, will help both the teacher and students cultivate the expectation for learning goals as a routine of most lessons. The lesson plan can be the place to note how the teacher wants to return to the learning goals at the end of a lesson as a way of checking in with students about what they are learning. Putting a student in charge of reminding the teacher to share the learning goals at the start of a lesson or for an end-of-class routine can help share the memory burden, while also actively engaging students in the learning process.

Routines for reflecting on lessons at the end of the day or week can provide opportunities for notes on lesson plans that can inform revisions for future years. In a recent meeting with teachers to help us (the authors) better understand how they develop their lesson plans, two teachers talked about their approaches for updating lesson plans. Both teachers used Google Docs to document their daily lesson plans, creating one document with all the lesson plans for a unit. At the end of each day they would both go back to their plans and either make changes for how they would use it next year or add comments to the document to remind them of potential revisions when they return to it the following year. With slight differences in approach, both teachers had developed a habit of reflecting on the day's teaching and a way to capture that reflection to inform future teaching. Providing concrete suggestions, along with modeling from more experienced teachers, can help beginning teachers more quickly develop good routines for self-reflection.

Routines to Support Use of Classroom Discussions

Whole-class and small-group discussions are important sources of evidence of student learning. While experienced teachers will likely use a wide repertoire of approaches for structuring class discussions, beginning teachers may benefit from a smaller set of routines that they initially work on to build fluency through deliberate, focused practice, observation and feedback, and reflection.

Routines such as write-pair-share can be particularly helpful, since they can provide a written record of students' initial thinking that teachers can collect to review later, particularly if a discussion gets off track, and they do not hear from as many students as they had intended. Other strategies, such as using mini whiteboards for student responses to an initial question, allow the teacher to scan the room to see responses from all students, and then use that information to decide whom to call on first to share their thinking with the class. This approach conveys the expectation that all students should participate, but also can relieve the concern of not knowing how a student, called on at random, might respond.

Targeted professional learning on discussion routines, in conjunction with trying out new strategies and reflecting on their success with a mentor, provides space for the beginning teacher to identify which approaches work well for their context, content, and grade level.

Self-Assessment and Peer Feedback Routines

Among the various formative assessment practices, both self-assessment and peer feedback are consistently challenging for teachers, and therefore tend to be the least frequently utilized.[37] This may be an area of professional development to introduce to apprentice teachers later in the school year, once they have become more confident in using learning goals and success criteria, and eliciting and acting on evidence. They may benefit from more opportunities to observe how other teachers support students in self-assessment and peer feedback (either in person or on video), and also to listen to experienced teachers reflect on how they scaffolded students' use of self-assessment and peer feedback when they first began using these practices.

Beginning teachers need to identify whether their students have ever engaged in self-assessment or peer feedback, and they need to understand those previous experiences and the strategies used. They will need support to identify the appropriate tasks that would warrant self-assessment or peer feedback, and to determine how the information will be incorporated into the flow of a lesson. They will also need help in how to model acceptable and unacceptable feedback in the context of peer assessment, or how to model students' thought processes as they self-assess their own work. Below we present an extended example of how two teachers work with their students over the course of multiple weeks at the start of the year. This example demonstrates the complexity of setting up routines for student self-assessment and peer feedback and illustrates the level of thought the process entails. Depending on the age and previous experiences of students, establishing these routines may be something beginning teachers tackle during their second year of induction.

We have had several opportunities to observe Ms. Cárdenas (the second-grade teacher introduced in chapter 3) along with her teaching partner, Ms. Lozano. We observed both teachers use a classroom routine for students to provide feedback to a peer, called P-Q-S: students first gave a peer a "P" for a "put-up" or praise, followed by "Q" for a question to probe or help the peer understand the work; and finally "S" for a suggestion or next step that the peer can work on. When we observed the classes, the school year was halfway through and the students were very familiar with the P-Q-S approach. As observers, we could appreciate that this routine took some effort to establish, but through an interview with these two expert teachers, we had an opportunity to really appreciate the commitment that they made to helping students understand and internalize the routine to maximize its effectiveness. They start by modeling this approach in student-teacher conferences, then they discuss and practice each step separately before asking students to put it all together.

Once students are familiar with their teacher providing feedback in the form of the P-Q-S routine in a teacher-student conference, they then talk about it some more and begin to practice each part in student pairs.

> And so, what we do is we take feedback that we've given a student, and together as a class we'll look at it closely, and analyze the writing, and ask them "What do you notice?" "What do you see?" in the feedback that the teacher has given a student. So, students will begin to point out—"Oh, I notice that the teacher starts with giving a put-up, recognizing something we've done really well, and then asking a question—it could be a clarifying question or a question just to get us to think about our work—and end with a suggestion, a next step, something we can work on.[38]

As they begin to have students use this structure for peer feedback, they talk about what it means to give a peer a put-up, and then they practice just that skill in isolation for several lessons. When students are comfortable with that, they move them to giving a put-up and asking a question, with opportunities to practice and rehearse asking questions. Finally, students are supported to engage with the full P-Q-S routine. As observers, we appreciated the skill with which both teachers used the P-Q-S strategy with their students. The interview provided a much more nuanced perspective than could be gleaned from the observation alone. Beginning teachers will benefit similarly from not just observing their mentors and other teachers in the school, but also having those more experienced teachers talk explicitly about how they helped the students develop the routines in the first place.

Routines to Support Collecting Evidence of Student Thinking

One final routine for consideration for professional development opportunities for beginning teachers is the use of teacher checklists in class to support student observations. We do not mean keeping records of the number of questions completed or who participated in discussions, but rather a checklist as a concrete reminder of what to listen for or observe as evidence of student understanding. For example, when Ms. Cárdenas was working with her second-grade class on decomposing numbers, she recorded what kind of strategy each student used to solve the problem: whether they used manipulatives or drew a diagram, used a guess-and-check approach, or had a more systematic approach to the problem. These notes later allowed her to plan for the following day's lesson and to think about warm-up problems that might help some students still working with concrete manipulatives develop a deeper understanding. Even as an experienced teacher, she still relied on observation notes to help her keep track of where students were in their learning, to get a sense of the range of strategies students were using, and to help her identify two or three students to share their approach the following day.

Checklists can provide a concrete tool for teachers to use during a lesson as a means of keeping them focused on what is critical evidence of student learning that they can use to inform next steps. Beginning teachers can get distracted by the minutiae of keeping a classroom running smoothly and forget to keep note of what students are saying or doing. A less experienced teacher might be supported by a mentor to anticipate likely student responses and then formalize those anticipated observations into a checklist as part of lesson planning, or the teacher might be supported to develop such tools as part of common planning time.

Many of the examples of formative assessment practice that we have used in prior chapters show how frequently teachers use one-on-one conferences with their students to elicit evidence of their thinking and to provide feedback to them. Being able to have these kinds of conferences without being interrupted means that the other students need to have well-established routines so that they can continue learning without the direct assistance of a teacher. Here is how one teacher described the routines she had put in place for this purpose:

> It's important to be able to establish routines in the classroom in which students become very independent . . . [we] have visuals and reminders for students to know what to do should they need help. Ways they can go about helping themselves. Using their peers as a resource, thinking of tools in the classroom that might help them during that one moment that they might need help. While students really go about their work and become more independent then we are able to spend more time to meet one-on-one with students.

Observing peers and having opportunities to talk with them about explicit routines and structures and how they were established are beneficial to beginning teachers.

OBSERVATIONS AND FEEDBACK OPPORTUNITIES

In chapter 7 we introduced the *Formative Assessment Rubrics, Reflection and Observation Protocol* (FARROP) as a knowledge representation that preservice teachers could use to help them understand the ten dimensions that, in combination, constitute formative assessment practices.[39] The FARROP also has value for beginning teachers as a structure for observation and feedback, both from their mentors and from other experienced teachers in formative assessment. It may be beneficial to focus observations on specific FARROP dimensions that align with the focus of ongoing professional development.

Using video-capture technology can make the logistics of releasing the observer from his or her class easier and allow for more frequent observations. In addition, the video record can be used in discussions with a mentor to support closer examination of particular parts of the lesson, for feedback and for the beginning teacher to engage in self-reflection. A mentor can also review a video of a more experienced teacher using a specific aspect of formative assessment practice with the beginning teacher. This process may provide opportunities to explicitly discuss the ways in which that teacher established norms and routines with the students beforehand that allow for effective implementation of the practice.

Reducing teacher turnover, which has the effect of increasing overall teacher experience within a school, has a positive impact on students' academic achievement as well as on other, nonacademic factors, such as attendance. Teachers have the steepest gain in effectiveness during their initial years in the classroom, but professional growth continues throughout their careers.[40] These gains in effectiveness are more likely when teachers are working in a collegial environment and have stability in their teaching assignments, with limited mobility across grade levels, subject, or district. Induction programs have emerged as a potential answer to the question of how to reduce teacher turnover in schools.

Mark Windschitl and colleagues argue for the need for coherence from preservice to teacher induction so that core ideas about teaching, critical practices, and tools can be developed and refined by both experienced and novice teachers.[41] In this chapter we proposed a set of approaches and strategies for communities of teachers to engage in to build on their preservice experiences. We focused on the ways in which common planning time could be used to support lesson planning and the review of student work, and on how a series of classroom routines could be introduced and developed over the course of a two-year induction program to help beginning teachers develop collaborative and respectful classroom environments. The habits of mind of inquiry, deliberate practice, and critical reflection are essential as beginning teachers apply what they have learned in preservice education and from their more experienced peers, in order to develop their own professional vision and practice.

SUMMARY: THE BIG IDEAS OF CHAPTER 8

- Teachers beginning their first year of full-time teaching enter into a new community of practice with greater autonomy for their students. Induction programs support teachers in this transition out of preservice.
- Comprehensive induction programs include high-quality mentors, common planning time, ongoing professional development, and observation and feedback opportunities.
- Weaving formative assessment into induction programs is essential to help beginning teachers transition from the externally supported phase of learning in preservice to functioning as more autonomous professionals.
- Common planning time allows for a focus on shared lesson planning approaches that explicitly embed formative assessment practices, such as the review of student work as a lens into classroom teaching and learning. Common planning time can also be used to share ways in which formative assessment can deepen the review process.
- Initial professional development should support beginning teachers in developing a set of formative assessment classroom routines that allow them to unpack what can look like a seamless practice into tangible steps that they can begin to incorporate into their own classroom.
- Opportunities to observe and be observed, with self-reflection and feedback, are also critical for beginning teachers to deepen their formative assessment practices.

CHAPTER 9

Deepening Teacher Expertise Through In-Service Experiences

Are good teachers born or made? Is it the case that talent, an innate capacity, is hardwired into individuals and supersedes the expertise that teachers might develop over thousands of hours across an entire career? Some have argued that talent cannot be overlooked, especially in areas like music and art, whereas others claim that it is motivation, interest, and practice that give rise to expertise independent of talent, and argue that there is no persuasive evidence to suggest that talent is a prerequisite for expert levels of performance.[1] A review of teaching research confirms the claim that teachers continue to develop increasing levels of expertise once they leave their induction phase and do not remain stagnant for the rest of their professional lives.[2] The development of teachers' expertise is not independent from the context in which they teach.[3] As David Berliner notes, "We too often think of expertise as a characteristic of a person, when psychology has repeatedly taught us that such characteristics are typically an interaction of the person and the environments in which they find themselves."[4]

This chapter focuses on the continuous development of formative assessment expertise, after teachers have completed the induction phase and have moved into their in-service experiences, and the kind of environments and opportunities that provide felicitous support. During the in-service phase, teachers become more conscious of their practice, are better able to make judgments about what they do in the classroom and how they do it, and are increasingly equipped to make decisions about ways to improve. It is the time when teachers take more control over their own learning. We continue to adopt a sociocultural approach to in-service learning, as described in chapter 2, in which learning is socially mediated by the context in which it occurs, including by the actions of others toward the learner that facilitate progress.

The chapter is organized in three main sections. First, we outline what we mean by expertise with reference to ambitious teaching and formative assessment. Next, we discuss the nature of environments in which teachers work that enable their ongoing professional learning toward increased expertise. Finally, we describe the opportunities that teachers can avail themselves of as they move along the continuum to becoming experts in formative assessment.

WHAT DO WE MEAN BY EXPERTISE?

In chapter 1, we outlined the characteristics of ambitious teaching and effective formative assessment, and proposed that both were grounded in disciplinary knowledge. Here we elaborate these characteristics with research findings on teacher expertise. John Hattie synthesized over 50,000 studies of the effects of influences on student learning and concluded that, beyond what students bring to the table, the teacher is the single most powerful influence (over home, principals, schools, or peers) on student learning.[5] He suggests that too much emphasis has been placed on differentiating between novice and experienced teachers rather than on distinguishing between experienced and expert teachers. Experience does not necessarily equate to being an expert. In a review of the literature on the distinctions between experienced and expert teachers, Hattie and Richard Jaeger considered dimensions that make up expert teaching. They concluded that expert teachers:

- Have high levels of knowledge and understanding of the subjects they teach and know the most important ways in which to represent their subjects for students; they have high levels of content knowledge for teaching
- Guide learning through classroom interaction; student questioning is high and engagement is the norm
- Monitor learning and provide feedback that assists students to progress; they are skilled at monitoring the current status of student understanding, are flexible in their responses to students, and gear their feedback to the students' current learning status
- Attend to the more attitudinal attributes of learning (especially developing self-efficacy and motivation); they are able to create an optimal

climate for learning that generates an atmosphere of trust in which it is understood that mistakes are sources of new learning
- Have a positive influence on a wide range of student outcomes, including summative test scores, students making an investment in their learning, having respect for themselves and others, and the disposition to become active, competent and thoughtfully critical participants in our increasingly fast-changing and complex world[6]

A further research program connected to the National Board for Professional Teacher Standards hypothesized prototypical features of expertise, which added to the list above: better adaptation and modification of goals, better skills at improvisation, more challenging objectives, better ability to read cues from students, and more respect for students.[7] When results from this research program were analyzed, the greatest differences between expert and nonexpert teachers were the degree of challenge offered to students, teachers' ability for deep representations of subject matter, and teachers' skills in monitoring learning and providing feedback. In this vein it is worth noting that National Board certified teachers outperformed their noncertified peers on every prototypical feature, with statistical significance achieved on eleven of the thirteen comparisons of the features.[8] It is also noteworthy that a recent research study found that most students—and especially students of color, students from low-income families, students with mild to moderate disabilities, and English language learners—spent "500 hours per school year on assignments that were not appropriate for their grade and with instruction that didn't ask enough of them."[9]

In preservice programs, teachers are introduced to formative assessment practices in the context of ambitious teaching. Expertise in teaching is inherent to effective formative assessment. Indeed, many would say, "Isn't formative assessment just good teaching?" While we can consider good teaching a necessary condition for formative assessment, it is not a sufficient one. At the same time as teachers are developing their expertise in teaching, if they are to continue to move along a continuum of expertise in formative assessment, it seems clear that they will need to focus on several dimensions that undergird expert teaching in ways that are specific to formative assessment.

In order to develop expertise in formative assessment, there are five areas of practice on which teachers can focus. First, they will continue to extend their subject matter knowledge, particularly about the representations of knowledge of the discipline so that they are able to identify clear goals and success criteria and create learning opportunities to elicit students' thinking. A commensurate increase in their pedagogical content knowledge will be necessary to develop skills in responding to student thinking as it evolves toward desired learning goals. Second, they will need to cultivate increased expertise in eliciting and interpreting evidence of the current status of student's learning and in guiding their learning through interaction. Paul Black and Dylan Wiliam, in their landmark review of formative assessment research, referred to this process of eliciting and using evidence of learning as "the heart of pedagogy."[10] Third, teachers will increasingly refine their skills in providing feedback that moves learning forward, a nontrivial skill involving sensitive interpretation of evidence in combination with sufficient disciplinary knowledge to help students close the gap between their current learning status and the intended learning goals. Fourth, teachers will focus on engendering feelings of self-efficacy and motivation among their students by supporting them to use feedback and to generate their own internal feedback through self-assessment. Finally, teachers will need to hone their skills in creating a climate of trust and respect in their classrooms so that students are willing to share their thinking and learn productively with and from each other.

In the next section, we consider the kind of environments in which teachers work that support their professional learning and continued growth as teachers.

ENVIRONMENTS THAT SUPPORT THE DEVELOPMENT OF EXPERTISE

We begin with a personal experience that foregrounds the kind of environment that shapes both teachers' motivation and capacity to engage in continuous learning. A large number of teachers were recruited to take a nearly yearlong course on formative assessment. The course consisted of online learning, individual reading and reflection, and team collaboration. Not surprisingly, given how busy teachers are, not all of them completed the course. When asked to complete a survey about noncompletion, the majority of participants who dropped out of the course cited "lack of support" as the reason for their withdrawal. A few teachers who were not part of learning communities soldiered on alone, but they were not the norm.

To feel motivated and committed to course completion, participant teachers needed support from their peers and their administrators. In chapter 1, we discussed the challenging goals that teachers have to meet in an increasingly fast-paced and changing world. Whereas at one time it might have been possible, although not necessarily desirable, for teachers to go it alone, now the work of teaching is too complex to do without support from others, including from district and school leaders. Indeed, one of the primary reasons that teachers cite for leaving the profession is lack of school-based support.[11]

District and School Leaders

A major contribution that leaders can make to developing expertise in formative assessment is to commit for the long haul. Formative assessment cannot be treated by leadership as the fad of the month or the current initiative that gets the most attention until another one comes along. Instead, supporting continuing expertise toward an expert status is achieved when leaders regard formative assessment as the way we do business, the DNA of classroom practice, and consistently provide the motivation, commitment, and structures that support teachers to continuously improve their formative assessment practice. An assistant superintendent puts what is needed this way:

> To really implement this systemically you have to take the time to do it from the foundational work first, and you have to stay the course. You have to have leadership who has an understanding of [formative assessment] and who also is very supportive of it. Not just giving lip service to it but actually involved in the work, involved in the conversations, able to ask those questions. Those questions that will drive the work to the next level.[12]

Another superintendent advised district leaders to "really think strategically about the support structures. I think we underestimate the amount of support teachers need. And we really felt that our support might feel intrusive. We have since learned that no, indeed they welcome the support. It does not feel intrusive."[13]

Support from leaders does not feel intrusive when it is provided in a professional climate, sharing the same characteristics as the kind of classroom culture that is conducive to student learning. Professionals develop expertise by making mistakes and learning from them, by receiving constructive feedback from leaders, and by being given inviolable time to engage in deep learning in collaboration with others. District and school leaders set the tone and create the conditions for a professional learning environment in which teachers are able to undertake the continuous development of expertise throughout their careers.

This tone and conditions for ongoing teacher learning in formative assessment are well captured by this school leader in his statement: "It's important for administrators to serve in role that's not easily quantified or noted in the research: Encourager."[14]

To reach an expert level of practice, teachers never stop learning. Good leaders know this and regard providing encouragement and an environment for continued professional learning as a cornerstone of their work.

Features of a Supportive Professional Learning Environment

In addition to leaders creating the ethos and structures, an environment conducive to the development of expertise comprises learning opportunities with a number of features, recently summarized by Linda Darling-Hammond and colleagues.[15] From a review of thirty-five methodologically rigorous studies, their summary identified seven widely shared features of professional learning, which we first introduced in chapter 2. To recap, professional learning:

- *is content focused*, which includes an intentional focus on discipline-specific curriculum development and disciplinary pedagogies
- *incorporates active learning*, and is centered on engaging teachers in trying out new strategies, using artifacts, interactive activities, and other strategies to provide deeply embedded, highly contextualized professional learning
- *supports collaboration*, creating spaces for teachers to share ideas and collaborate in their learning, often in job-embedded contexts
- *uses models of effective practice*, including lesson plans, unit plans, samples of student work, observations of peer teachers, and video or written cases of teaching
- *provides coaching and expert support*, involving the sharing of expertise about content and evidence-based practices

- *offers feedback and reflection*, frequently providing built-in time for teachers to think about, receive input on, and make changes to their practice by soliciting feedback and reflection
- *is of sustained duration*, with adequate time to learn, practice, and implement[16]

Although these characteristics are relevant to all phases of the continuum, they take on a different hue as teachers gain experience. After the preservice and induction phases, teachers continue to deepen their disciplinary knowledge, both in terms of the content standards and associated analytical practices, and how student learning progressively develops in relation to specific topics within the discipline, including common misconceptions and challenges students typically experience. Deeper disciplinary knowledge drives their expertise in establishing learning goals and success criteria, their understanding of what constitutes evidence, and their developing skills in evidentiary reasoning. They also deepen their content knowledge for teaching, which, when combined with disciplinary knowledge, provides them with the security and flexibility to respond to students' emerging ideas, which, as we learned in chapter 1, is a hallmark of ambitious teaching.

At earlier phases of the continuum, how teachers engage in active learning is largely determined by others who have responsibility for supporting their professional learning. At the in-service phase, consistent with current ideas in the professional learning literature, teachers make their own decisions about how they want to engage in active learning. A recent report from Learning Forward and the National Commission on Teaching & America's Future calls attention to teachers' own decision-making in ongoing professional learning:

> In the context of professional learning, teacher agency is the capacity to act purposefully and constructively to direct their professional growth and contribute to the growth of colleagues . . . Teachers who have agency are aware of their part in their professional growth and make learning choices to achieve those goals.[17]

Similarly, a mixed-methods study used both survey and interview methodologies to understand the perspectives of state teachers of the year on professional learning.[18] One striking finding was that while 77 percent of teachers had the opportunity to set their own professional learning goals for the year, only 31 percent reported that professional learning opportunities were targeted for teachers of differing levels of experience or expertise. These data suggest a mismatch between the intentions of allowing teachers to direct their own learning and the realities of supporting that approach. Also, few teachers reported the opportunity to receive feedback on classroom observations from a colleague who taught the same content area.

Collaboration continues to be a staple in the development of expertise. However, at the in-service phase, teachers may exercise their agency by determining with whom they want to collaborate, selecting a peer or a group of peers, an administrator, or an external advisor based on who is the best fit for a particular aspect of practice that they want to explore and refine.

Collaboration can also offer teachers a chance to be coached by a trusted peer or school leader. At the in-service stage, the difference in coaching from previous phases lies in the teacher's own self-determination. The teacher invites coaching on a targeted aspect of practice and remains in charge of the coaching agenda throughout the process. In this context, feedback from a coach can provide occasions for self-reflection and, because at this point teachers have an increased awareness of their own practice, they can determine how they will use or not use the coach's feedback. Such invitations for coaching and decisions about if and how to incorporate feedback are part of teachers' own self-regulation, a characteristic of teachers' agency in professional learning at the in-service phase of the continuum.

Darling-Hammond and colleagues identify that "sustained duration" is a characteristic of effective professional learning. For teachers at the preservice or induction phase of our continuum, the idea of sustained duration contrasts with one-shot workshops, learning about a discrete classroom activity, or other episodic or fragmented approaches to teacher learning. Those who are responsible for the first two phases are charged with providing sufficient time to engage teachers in rigorous and cumulative learning that has the possibility to have an impact on practice. It is a truism that good teachers never stop learning, and certainly becoming an expert teacher in formative assessment requires sustained learning over several years on key aspects of the practice within the context of ambitious teaching. We are reminded of this by Olivia Lozano who, by common consent, is an expert in formative assessment. Ms. Lozano has been working with her partner teacher to develop their expertise over the past fifteen years, and as she observed in an interview with the first author:

> We first started by just crafting learning goals and success criteria and practicing that and how that felt in our lessons, and we would share our learning goals and share our success criteria. To this day we feel like we still need to share them with one another and get feedback because they're not always one hundred percent.[19]

Becoming an expert in formative assessment, as opposed to being a successful implementer of the practices, is a long-term prospect and requires commitment and collaboration, both on the part of teachers as continuous learners and school leaders as supporters of that learning, to be seamlessly integrated into ambitious teaching.

In the next section, we turn to some of the ways that teachers can hone their expertise in formative assessment to reach expert status over time.

DEVELOPING EXPERTISE THROUGH IN-SERVICE PROFESSIONAL LEARNING

In chapter 2 we introduced a framework for considering teacher learning in formative assessment along a continuum from preservice to becoming a teacher leader. As in prior chapters, we maintain that the cultivation of expertise in formative assessment during the in-service phase of the continuum is grounded in ambitious teaching and comprises three core, interrelated domains: formative assessment knowledge and skills, disciplinary knowledge, and habits of practice (figure 9.1 below).

During the in-service phase of our continuum, although teachers may seek external avenues for professional learning—such as extended workshops or lectures from experts in formative assessment—most of their opportunities to deepen understanding of formative assessment and its intersection with disciplinary knowledge will be school-based. Of course, teachers' habits of mind, hopefully inculcated during the preservice and induction phases of the continuum, will be a potent driver of their continued willingness to take advantage of school-based learning, which generally occurs in communities of practice.

FIGURE 9.1 Framework for cultivating expertise in formative assessment

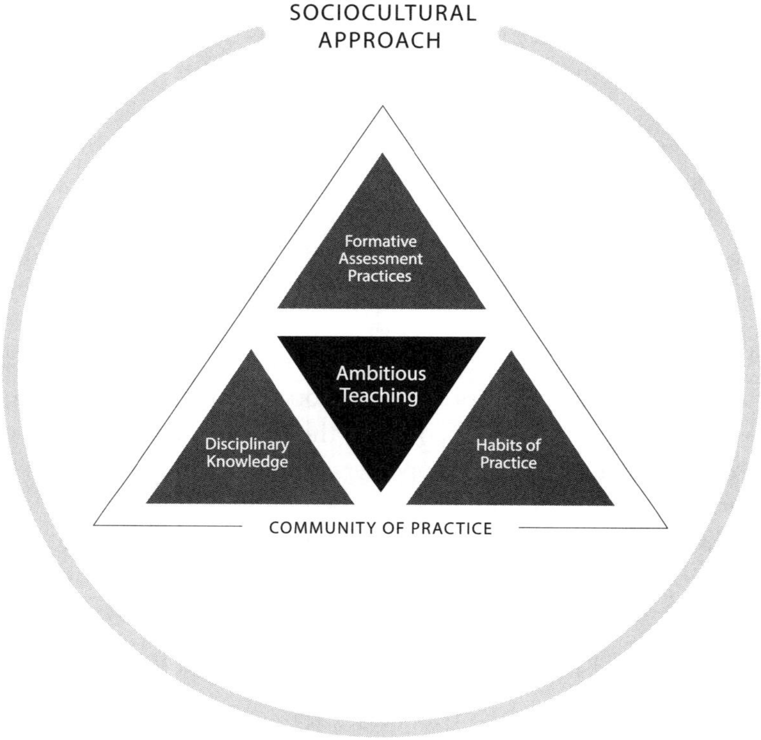

Communities of Practice

The term *community of practice* is usually attributed to Jean Lave and Etienne Wenger who argued that individuals learn in social contexts with other members of their communities who share common goals.[20] In a community of practice, group members interact regularly to learn from one another, focusing on knowledge exchange and growth, rather than on the completion of work tasks.[21] Learning is situated in the group's context, in members' personal experiences and in their relationships. At the in-service phase, a community of practice for teachers occurs in schools and classrooms, develops through relationships with other teachers, and focuses on areas of concern and interest to its members.[22]

A community of practice for formative assessment accords with Darling-Hammond and colleagues' summary of professional learning discussed earlier. The community is intentionally centered on learning and assessment; participants are actively involved in learning and collaborating with colleagues; peer teachers routinely discuss models of effective practice in the form of rubrics, samples of work, and videos and observations of practice; colleagues share expertise and seek and respond to feedback. Furthermore, there is no end to a community of practice; it is sustained through its members' continued commitment to developing their professional expertise in formative assessment, which, as we learned from the teacher experts quoted above, can be a journey of many years. Interviewed as part of the state teacher of the year research previously mentioned, a teacher said of a community of practice: "The power of teachers together, with time? It's mind-blowing and worth every penny."[23]

Tools to support continued learning within a community of practice can help to enhance expertise in formative assessment; we now consider two specific instances of such tools.

Tools to Support the Development of Expertise in Formative Assessment

In chapter 7, we described how observation protocols could support preservice teachers' formative assessment, for example, using the *Formative Assessment Rubrics, Reflection and Observation Protocol* (FARROP) to support the development of expertise among teachers in member states. Several implementations of the FARROP in the context of in-service have suggested that quality formative assessment practice, made explicit through the rubrics and benchmark examples of practice, provides a valued opportunity to examine and refine practice, as this testimonial from a participating teacher attests:

> I learned many ways to incorporate formative assessment into my classroom. I had many opportunities to work with my colleagues and learn more about how they were using formative assessment. It was a wondrous experience to watch instruction change.[24]

Clearly, this teacher had benefited from being observed by his peers and by receiving targeted feedback on the areas of formative assessment he wanted to focus on. He had also gained from reciprocally observing his peers. However, a caution is in order here. A protocol such as the FARROP is not a tool that teachers can use for a few weeks and then be done. Rather, it is a tool that becomes a mainstay for continuously refining formative assessment practices. Even if a teacher reaches the highest level across all dimensions of the rubric, observing and collaborating with similarly sophisticated peers to tease out further nuances of practice can offer continued learning opportunities. It bears repeating that without the habits of mind referenced in figure 9.1, teachers are unlikely to benefit from the use of tools and peer feedback.

Expanding Practice to Involve Students

Successfully engaging students in formative assessment practice is a feature of higher levels of expertise. As teachers become more confident in the teacher-oriented practices of formative assessment (setting learning goals and success criteria, eliciting and acting on evidence), they gradually move toward collaboration with students in ways that are increasingly nuanced, to the point that their formative assessment practice becomes essentially invisible, although still central to teaching and learning. In high-functioning formative assessment classrooms, teachers share responsibility for moving learning forward with their students; learning is recognized as a social process and becomes a joint responsibility.

In chapter 4, we saw a vivid example of an English language arts (ELA) teacher, Ms. Eilertsen, sharing responsibility with her AP students. She established learning goals for the students that were in line with the course requirements, but rather than telling them what the success criteria were, she reviewed with the entire class several models of effective essays and led a discussion about the qualities that made them effective, which eventually became the success criteria for the essay writing. As the students were drafting their essays, Ms. Eilertsen melded into the classroom community as one resource among the students who acted as resources for each other.

When each student decided on questions to help focus their peers' feedback, Ms. Eilertsen realized that many of the questions her students had generated were too focused on a narrow subset of skills and applied to any genre, rather than being substantive questions related to the genre in which they were writing, argumentation. She then intervened and scaffolded a discussion with students so that they collectively developed substantive questions likely to stimulate peer feedback that would genuinely assist improvement. Once the students received peer feedback, they used it in conjunction with their own self-assessment to determine how they would improve their essays. Ms. Eilertsen acted as a resource in the classroom, consulting with students about the feedback they had received and reviewing their written self-assessments. Instead of the more teacher-directed, transmission model that we discussed in chapter 1—which in the interests of future-ready students can no longer be the dominant classroom practice—Ms. Eilertsen operated more as primus inter pares; she was the senior member of a group, rather than the sole arbiter of what happened in her classroom in terms of learning and assessment.

How was Ms. Eilertsen able to develop this level of practice? Previously, we noted that teachers at the in-service phase of the continuum, particularly those with several years of experience, are able to regulate their own professional learning. Ms. Eilertsen is a case in point. She had participated in the course on formative assessment, mentioned earlier in the chapter, and on completion she wanted to enhance her formative assessment practice by giving her students a more involved role in the process. She was offered an opportunity to participate in another professional learning experience, this time focused solely on supporting students to become active agents in their own learning and assessment.

This professional experience required participants to be self-directing, without a leader or facilitator, and to engage in monthly cycles of inquiry with a small group of colleagues. The teachers were provided with a rubric, similar to the FARROP but addressing the constructs specifically related to students: self-assessment and peer feedback. The teachers took video (mostly with their smart phones) of their own classroom practice, which they shared with the other group members for feedback and reflection. Their ultimate aim was for their students to reach the highest levels of the rubric. For example, one of the dimensions of peer feedback at the highest level was that students "engage in productive reciprocal discussions about their descriptive feedback (e.g., asking clarifying questions, discussing how peer feedback relates to peer's own work, discussing suggestions for improvement/next steps)"; the highest level of one of the dimensions of self-assessment called for students to be able to "justify their self-assessment and independently set well-developed goals likely to lead to improvement (e.g., here's the evidence in my learning/work related to the goals and criteria that I used to set goals for improving my learning/work)."[25]

No one told Ms. Eilertsen that she had to participate in the inquiry cycles. Without prompting, she determined that student involvement was an area that she wanted to improve in her formative assessment practice, revealing the habits of mind (figure 9.1) that we have proposed are critical for continued professional learning throughout a teacher's career. In terms of the representations of formative assessment (again, see figure 9.1), she used a tool, the rubrics that described a trajectory for student involvement, and participated in learning experiences with her colleagues, characterized by observation, analysis, practice, feedback, and reflection.

One of the major advances on the road to expertise occurs when teachers are able to integrate all aspects of formative assessment into the everyday work of their classrooms. We saw that once Ms. Eilertsen had achieved competence in the teacher-oriented aspects of formative assessment, her commitment to focusing on the student role ultimately led her to a point of integration. Next, drawing from examples of practice in earlier chapters, we consider what is entailed in reaching this high level of expertise. As we will see, it is achieved by working with colleagues, but also demands considerable analysis and reflection on the part of individual teachers.

Integration of Practices

The definition of formative assessment that frames this book comes from the Formative Assessment for Students and Teachers (FAST) State Collaborative on Assessment and Student Standards (SCASS) of the Council of Chief School Officers.[26] The FAST SCASS members elaborated their basic definition by outlining a number of practices that comprise the process of formative assessment (see chapter 1 for a full description of the definition and practices). In earlier phases of the professional learning continuum, we expect that teachers will be focusing on individual practices, for instance, they may spend considerable time on decomposing questions to develop their questioning skills (see chapter 7), whereas more expert levels would see both teachers and students integrating and embedding these practices in a collaborative and respectful classroom environment.[27] Throughout our content chapters (chapters 3 through 6), there were examples of teachers integrating formative assessment practices into ongoing teaching and learning in their classrooms. In chapter 3, the example of a lesson plan from the Mathematics Assessment Project (figure 3.3) illustrates how a teacher plans for the integration of formative assessment practices in a lesson, ranging from sharing learning goals and success criteria, to identifying formative assessment opportunities in the learning tasks, to crafting questions to elicit evidence of learning during the lesson. Chapter 4 includes an example from Ms. Johannes' ELA class in which there is complete integration of all formative assessment practices, including peer feedback and self-assessment in her lesson. Similarly, in chapter 5, Mr. Rhodea integrates formative assessment in the flow of activity and discussions in his science class. This same situation is repeated in Ms. Closs's lesson in chapter 6; all the practices are evident while her students tackle the compelling social studies question, "Can we be both free and safe?" in their investigation of the tough decisions that leaders have to make in times of war. How did these teachers develop the expertise to be so accomplished in formative assessment? The answer is simple: through trial, error, feedback, and reflection.

Of critical importance in their effort were the habits of mind the teachers had developed to commit to continuous inquiry into their practice, to engage in deliberate practice, to collaborate with their colleagues in analyzing and reflecting, and to make incremental changes over time that led them to higher levels of expertise. Although they may not have worked in a community of practice in the same way that Ms. Eilertsen did (although we note that Ms. Johannes was part of the same inquiry cycle), they drew support from colleagues, while at the same time investing considerable effort and energy in their own analysis and reflection. For example, Ms. Closs carefully drafted her lesson plan to deliberately include all aspects of formative assessment. She then refined her lesson based on feedback from colleagues. When she taught the lesson, a colleague took video of it so that she could engage in her own analysis and incorporate what she learned from this to future lessons.

It is important to note that all these teachers worked in schools where professional growth was the norm, leaders supported a risk-taking environment, and teachers routinely received feedback from their peers, district coaches, or building administrators.

So far in this chapter, we have considered how teachers can enhance their skills in one of the triangles of our framework, formative assessment (figure 9.1), and how habits of mind motivate their continued learning. The premise of the book is that formative assessment practices are primarily rooted in the disciplines in which they take place. For this reason, the development of higher levels of expertise in formative assessment is a critical factor in teachers continuing to deepen their disciplinary knowledge. Also, recall from our earlier discussion of expert teaching, disciplinary knowledge is one of the main elements in achieving the status of expert. In the next section, we turn to how teachers can enhance their disciplinary knowledge at the in-service phase of our continuum to benefit formative assessment.

Disciplinary Knowledge

Disciplinary knowledge consists of the content standards and analytic practices of specific disciplines, an understanding of how students' learning typically develops in the discipline, and also the teachers' pedagogical content knowledge (PCK), which Lee Shulman, the originator of the term, referred to as "the special amalgam between content and pedagogy."[28] In a further elaboration, PCK has been summarized as teachers knowing "the structure of their disciplines, and this knowledge provides them with cognitive roadmaps that guide the assignments they give students, the assessments they use to gauge students' progress, and the questions they ask in the give and take of classroom life."[29]

The value of disciplinary knowledge to formative assessment is emphasized by one of the expert teachers quoted earlier in the chapter:

> As a new teacher, it was really hard for me . . . my content knowledge wasn't fully developed yet. That happened with time, and as I became a more experienced teacher, I became more familiar with the standards, then I was able to draw from that knowledge, in order to provide my students with in-the-moment, on-the-spot instruction that would help them to meet the learning goal for that class.[30]

However, it is not a given that teachers' disciplinary knowledge will automatically increase to high levels of expertise as a result of experience. Experience will provide teachers with some insights about how students learn in a particular discipline, but it does not guarantee the level of disciplinary knowledge that we view as necessary for expert formative assessment implementation. For example, recall the experienced mathematics teachers in chapter 4, who participated in a research program on student misconceptions, over one-third of whom, prior to the project, had not been aware of the breadth of student misconceptions.

Jim Minstrell and his colleagues' research points to the need for disciplinary knowledge, and more nuanced interpretations of student learning beyond "got it, didn't get it," in order for teachers to answer the questions:

- What and how are my students thinking/learning in relation to the learning goal?
- What are the strengths and problematic aspects of their thinking? What do they need next to deepen their learning?
- What learning experience or feedback will address the needs I just identified?[31]

Being able to answer these questions is to a great degree dependent on disciplinary knowledge. Minstrell and colleagues give an example of how science teachers can combine disciplinary knowledge with interpretive skills in formative assessment. Teachers highly skilled in interpretation noted that inexperienced physics students typically expressed speed as proportional to the net force acting on the object: when the object was speeding up, the net force was getting larger and larger, and when the object was moving with constant velocity, the net force was constant. They also pointed out that students were likely correctly distinguishing between constant speed and acceleration. In contrast, the less skilled interpreters tended only to note that the students were wrong about the net force needed, and their response to the students was to recite the correct relation between force and motion.[32] The highly skilled interpreters would be in a better position to provide an effective pedagogical response, including feedback, that engaged students' thinking and gave them an opportunity to actively construct the next steps in their own learning. The less skilled interpreters removed any opportunity for the student to advance their own learning, and potentially short-circuited learning by providing the correct relation between force and motion without any explanation of how it differed from the students' own thinking. To achieve high levels of expertise in formative assessment, then, teachers must deepen their content knowledge, which includes developing horizon knowledge, discussed in chapter 1, their PCK, and their knowledge of how learning develops in a domain, all of which contribute to their capacity to interpret students' thinking and respond in ways that are intended to move learning forward.

It is fair to say that good teachers never stop deepening their disciplinary knowledge. They cannot possibly learn all they need to know during preservice and induction to equip them to become sophisticated practitioners of formative assessment. We expect that during preservice learning teachers will be introduced to and consider in some depth the standards that they are responsible for teaching. The induction phase, when they have external support to consider disciplinary knowledge in relation to their own students and their own practice, should be a time when that knowledge continues to increase. To achieve high levels of expertise in formative assessment during in-service will require teachers to actively seek out ways to work with colleagues to deepen their knowledge of content and analytical practices, the typical and atypical pathways that student learning follows, and the common misconceptions that students might have and challenges they might experience in relation to specific disciplinary topics.

Collaborating with colleagues within a community of practice is a fruitful avenue for extending the disciplinary knowledge described above. An example of how effective a community of practice can be illustrated by two teachers who were working with their peers on refining their skills in creating learning goals and success criteria. One of the teachers had observed that another teacher in the community of practice was strong in this area and engaged her in an email exchange. She first shared her concern about including slope as a rate in her learning goal for her mathematics lesson because she wanted her students to come to that understanding through their own investigations and did not want to tell them prematurely and preempt their discovery. Her colleague responded that she had struggled with the same problem of "discovery" and was able to share what she had learned, suggesting that she use words like "relate" or "connect" so that students would be looking for a relationship from the outset of the lesson. The teacher followed her colleague's advice, and after she had taught the lesson, she emailed, "You are the QUEEN of learning goals!" She went on to describe how the lesson had gone, noting that the lesson was more focused, and students were still working on the exploration. As she questioned students about the connection between slope and rate, she was pleased to learn that they could explain what was happening in terms of time and distance. She ended her email by writing, "collaboration is key!"[33] While framing learning goals might seem a small point to focus on, it represents the stitches that weave together the strands of disciplinary knowledge to form a deep overall understanding over time.

As we noted in chapter 7, Black and Wiliam called for "sound models of students' progression in the learning of the subject matter" so that teachers could interpret and respond to assessment evidence in a formative way.[34] Progressions invite a developmental view because they lay out how learning develops over a more or less extended period of time, beginning with rudimentary forms of learning and moving through progressively more sophisticated states. In earlier chapters we suggested that learning progressions can assist teachers to develop their disciplinary knowledge and we return to that idea, this time in the context of in-service learning.

Regrettably, there are few research-based and validated progressions, but this situation should not prevent teachers from using ones that exist. When investigating progressions, teachers can map their own students' progress to the progression, analyzing how well the progression reflects what they are seeing in their classrooms. Such analysis has the potential for teachers to develop a deeper understanding of their students' learning, which in turn can benefit their formative assessment practices, particularly their interpretive skills and their pedagogical actions in response to evidence. In addition, we have seen significant value when teachers collaborate on developing learning progressions, either within or across multiple grades. We describe a process below but recommend strongly that this is work best done collaboratively.

Standards are not progressions, although most current college- and career-ready standards are more coherent in describing a trajectory of learning than many previous state standards. However, content standards describe learning goals at the end of a grade level or a set of grade levels, rather than identifying the intra-grade development of underlying knowledge, concepts, and skills necessary for meeting these goals. For example, foundational skills such as understanding and using sequencing language are presupposed in standards that require students to keep track of meaning in a text.[35] Teachers can collaboratively develop intra-grade progressions for more than one grade level, a process which has considerable payoff in terms of enhancing disciplinary knowledge. By way of testimonial to the process, middle school social studies teacher Jason Riley said that developing and using progressions "has changed the way I think about how I plan instruction and how I use formative assessment."[36]

To develop progressions, teachers first collectively generate ideas about what they think the incremental steps are between the end of one standard and the beginning of the next, or between groups of related standards. Then they review the progression, keeping in mind questions such as, "Are the main building blocks between standards addressed?" and, "Is this a realistic representation, based on the knowledge we have so far, of how students learn the content of this standard?" At this point they can refine the progression in light of their responses to the review questions. Once a defensible progression has been established, teachers can put their progression into practice for teaching and formative assessment. After some experience using the progression, they will be in a position to evaluate the degree to which it represents what happened in reality, and can make further refinements, if necessary.[37] Obviously, teachers cannot do this for every standard at their grade level all at once. But incrementally, spurred by a commitment to inquiry, they will be able to build up a set of progressions. Not that these progressions will ever be carved in stone. Instead, they are representations that are subject to revision as teachers work together to analyze how they play out in practice with different groups of students over the years. In addition, they can be a means of communicating guild knowledge with more novice members of their group to help them predict and anticipate the range of student responses to key learning goals.

Collaborating with colleagues to plan lessons together and evaluating the effectiveness of the planning once a lesson has been completed, including a consideration of the evidence obtained and the responses made, can also augment disciplinary knowledge. Ms. Lozano and her teaching partner, quoted earlier, cite analyzing student work as a core experience in increasing disciplinary knowledge, particularly in relation to misconceptions and challenges that students might experience in specific domains. They also routinely discuss how they responded pedagogically to the work and how well their responses moved learning forward, which in some instances lead to reconsidering their responses in terms of what might have been more effective.

We also suggest that teachers have a responsibility to keep up with research that pertains to the structure, organization, and nature of thinking processes within disciplines, as well as with research into how students learn in specific disciplines. We do not mean that teachers should necessarily read slews of scholarly papers, but there is a good deal of professional literature written for practitioners that teachers could consult to expand their disciplinary knowledge. A community of practice provides a useful forum for reading and discussing articles on disciplinary topics and reflecting on them in relation to the teachers' own practice.

Another area of knowledge that we think is important to take into account during the in-service phase is knowing about students' funds of knowledge as a means to invite in the knowledge and experience students bring from their homes and communities. This both supports learning and enables greater insights for teachers into student learning through formative assessment. We anticipate that in the preservice phase of our professional learning continuum, candidate teachers will be introduced to the concept of funds of knowledge, but that during the in-service phase it will take on greater salience in formative assessment.

Funds of Knowledge

Students' prior knowledge in a discipline is important to build on in developing new learning. Prior knowledge includes not just the academic knowledge students have acquired, but also the knowledge that they bring from their homes and communities—their funds of knowledge. The term derives from Luis Moll and colleagues, whose research revealed that teachers generally only know their students from their classroom performances, rather than knowing each student as a "whole person." Knowing a student as a whole person requires taking into account the student's home-based context.[38] Moll and colleagues advocated drawing on students' funds of knowledge not to merely reproduce household knowledge in the classroom, but rather to legitimize students' experiences as valid, and to build on familiar knowledge bases that students can manipulate to enhance learning in subject matter content in school.[39] In essence, they proposed using students' knowledge acquired in their homes and communities in ways that enhance students' sense of themselves as "knowledge-makers and knowers."[40] In this example from a science class on photosynthesis, we see how a student has been invited by her teacher to combine her lived experiences with the knowledge she has acquired in school to develop her understanding:

> I now know that plants don't suck up food from the soil. I was re-potting plants with my Gran and it was really, really difficult

> getting them out of the pots. They were stuck tight in the soil. The roots are really tight and there's no gaps. So they can't be getting food from there. It must be from photosynthesis.[41]

In this situation, the teacher had created space in the lesson for students to share their thinking, and for this student that meant making connections to what she had thought about when repotting plants with a family member. As a result, the teacher had greater insights into the depth of this student's thinking about photosynthesis, to which she could respond pedagogically. Furthermore, it represents an example of "interthinking"—an idea introduced in chapter 1. This student's peers heard her account and had the chance to either rethink or confirm their ideas in response.

What teachers see their students doing on classroom learning tasks may not reflect what they are capable of doing.[42] For this reason, teachers must know and value who their students are at a deep level, which includes knowing about the beliefs, values, languages, and practices of the communities to which their students belong. As we saw in the previous example, sophisticated teachers take into consideration the students' home experiences in a formative assessment context. Students can be advantaged when teachers make connections from the students' home knowledge and experiences to the ideas they are learning about in school. For instance, in a science class, a teacher elicited a student's thinking about germination, and discovered that his experience included watching his mother sprout seeds by soaking them overnight and then packing them in a cloth, which she put away in a dark place for couple of days. From his observations, the student had concluded that seeds could grow in places where there was hardly any air. In response, the teacher helped him understand seed germination processes, and what kind of gas plants need to survive.[43]

Knowing who their students are may seem like a daunting prospect for teachers. To this end, Moll and colleagues suggest that teachers become ethnographers of their students' home communities. With all the other demands on teachers, it is easy to imagine that an ethnography might seem like a bridge too far. However, in a recent discussion on how teachers might access students' funds of knowledge, one teacher pointed out that she could have learned so much if she had "only bothered to ask." Bothering to ask can take many forms, ranging from asking students what they already know about a particular topic from their home community, to informal questionnaires and interviews with families. The habits of mind, particularly a commitment to inquiry, will serve teachers well as they continue to grow in their formative assessment practice, particularly as they see how taking their students' funds of knowledge into account can affect how they approach their discipline and their students.

The ideas we have suggested for the continuous development of expertise in formative assessment during the in-service phase of our continuum are by no means exhaustive. Rather, they are intended as pointers to how teachers can work together in the interests of increasing their expertise in formative assessment. No doubt, teachers who possess the habits of mind for continued learning will find their own ways to boost their knowledge and skills in their quest for expertise in formative assessment.

SUMMARY OF THE BIG IDEAS OF CHAPTER 9

- District and school leaders are responsible for creating conditions conducive to teachers' continued professional learning.
- Being an experienced teacher is not the same as being an expert teacher.
- While teachers are developing their expertise in teaching during the in-service phase, they need to focus on several dimensions that undergird expert teaching in ways that are specific to formative assessment.
- The features that characterize effective professional learning in previous phases at the earlier stages of the continuum are equally relevant at the in-service phase.
- In the in-service phase, communities of practice occur in schools and classrooms, develop through relationships with other teachers, and focus on areas of concern and interest to their members.
- During the in-service phase, teachers become increasingly skilled at seamlessly integrating formative assessment into ongoing teaching and learning.
- A hallmark of developing expertise in the in-service phase is that teachers become more increasingly self-directed in their own professional learning.
- Teachers striving for expertise become more aware of students' funds of knowledge and incorporate them into their teaching and formative assessment practice.

CHAPTER 10

Teacher Leadership for Formative Assessment

During the self-regulation phase of our professional learning continuum for formative assessment, teachers take more control of their own in-service learning. We envision that it is at this point that a number of teachers will expand their capacities and influence by adopting a teacher leadership role. At this phase of the continuum, teachers have become accomplished in ambitious teaching practices (see chapter 1), which are grounded in disciplinary knowledge and encompass formative assessment. They are now well positioned to support their peers at the induction and in-service phases of the learning continuum who are still developing their knowledge and skills.

A commonly held view of teacher leadership is that it is the process through which teachers—individually or collectively—influence their peers, principals, and stakeholders to improve teaching and learning practices in support of increased student learning and achievement.[1] Being a teacher leader is different from other leadership roles within a school, for example, those assumed by principals, vice principals, or directors of curriculum. Instead of having positional authority, teachers become leaders by being continuous learners, by gaining respect from their peers, and by using group skills and influence to improve the practice of their teacher colleagues. They model effective practice and support collaborative team structures within their schools.[2] In addition, teacher leaders are learning and achievement oriented, willing to take risks, and ready to assume responsibility.[3]

Teacher leadership is not a new idea. Teachers have assumed both formal and informal leadership roles in schools for at least two decades.[4] Yet, when asked about leadership roles teachers will often say, "I am just a teacher."[5] This response belies many teachers' potential to become teacher leaders and influence policy and practice in their schools and districts. At the self-regulation phase, once teachers have acquired considerable knowledge and skills in formative assessment and are recognized for those skills by their peers, they are ready and fully capable of new leadership roles to support formative assessment school- and districtwide. Often missing in schools and districts, however, is the imagination to envision new ways of working and leading. Hybrid roles are starting to appear in schools, where teachers have classroom responsibilities for part of the day and spend the rest of the time supporting other teachers. These roles offer positive benefits by maintaining the teacher leaders' classroom connections while allowing them to have impact more broadly within their schools.[6]

In this chapter, we first consider what a leadership role for teachers entails and its value to teachers, their colleagues, and their schools. Next, we discuss the attributes of a culture that enables teacher leadership. This is followed by a detailed description of the various roles and activities they can undertake with their colleagues to engage them in inquiry, deliberate practice, and critical reflection. Finally, we highlight the skills and qualities that teachers need to be successful in a leadership role.

WHY TEACHER LEADERSHIP?

Today, school leaders must assume responsibility for an ever-widening range of areas—from instruction to management to strategic development—such that no individual can successfully lead a school without support from others.[7] Teacher leaders, working in collaboration with the principal, can support improvements in instruction and promote practices among their peers that lead to improved student outcomes. Principals can maximize their effectiveness by harnessing the talents and expertise of teachers in leadership roles.[8] A case in point is Norma Silva, principal of an elementary school in Los Angeles, who decided to create teacher leadership roles to meet learning needs that she observed in the school. These two teacher leaders have their own classrooms, but they take on additional responsibilities that include providing demonstration lessons and being released about twenty percent of the time to work with their peers. Acknowledging how the teacher leaders enhance her own leadership capacity, Ms. Silva commented:

> There are teachers whose expertise is visible solely to the eyes of the principal. Structures can be created to make that expert teaching

> visible to support teacher development more broadly as a school. For instance, during PE, same grade-level teachers can visit the teacher leaders' classrooms to see demonstration lessons. During a debrief session, beginning and developing teachers can discuss the lesson, teacher moves, and next steps. In addition, teacher leaders coach their peers in the same focus area during their classes' PE time. During common planning time, teacher leaders collaborate with beginning and developing teachers by supporting the planning of their next steps in teaching. Through these structures, the teacher leaders help me build the school's internal capacity to sustain professional learning throughout the school year.[9]

Most notable in the quote from Principal Silva is her recognition of teacher expertise and her desire to make it visible to other staff in the school by creating a structure that will provide opportunities for teachers to observe and be observed by peers.

There are also benefits for teachers from assuming leadership roles. Some teachers are reluctant to leave their classrooms entirely to become school leaders (for example, taking on a principalship), but feel that they are at a point in their careers when they would like to apply their expertise in support of their peers in a more formalized way. Not only does the opportunity for leadership help their colleagues, but it also provides teacher leaders with challenge, personal accomplishment, and job satisfaction, which are important components in retaining expert teachers. One of the teacher leaders who works with Principal Silva put it this way:

> I see becoming a teacher leader as a hybrid between two of the things I enjoy most. One being in the classroom teaching and the other continuing to develop my own skills as I help develop others. I'm fortunate to be at a school that has a different mindset around what teacher leadership is. Here, the administrator recognizes that the most important place to be is the classroom. She also recognizes the importance of teachers fostering growth amongst each other. This creates an environment of learning for all.[10]

Descriptions of career trajectories or pathways and models of innovative approaches for using teacher leaders have been proposed, but to date, little compelling research has been undertaken about the effects of teacher leadership.[11] However, the value of teacher leaders is bolstered by an intersection with divergent literature showing that traditional top-down structures inhibit teacher leadership, and consequently school improvement, and by research on high performing schools that suggests schools with cultures of collaboration and professional inquiry have success in improving student learning.[12] These studies point to the potential for teacher leadership being best realized in contexts that are characterized by more horizontal and less hierarchical leadership structures, and that maintain a focus on collaboration and reflective practice among colleagues.

A study of attitudes toward teacher evaluation and professional support provides additional insight into the value of teacher leaders.[13] Study participants were State Teachers of the Year, who were already recognized as successful practitioners, and were vocal in their desire to continue their own learning while supporting the learning of their peers. Teachers highlighted one challenge in particular, concerning receiving meaningful feedback grounded in specific content areas: principals and assistant principals often lacked "recent and relevant classroom teaching experience."[14] In contrast, peer observations were viewed as opportunities for "helpful feedback to be provided to teachers about their practice and their content."[15] One teacher noted, "teachers helping teachers has arose [sic] due to the vacuum of any other real support, and it has been authentic and beneficial."[16]

Further support for the role of teacher leader comes from findings that when teachers consult with peers and jointly reflect on practice, their belief in their own abilities and their capacity to successfully solve teaching and learning problems is enhanced. Peer consultation also encourages improvement through collaboration and an inclination toward taking action on the part of teachers.[17]

With this background on teacher leadership, let us now consider how a school culture can be shaped to provide fertile ground for teachers to take on leadership roles.

A CULTURE FOR TEACHER LEADERSHIP

While in every school there may be "a sleeping giant of teacher leadership, which can be a strong catalyst for making change," the giant is unlikely to be awakened without a culture that stirs it.[18] Several factors contribute to a stirring culture, beginning with the attitude and example of the principal. A prerequisite for teacher leadership is a principal who does not believe that authority resides solely in her or his position, but instead allows colleagues to assume roles as leaders and create collective leadership within a school.[19]

Principal Silva's quote earlier provides an example of how a principal does not assume that she alone has all the requisite expertise to support the learning of every teacher in her school. She expresses the value she places on teaching professionals by establishing mechanisms that encourage peer observations and post-observation conversations to reflect on their lessons. In doing so, she is promoting a schoolwide focus on learning, inquiry, and reflective practice.

Principal Silva established the teacher leader roles. However, in a school culture characterized by collaboration and shared responsibility, the initiative could be taken by the teachers directly. For example, a teacher could propose the formation of a teacher learning community to discuss problems of practice, or suggest a different approach to class scheduling that would allow for more common planning time.

Teacher leader and school leader roles need to be clearly defined, including their shared leadership responsibilities. For example, if teacher leaders are engaged in formative observations (not part of evaluation processes), teachers need to be able to trust that the teacher leaders will keep conversations and observations confidential, and principals have to respect that confidentiality. Principals also need to ensure that the responsibilities of their teacher leaders are central to the teaching and learning processes, rather than focusing on administrative or managerial tasks. Being a department chair or a grade-level chair could potentially be a teacher-leader position supporting ambitious teaching and integrated formative assessment across departments or grades. Unless, of course, those teacher leaders are overburdened with responsibilities (planning field trips, ordering classroom materials, and the like) that limit their time to focus on teacher practice and student learning.

Norms of collaboration, teamwork, professional inquiry, and reflective practice within the school that permit teachers to adopt a leadership role are established and nurtured by the principal. There is a multiplier effect for these norms, as teacher leaders promote them through building trusted relationships with their peers and engaging them in group processes to reflect on their teaching, discuss their classroom practice, and advance shared goals.

In a culture characterized by collaborative norms, teachers do not regard themselves as classroom subcontractors within a school, but rather recognize the value of collaboration, learning with and from others for the benefit of their students and their own professional satisfaction. With the example from school leaders like Principal Silva, who unlock access to expertise already residing in their schools, teachers see the value of teacher leaders to facilitate their professional learning in a variety of ways, and do not regard them as another layer of hierarchical authority.

When the sleeping giant of teacher leadership is awakened, it is very likely that teachers who have the expertise in teaching, learning, and formative assessment to support their colleagues may still need assistance in honing the skills of leadership.[20] As expert teachers, they will have developed many of the skills that will serve them when working with adults, for example, creating a safe space for learning and active listening and providing feedback. However, working with adults is different from teaching students; classroom teachers beginning a leadership role may not yet have the skills to lead discussions, mediate, provide feedback to their peers, identify the needs of their colleagues, and build ownership and action in support of student learning. The principal and other school leaders can be a source of assistance in refining these skills, through modeling, feedback, and encouragement. Seeking perspectives of those being supported by the teacher leader is also a useful way to evaluate their efforts and to identify areas for improvement. This kind of feedback can be solicited by school leaders and by the teacher leaders themselves. At the risk of stating the obvious, the school's collegial culture will be a determinant of how well the feedback is both given and received.

There is no single model of teacher leadership for formative assessment. Teachers can assume many different leadership roles, from being a mentor to colleagues at the induction phase of the continuum to being formally designated as a districtwide formative assessment specialist for colleagues at the in-service phase. However, as we discussed in chapter 2, our approach to professional learning at each phase of the continuum is a sociocultural one, focused on the social construction of learning through interacting with others and being supported by more skilled colleagues. In this regard, all the different forms that leadership can take include working within a community of practice to assist peers in developing knowledge about and skills in formative assessment practice, and expanding and deepening their disciplinary knowledge through inquiry, deliberate practice, and critical reflection.

In the next section, we go into detail about specific activities that teacher leaders can undertake to support formative assessment practices school- or districtwide.

TEACHER LEADERS' ROLES AND ACTIVITIES

Professional learning experts Cindy Harrison and Joellen Killion offer a sample of roles and activities for teacher leaders.[21] We draw from this sample to consider how teacher leaders can engage in specific activities to enhance their peers' formative assessment knowledge and skills. These roles are not intended to be mutually exclusive; a teacher leader may be involved in one or more simultaneously. We consider six roles: resource provider, instructional specialist, curriculum specialist, classroom supporter, learning facilitator, and mentor.

Resource Provider

Teacher leaders may support their colleagues as providers of formative assessment resources, which can then serve as a springboard to a range of activities such as discussion groups or other forms of exploration of ideas. There are many resources written for practitioners (books, articles, and websites) that provide accessible information about formative assessment practices along with examples of how teachers have implemented them. For instance, teachers' formative assessment knowledge and skills can be significantly increased when they can examine examples of effective learning goals and success criteria, high-quality feedback, and students' self-assessment and peer feedback skills. Furnishing teacher colleagues with these resources means that teacher leaders must keep up with new publications and make decisions about which are likely to be most helpful to their colleagues. At the same time, they will be augmenting their own formative assessment knowledge, which is important for their leadership role.

Teacher leaders can encourage learning from resources by convening discussion groups that focus on a specific article or book chapter, and presenting some guiding questions for discussion. One important question to be considered within each discussion group is, "How does what I have learned about formative assessment impact my daily classroom practice?"[22] In discussing written materials, teachers may bring up specific areas that they would like more help with, for instance, how to ask better questions to gain insights into student learning, or how to provide formative feedback that is actionable without being too directive. These allow teacher leaders to target further assistance, possibly by observing teachers and giving feedback, collaborating on lesson planning, or brainstorming questions for a particular lesson and discussing which ones would be most likely to generate evidence of student thinking.

Instructional Specialist

Another role for teacher leaders is that of instructional specialist, whose aim is to help teachers engage in ambitious teaching. In chapter 1, we discussed ambitious teaching as a model for pedagogy that exemplifies the teaching practices necessary to realize broad educational goals in support of individual and collective well-being in our rapidly and profoundly changing societies.[23] Recall that ambitious teaching is grounded in a deep understanding of subject matter, involves engaging students in interaction and the active construction of knowledge, and is adaptive to students' needs. Formative assessment, which is itself a high-leverage practice, is seamlessly integrated into ambitious teaching. A role for teacher leaders, then, is not only to assist colleagues with implementing formative assessment, but also to shore up their ambitious teaching practices so that the benefits of formative assessment can be maximized, and students' learning experiences can be enriched.

The role of a teacher leader as an instructional specialist may focus on changing the nature of classroom tasks or discourse practices to allow for greater formative assessment opportunities. For instance, assisting their colleagues to provide better feedback to students will be challenging if a predominant form of classroom pedagogy is to assign in-class work that is closed-ended in nature and requires only correct answers. Also, in classrooms where the prevalent method of questioning is initiation (teacher asks a question that requires one correct answer), response (student responds with either the correct or incorrect answer), and evaluation (teacher indicates whether the answer is correct or incorrect), occasions for eliciting evidence of student thinking are significantly reduced, therefore diminishing the prospect of deep learning on the part of the students. A hallmark of ambitious teaching is discourse-based learning that involves students in talking about their ideas, explaining their reasoning, critiquing the reasoning of others, and engaging in argumentation. If classrooms in a school are dominated by closed-ended assignments and questions and teacher talk, teacher leaders will most likely want to support their colleagues in changing these fundamental aspects of practice, possibly even before concentrating on the formative assessment opportunities that are available from open-ended assignments and questions and student discussions.

Among the activities that teachers might engage in with their peers are: lesson planning to ensure ambitious teaching practices are incorporated and formative assessment opportunities are clearly embedded in the lesson, observing peers and providing feedback on how well they promote dialogue among their students, and helping colleagues with classroom organization and management so that they can engage in substantive conversations with individuals or small groups to elicit evidence of student thinking. Whatever the activity, the goal is to develop teachers' capacities for ambitious teaching while simultaneously improving their abilities to implement formative assessment in their classrooms.

Curriculum Specialist

There may be curriculum specialists in a district who, by definition, have deep disciplinary knowledge, but who no longer have formal classroom responsibilities. Here, however, we are referring to teacher leaders who still have classroom responsibilities and who are recognized as having an expert understanding of the discipline that they teach and of how students learn in that discipline. In this context, a teacher leader with a curriculum specialist role focuses primarily on helping teachers develop rich disciplinary knowledge in support of formative assessment practices.

For teacher leaders to support their colleagues' formative assessment practices effectively, they need a deep well of disciplinary knowledge that supports their use of formative assessment. Disciplinary knowledge encompasses: understanding how a particular discipline is structured; knowing how students learn disciplinary content; using appropriate ways to develop emerging student ideas within a discipline; and acknowledging the importance of horizon knowledge, an understanding of how disciplinary topics or ideas are connected over the span of the curriculum.

Teacher leaders with a curriculum focus can help their peers analyze content standards, relate the standards to the curriculum, review or develop learning progressions, and examine student work.

Analyze content standards In the chapter devoted to preservice learning, we stressed the importance of teachers becoming knowledgeable about the content standards adopted by their state jurisdictions. This is only the first step in acquiring disciplinary knowledge, but it is one that new teachers at the induction phase (and even some teachers at the in-service phase) will not have fully mastered. One of the activities of a teacher leader–curriculum specialist, therefore, will be to help colleagues develop a deeper understanding of the standards, emphasizing how to think about what is entailed in meeting specific standards and how to plan a sequence of lessons aimed toward achieving them. In addition, because current grade-level standards tend to be vague about what happens to students' learning as it moves between end-of-grade levels, teacher leaders will need to assist their peers in understanding intermediary steps between standards, at a level of detail that facilitates unit and lesson planning.[24] Developing a deeper understanding of standards and the intermediate steps between them can be undertaken through consultation with individual teachers, at grade-level meetings, and at across-grade-level meetings so that teachers can enlarge their view of the progressions among standards.

Relate standards to curriculum Another important aspect of working with standards is to understand how they relate to specific curricula adopted by a school or district. Sometimes this is not clear to teachers, so helping match the curriculum they are teaching with the standards they need to meet will benefit both their disciplinary knowledge and their curricular understanding. This can be accomplished through individual consultations or in grade-level group meetings.

Once teachers have a better understanding of their curriculum and its relation to standards, they will have greater confidence following a curricular sequence and structure and will be more able to use it to support adaptive teaching. If the curriculum is viewed as a prescribed series of activities, the scope for adaptive teaching based on formative assessment is decreased.

Responding to evidence as it emerges in a lesson often requires changes to the teaching plan, which a deep knowledge of the curriculum can support without teachers feeling insecure about deviating from the specific learning tasks that a curriculum requires. They can continue to advance learning toward curricular goals without losing momentum in the demands of curriculum coverage. The balance between adhering to the specificity of the curriculum and responding to students' emerging understanding can be challenging, but with sensitive support from a teacher leader through curricular analysis, lesson planning and reflection, and observation and feedback, teachers can maintain an equilibrium between these two seemingly competing needs.

Review or develop learning progressions Another aspect of disciplinary knowledge that teacher leaders can help their peers acquire and deepen is how students' thinking is likely to progress in relation to specific topics. Part of understanding a progression of learning is seeing the steps students need to go through to reach the goals of the standards, figuring out what kinds of learning tasks can help them move ahead through those steps, and anticipating the sorts of difficulties and misconceptions they may experience along the way.[25] Activities that teacher leaders can engage colleagues in to better understand progressions of learning include examining a range of student work related to learning a particular concept and discussing what it shows about student thinking, including what misconceptions are revealed. Questions that target misconceptions, such as those identified in chapters 3 and 4, can also generate rich discussions among teachers and help them to recognize that students often have logical but less than fully developed ways of reasoning. Teacher leaders can help their colleagues develop their own questions to target partial understandings that students might have about particular topics, providing feedback on initial question drafts and discussing potential revisions to a question after one or more teachers have tried it out with students.[26]

It is also useful to select multiple pieces of student work to place in a progression from least to most sophisticated so that teachers see how understanding of the concept develops. Discussing the progression can also assist teachers in articulating what the work shows students at each stage *can* do, and what will help them move to a deeper level of understanding, rather than simply evaluating answers as correct or incorrect. Analysis of student work in the form of a progression can also assist teachers in evaluating how well the students' tasks promoted the targeted learning and considering modifications that might need to be made to accelerate student progress.

Examine student work When their colleagues are analyzing student work, teacher leaders can guide conversations to consider appropriate next steps for individual students, groups, or the entire class. These conversations could focus on identifying what the students already understand, how they are thinking about phenomena and concepts they are studying, and what might be fruitful next steps in learning. These kinds of conversations are helped by taking into account the sequence of development they have established; placing the work in a progression from least to most sophisticated could suggest what the next step in students' learning should be.

Classroom Supporter

Another role for teacher leaders is to work collaboratively in their colleagues' classrooms, providing demonstration lessons or acting as a coteacher or observer to provide formative feedback to the teacher. A high level of trust and positive working relationships both among teacher peers and between teachers and school administrators is required for teachers to open up their classrooms to teacher leaders, to try out new ideas with the possibility of failure being observed, and to make themselves vulnerable by admitting that they are struggling with an aspect of formative assessment practice or do not understand part of the curriculum. One teacher leader reflected on the value of being observed by other teachers and supporting teachers in their classrooms:

> My position allows for me to use my own classroom as a demonstration class for other teachers to watch, learn, question and discuss learning practices. I wanted to be in a leader position to be able to share my knowledge of education, ideas, and examples that will make a better impact on our students. As educators we have a commitment to our students and having a leadership role helps me support teachers in their classrooms without teachers [getting] the feeling that they are being evaluated.[27]

In-class support could involve demonstrating a lesson that highlights some of the aspects they have focused on in previous professional learning activities, such as helping students understand what meeting the learning goal and success criteria entails, asking productive questions that propel a discussion among students to support their learning (while also providing insights into how they are thinking), or providing substantive oral feedback to students. Prior to the lesson, it is important for the teacher leader and the peer to be clear about what the focus of the demonstration will be, and what the peer should anticipate. After the lesson demonstration, a debriefing conversation can be an occasion for the teacher leader to respond to questions and observations the peer may have, as well as think about how the peer might build on what has been demonstrated in her own lessons.

Teacher leaders can also provide in-classroom support to their peers by coteaching with them. Coteaching will obviously require joint lesson planning, followed by teaching the lesson together and focusing on improving an aspect of practice. For instance, if the target of the teacher leader's support is to help the peer ask better questions that provoke a range of responses from students, they both might plan some questions prior to the lesson, but then jointly orchestrate a discussion, encouraging students to clarify, compare, challenge, and defend their various views to one another. To orchestrate a discussion of this kind requires the teacher to play a variety of roles, ranging from being a boundary setter for rules of argumentation, a challenger, a provocateur, or a summarizer. The overall success of the discussion is dependent on the power of the opening questions, and then on the capacity of the teacher to listen, to interpret the responses, and to steer the discussion by summarizing or by asking further questions.[28] When orchestrating a discussion together, the peer might begin with the opening question, followed by the teacher leader stepping in with a summary or follow-up question, after which the peer continues steering the discussion in productive directions. If the direction taken proves not to be productive, the teacher leader can intervene and redirect the conversation so that it is back on track. This kind of back and forth can continue so that the peer's skills are consistently shored up and reinforced by the teacher leader throughout the discussion.

Coteaching gives peers a very different experience from observing a demonstration lesson by the teacher leader. The peer is involved in deliberate practice, in real time, with a form of scaffolding from the teacher leader as the lesson evolves. The teacher leader, with a light touch, can elevate her peer's practice so that she experiences the subtleties of what is involved in eliciting a range of responses from students both to develop their understanding and to gain insights into their thinking. This experience is further enhanced by a post-lesson reflection when they discuss what the peer learned from the experience, how it was different from her regular discussions, and what future plans might entail. Of course, both the coteaching opportunity and the post-lesson reflection are dependent on the habits of practice, inquiry, deliberate practice, and critical reflection, which are buttressed by the collegial and collaborative ethos created in the school, largely by the principal.

A further way that teacher leaders can provide in-class support is by observing a peer teach and then providing feedback intended to help the peer reflect on an aspect of formative assessment for the purpose of improvement. Such an observation should comply with the agenda of the observed, not the observer. A simple example: The observed teacher specifies focus of observation such as wanting to increase wait time between asking a question and soliciting the students' response. The observed teacher specifies what counts as evidence and provides the teacher leader with a stopwatch to log wait times. The observed teacher owns any notes made during the observation.

In previous chapters, we have discussed the *Formative Assessment Rubrics, Reflection, and Observation Protocol* (FARROP), which makes explicit the characteristics of stronger and weaker formative assessment implementation along ten dimensions of practice.[29] The FARROP, or a similar protocol, can be used as a tool by teacher leaders for structuring observations and feedback in support of a peer's deliberate practice. Again, the observed teacher would determine the focus of the observation based on one or two of the dimensions of formative assessment included in the FARROP. Without making any form of judgement, the teacher leader observes the lesson focusing only on the dimensions of interest to the peer, and noting only what happened in the lesson, capturing any direct speech when it is informative. After the lesson, the teacher leader reviews her evidential notes and makes a determination, based on the preponderance of evidence, where the teacher's practice in these dimensions falls on the rubric scale: beginning, developing, progressing, or extending.

Following the observation, the teacher leader gives feedback to the observed peer, first discussing where she thinks her peer falls on the rubric, providing examples of specific practice from her notes to explain the rationale for her placement. At this point, the peer may have questions or want further clarification or more examples to substantiate the rationale. Next, the teacher leader provides suggestions for improvement that are specific, actionable, and thought provoking. Importantly, the feedback should not be construed as telling the peer what to do—it is not intended as a remedy, but rather an opportunity for reflection on the part of the peer on how she might use the feedback for improvement. It may be that the peer asks the teacher leader for assistance, possibly in-class support, help with lesson planning, or more guidance about how to improve, but the agenda needs to remain under the control of the observed teacher.

Providing feedback to colleagues is an entirely different enterprise than providing feedback to students. It may be that teacher leaders will need support from school leaders in developing their feedback skills, possibly by rehearsing what they are going to say to the peer they have observed and being given pointers for how they could improve, or even soliciting the observed teacher's perspective on how effective the feedback was. Just as students need to understand the difference between criticism and feedback, so, too, do many teachers. In addition to the quality of the feedback provided, the degree to which the school has a collegial culture will help determine whether the feedback is received by the observed teacher as supportive and constructive.

Learning Facilitator

Facilitating professional learning opportunities among teacher colleagues is another role for teacher leaders. In this role a teacher leader considers both content (what tasks, subjects, and problems are being addressed) and process (including how topics are discussed, the style of interaction, procedures, and group norms and dynamics).[30] To successfully adopt this role, they will need to understand what makes effective professional learning. Effective learning is embedded in the teacher's job and focused on student learning and formative assessment, but it also incorporates active learning and builds strong working relationships among teachers.[31] In their facilitator capacity, teacher leaders incorporate these attributes as they work with their colleagues in various ways. One aspect of the role should be noted across examples: learning facilitators *facilitate* learning. In this regard, they do not adopt didactic roles, lecturing to their colleagues, giving directions, and telling them how to do things. Instead, they operate from the values of collaboration, learning, and partnership to advance their peers' learning, helping them to own their learning completely.

Teacher leaders can facilitate teacher learning in various ways, such as developing a professional learning community, using a lesson-study approach to support learning, or engaging peers in a video lesson study.

Professional learning communities Teacher leaders may take responsibility for convening and guiding professional learning communities, a specific instance of a community of practice (see chapter 2), where groups of teachers come together to focus on a topic of mutual interest with regard to formative assessment practice. As a facilitator, the teacher leader might develop an agenda in consultation with colleagues, help create and maintain meeting expectations (for example, everyone pays attention and everyone acknowledges that each participant is a learner), and keep the conversation on target so that meeting goals are accomplished.

Teacher leaders may also structure a professional learning community so that teachers engage in ongoing cycles of learn-practice-reflect-revise to improve their formative assessment practice.[32] The teachers learn with and from each other by sharing ideas about formative assessment. They practice putting what they have learned into action, then meet again to share their experiences, receiving advice from colleagues about how to overcome any challenges they encountered. Based on their discussion of their practice experience, teachers revise their plans and try their new learning out in their classrooms. Throughout the cycle, the facilitator remains neutral about opinions and ideas that are expressed by the group, unless, of course, group members wish to draw on the teacher leader's expertise. The facilitator's job is to guide the group to achieve its goals, not tell them what to do or how to do it, and to provide leadership without dominating the group process.

Lesson study Another way that a teacher leader might facilitate professional learning is through a group lesson study, following a model developed in

Japan.[33] Typically, the lesson study focuses on an aspect of practice or a research question that the group wishes to investigate. The teacher leader facilitates a small group of teachers to create a lesson plan that incorporates the focus of their inquiry, for example, using success criteria as a way to structure peer feedback. One member of the group subsequently teaches the lesson while the other teachers, along with the teacher leader, observe. Then they reconvene to discuss their observations under the teacher leader's guidance. In light of the discussion, the lesson may be modified and then implemented a second time by another teacher in the group. After a second round of discussion, the group is reconvened by the teacher leader, who facilitates a discussion about what the group has learned from the process.[34] The teacher leader's expertise in formative assessment will enable her to guide the discussion in such a way as to keep the focus on the objective of the lesson study, while supporting her colleagues to work effectively and make their own suggestions for improvement.

Another very productive way that teacher leaders can facilitate learning is to involve peers in a video lesson study. Many good videos of formative assessment practice are available (e.g., from the Teaching Channel) and could be carefully selected to highlight specific aspects of formative assessment. A teacher leader could assemble a set of questions to guide the video viewing, for example, "What structures and routines has the teacher put in place to support formative assessment? What do you notice about the questions the teacher asks? What are the features of the teacher/student interaction during the time the teacher is providing feedback to the student?"

These examples of teacher leaders as learning facilitators are by no means exhaustive. Teacher leaders and their colleagues will find many ways in which learning can be facilitated in their own contexts.

Mentor

In chapter 8, we described the mentor roles that teachers take to support early career teachers, so we will not reprise those details here. However, we want to underscore that teacher leaders have both the expertise and the skills and qualities, which we discuss in the final part of the chapter, to be very successful as mentors. School leaders and teacher leaders will have to decide, based on the needs of the teaching faculty as a whole, where their support is best targeted, which may not be as mentors to new teachers.

Other experienced teachers can act as mentors in their place. Teacher leaders are a finite resource in a school, and overburdening them, spreading them too thinly, or not directing their attention in focused ways, will not make the best use of their expertise.

While a teacher leader may not undertake all the roles we have described, to engage successfully in any one of them requires knowledge and skills beyond demonstrating ambitious teaching in their own classrooms, having well developed expertise in formative assessment, and having acquired deep disciplinary knowledge. In the next section, we consider some of the skills and qualities that equip teachers to be successful in their leadership roles.

TEACHER LEADER SKILLS AND QUALITIES

Catalyst

Being a catalyst entails mobilizing and energizing others with the goal of improvement. To do this, teacher leaders feel secure in their own work and have a strong commitment to continual improvement, always looking for a better way to do things.[35] They are resilient in the face of challenge and difficulty, and they are willing to persevere, finding ways to overcome obstacles for the benefit of improvement. For example, in a school where a nucleus of teachers who are already focused on enhancing their skills in formative assessment face challenges from colleagues who see it as "just the latest fad," a teacher leader would marshal support from the reluctant teachers, finding ways to help them understand the benefits of formative assessment and engendering feelings of security about making changes. And the teacher leader would be persistent in her efforts!

Personal Effectiveness

Teacher leaders understand their own personal strengths and leadership style and capitalize on them to develop trust and credibility with their colleagues, using warmth, empathy, and humility. They have effective communication skills and use them in support of their peers.[36] In situations where teachers are reluctant to ask for support because of their feelings of vulnerability, a teacher leader will take the time to build relationships before engaging in any of the activities we have described. Through a relationship-building process, the teacher leader's colleagues would come to understand that she is not going to sanction them, or tell them what to do, or fix their problems, but rather is there to provide support because she genuinely cares about them and the students they teach.

Teamwork

The ability to work with others is a key skill for teacher leaders. In this regard, they understand and can implement group processes, they effectively manage group dynamics, and they can actively engage diverse opinions and experiences to produce desired outcomes.[37] For instance, when teacher leaders are facilitating activities such as analyzing student work with their colleagues to determine what students can do and potential next steps, they will employ teamwork skills to ensure everyone is able to participate, everyone's opinion is listened to and respected, and that all participants conclude the activity feeling that it was worthwhile and beneficial to their formative assessment practices.

Leadership

In addition to teamwork skills, teacher leaders need leadership skills, since they are often necessary to promote effective teamwork. Leadership from teachers stems from a desire to help others, and entails engaging, inspiring, and motivating others toward improvement.[38] Imagine a situation where a teacher has asked a teacher leader to observe her practice on a dimension of the FARROP and provide her with feedback. The observed teacher is disappointed with the feedback, because she believed she was at a more sophisticated level than the evidence from the observation revealed. Even though the observed teacher feels dejected, the teacher leader can encourage her, motivating her to think about her practice and involving her in joint planning of concrete ways she can move forward.

Openness

Teacher leaders work with others in a spirit of openness and respect for other's ideas, always willing to explore productive pathways toward improvement. They combine this openness with flexibility and creativity and use these qualities to explore productive pathways toward improvement, deftly adapting and adjusting as the need arises.[39] For instance, in a situation where the teacher leader believes some of her colleagues would benefit from reorganizing their physical classroom environment to facilitate group work among their students, but they are reluctant because they think they will "lose control" if they reorganize, she would find creative ways for them to support more student collaboration in their current classroom organization.

Vision

Teacher leaders must have sufficient vision to identify where support for formative assessment might be best provided, rather than just waiting to be approached by others. They also need the ability to see how their support fits into the larger goal of formative assessment.[40] For example, a teacher leader might become aware, through informal conversations with her colleagues, that some of them are experiencing problems with engaging students in productive self-assessment. With this information, he takes the initiative and suggests that they form a group to work on helping students understand how to self-assess. He recognizes that they need assistance in communicating the purpose of self-assessment to students, and he helps the teachers practice these communication skills. He also supports teachers to develop skills in giving feedback to students about their self-assessment efforts to help them calibrate their judgments, without which the self-assessment process can be undermined.

Risk-taking

Teacher leaders are willing to take risks in order to reach lofty and meaningful goals, even when there is a possibility that what they are doing may fail. They model resiliency and motivate others to take risks to achieve desired results.[41] Consider a situation in which teachers in a school have been working on incorporating formative assessment into their lessons for some time. They have asked the teacher leader to observe and provide feedback, and from this, she realizes that the teachers have not made some of the fundamental changes in their classroom practice to allow them to be successful involving their students in formative assessment. She notices specifically that the teachers are not spending enough time to ensure that their students understand what meeting the lesson learning goals entails, they are not giving the students time to use feedback, they often curtail student conversations so that the students do not have sufficient chance to build on each other's thinking, and they are providing insufficient guidance to students on how to self-assess. Helping her colleagues make these changes is a big undertaking, but one she believes is necessary for improving students' experiences with formative assessment. She does not shy away from this challenge, but instead embraces it wholeheartedly, even though there are likely to be many bumps along the way.

Positive Affect

When teacher leaders display optimism, enthusiasm, and confidence, they can lead others to think creatively and work together to solve problems.[42] A positive affect can help mobilize peers toward improvement and sustain them when the going gets tough. For example, in the situation described above, with teachers attempting major changes to their classroom practice, there will likely be times when they are frustrated and want to give up. In these circumstances, the teacher leaders' positive affect can be a source of assurance for her peers and motivate them to engage with her in creative problem solving to overcome any challenges they are experiencing.

Continuous Learning

Among the most important qualities teacher leaders have is the desire for continuous learning. They have enough humility to recognize that they have not reached the end of the road in terms of developing expertise. Instead, they understand that they always have something new to learn, and they are willing to step outside of their comfort zones in the interests of increasing their knowledge and skills. They are always open and ready to learn more about the discipline, about formative assessment within the discipline, and about ways to implement formative assessment in different contexts with a diversity of students. In their leadership capacity, they demonstrate lifelong learning, always seeking out better ways to teach and implement formative assessment effectively, and better ways to support their colleagues to do the same. Teacher leaders have the confidence in their own capacities to acknowledge that they learn from their peers during all the activities they undertake, letting them know that they, too, have expertise to share for the benefit of others.

Teacher leader is a role whose time has come. Leadership offers opportunities for teachers to build the professional capital in their schools by enhancing all teachers' capacity to be effective in their classrooms. They also support school leaders, who may have limited time or expertise in certain areas, by engaging teachers in a range of professional learning activities, by observing them and providing feedback, and by giving lesson demonstrations. Teacher leaders also help develop a culture of collaboration and foster a sense of self-efficacy and motivation among their colleagues. Finally, assuming a leadership role can provide expert teachers with expanded responsibilities that meet their desire to grow as teachers and leaders.[43]

CHAPTER 10: SUMMARY OF BIG IDEAS

- Teacher leadership roles provide a way for teachers to remain in the classroom while influencing the work of their peers to improve formative assessment practices and support increased student learning.
- Teacher leaders will be more successful in a school where the principal establishes and nurtures a climate of collaboration, teamwork, professional inquiry, and reflection.
- Teacher leaders can take on a wide variety of roles, including but not limited to resource provider, instructional specialist, curriculum specialist, classroom supporter, learning facilitator, mentor, and learner.
- Teacher leaders have a specialized set of skills in pedagogy and formative assessment, as well as skills for working with adults, but they will also need support from both peers and school leaders to refine these skills.
- Teacher leaders are motivators, encouragers, team-builders, and seekers of feedback from their peers on how they can best support them and the work they are doing with students.

Conclusion

In this book, we have described and illustrated a continuum of professional learning for discipline-based formative assessment, in the context of ambitious teaching, from preservice through induction to in-service and potentially teacher leadership. We have examined examples of practice in mathematics, English language arts, science, and social studies. We have seen how expertise can be developed across the phases of the continuum. Initially, preservice programs stipulate what teachers need to learn, but during induction programs, and particularly during the in-service phase, teachers will have much more freedom to identify aspects of their own practice on which to focus. Teachers never stop learning how to teach at any phase of the continuum.

We discussed in chapter 1 that we can no longer provide students in school with the knowledge and skills that they will need for a lifetime of employment, which was once the goal of schooling, generally accomplished through standardization and compliance. The world is changing too rapidly for that to be a possibility. Just as the goal of teaching is now to equip students with competencies—critical, creative, and metacognitive thinking—so that they can continue a lifetime of learning for societal and personal benefit, so too must teachers continuously evolve in their practice. They will always need to be ready to meet the challenges of educating today's children.

The professional learning continuum we have proposed affords teachers the opportunity to keep learning at different stages of their careers and in different ways that are fitted to their professional status. A characteristic of each phase of the continuum is that teachers situate themselves in a learning community and collaborate with peers and more "knowledgeable others," such as teacher leaders, to continuously keep learning.[1] While we have not provided a chapter specifically for school and district administrators, we hope those in such leadership roles can glean some of the mind-sets, values, and systems that would be necessary to support teacher learning as described in chapters 8 through 10. In brief, concrete actions that school and district leaders can take are:

- Demonstrating that they understand and value formative assessment, and when they do not, to take on a role as learners themselves
- Supporting teachers to learn about and have opportunities to experiment with aspects of formative assessment
- Providing and protecting time for teachers to engage in peer observations, meet in learning communities, and participate in other learning opportunities with peers outside of their teaching responsibilities
- Identifying and supporting teacher leaders to take on roles that extend beyond their classroom responsibilities
- Recognizing progress made by teachers at all stages of the learning continuum and celebrating their achievements[2]

Recently, a paper from the American Federation of Teachers (AFT) quoted Andreas Schleicher, director of education and skills at the Organisation for Economic Co-operation and Development, who observed that "collaboration doesn't just fall from the sky." In response to his observation, the AFT paper made clear that "we must create structures and strategies where everyone works together to improve teaching and learning."[3] That is exactly what we have aimed to do in this book with respect to improving teaching and learning through discipline-based formative assessment. We sincerely hope we have succeeded.

APPENDIX

FARROP Learning Goals Rubric

Learning Goals are developed within the context of a larger progression of student understanding (**learning progressions**). Research indicates that students who can identify and understand the learning expectations for a lesson or set of lessons are better prepared to support one another and to take responsibility for their own learning. The goals for a single lesson (or series of lessons) should be clearly identified and communicated to students or codeveloped with students and should help students make connections among lessons within the larger sequence, progression, or the broader purpose for learning. Learning goals should be aligned with state or district grade-level standards; however, this dimension focuses on how the teacher identifies or codevelops the learning goals for a particular lesson, communicates them to the students, uses them in a way that supports learning, and helps the students to understand the trajectory of the lesson.

N NOT OBSERVED	B BEGINNING	D DEVELOPING	P PROGRESSING	E EXTENDING
The teacher does not present learning goals to students in any form.	The focus of the lesson is presented in isolation without connecting with previous or future learning or to a broader purpose for the learning.	The focus of the lesson is presented with only *isolated references* made to previous or future learning or to a broader purpose for the learning.	The focus of the lesson is clearly presented *in terms of previous or future learning*. A larger sequence of learning is identified and the teacher shares where the current lesson fits within the larger sequence or with a broader purpose for the learning.	The focus of the lesson is presented as part of a *coherent sequence of learning with meaningful connections* made to previous or future learning so that students clearly understand the connections or a broader purpose for the learning.

(Continued)

N NOT OBSERVED	B BEGINNING	D DEVELOPING	P PROGRESSING	E EXTENDING
—— *or* —— The teacher only presents an agenda for the day or lesson activities —— *or* —— The teacher describes the task in place of sharing the learning goals.	—— *or* —— Superficial procedural connections are made or a topic is identified without specific goals. —— *or* —— The content of the learning goals is highly inappropriate for the students. —— *or* —— The learning goals are expressed in language that is not accessible to students.	The learning goal focuses on what students should know or understand by the end of the lesson. The content of the goal is *appropriate* and expressed in language *accessible* to students. The teacher does *not* provide opportunities for students to internalize the goal.	The learning goal focuses on what students should know or understand by the end of the lesson. The content of the goal is appropriate and expressed in language that is accessible to students. The teacher *provides opportunities* for students to internalize the goal.	The learning goal focuses on what students should know or understand by the end of the lesson. The content of the goal is appropriate and expressed in language accessible to students. The teacher provides opportunities for students to internalize the goal and *checks for student understanding* of what meeting the goal entails.
		The teacher presents the learning goal to students but makes *no verbal or direct reference* to the goal at any appropriate time during the lesson.	The teacher *presents or codevelops* the learning goal with the students (although it may not be a clear, meaningful process) and makes verbal or direct references to the goal at some appropriate time during the lesson.	The teacher *clearly, meaningfully, and/or rigorously* presents or codevelops the learning goal with the students and makes meaningful, appropriate references to the goal during the lesson.
		Neither the students nor the teacher return to the learning goals at any point during the lesson.	The teacher makes *some reference* back to the learning goals throughout the lesson, in a way that *superficially* focuses student attention on the purpose and trajectory of the lesson, but students make *limited use* of the goals during lesson activities.	The teacher makes *multiple meaningful and appropriate verbal references* to the learning goal throughout the lesson, *summarizes* progress toward the goals throughout the lesson, helps the students to understand the *trajectory* of the lesson, and/or invites students to *explain progress* made toward the goal at the end of the lesson. Students make use of the goals in conversation with each other or when reviewing their work.

Notes

Introduction

1. Gregory J. Cizek, Randy E. Bennett, and Heidi L. Andrade, "Formative Assessment: History, Definition, and Progress," in *Handbook of Formative Assessment in the Disciplines*, ed. Heidi L. Andrade, Randy E. Bennett, and Gregory J. Cizek (New York: Routledge, 2019); Margaret Heritage and E. Caroline Wylie, "Teacher Preparation in Mathematics," in Andrade, Bennett, and Cizek.
2. Margaret Heritage, *Formative Assessment: Making It Happen in the Classroom* (Thousand Oaks, CA: Corwin Press, 2010); E. Caroline Wylie and Christine J. Lyon, "Supporting Teacher Assessment Literacy: A Proposed Sequence of Learning," *Teachers College Record* (October 30, 2017), http://www.tcrecord.org/content.asp?contentid=22193.
3. Organisation for Economic Co-operation and Development, *Teachers Matter: Attracting, Developing and Retaining Effective Teachers* (Paris: OECD, 2005), https://www.oecd.org/education/school/34990905.pdf.
4. Robert Glaser, "Changing the Agency for Learning: Acquiring Expert Performance," in *The Road to Excellence: The Acquisition of Expert Performance in the Arts and Sciences, Sports, and Games* (Hillsdale, NJ: Lawrence Erlbaum Associates, 1996), cited in David Berliner, "Describing the Behavior and Documenting the Accomplishments of Expert Teachers," *Bulletin of Science, Technology, & Society* 24, no. 3 (2004), 200–212, doi:10.1177/0270467604265535.

Chapter 1

1. Andreas Schleicher, "Educating Learners for Their Future, Not Our Past," *ECNU Review of Education* 1, no. 1 (2018), doi:10.30926/ecnuroe2018010104.
2. Thomas L. Friedman, "The Biggest Threat to America Is Us," *New York Times*, July 3, 2019.
3. Schleicher, "Educating Learners for Their Future."
4. Lisa H. MacNeilley et al., "Opening Dialogue: Understanding the Dynamics of Language and Learning in the English Classroom," *Language* 74, no. 2 (1998), doi:10.1353/lan.1998.0252.
5. Organisation for Economic Co-operation and Development, *Education at a Glance 2018* (Paris: OECD, 2018).
6. Paul Black, Mark Wilson, and Shih-Ying Yao, "Road Maps for Learning: A Guide to the Navigation of Learning Progressions," *Measurement: Interdisciplinary Research and Perspectives* 9, no. 2–3 (2011), doi:10.1080/15366367.2011.591654.

7. Deborah Loewenberg Ball and Francesca M. Forzani, "The Work of Teaching and the Challenge for Teacher Education," *Journal of Teacher Education* 60, no. 5 (2009); Magdalene Lampert and Filippo Graziani, "Instructional Activities as a Tool for Teachers' and Teacher Educators' Learning," *The Elementary School Journal* 109, no. 5 (2009); quoted in Lorrie A. Shepard, "Classroom Assessment to Support Teaching and Learning," *ANNALS of the American Academy of Political and Social Science* 683, no. 1 (2019).
8. Schleicher, "Educating Learners for Their Future."
9. Margaret Heritage and John Heritage, "Teacher Questioning: The Epicenter of Instruction and Assessment," *Applied Measurement in Education* 26, no. 3 (2013), doi:10.1080/08957347.2013.793190.
10. Mark Windschitl et al., "Proposing a Core Set of Instructional Practices and Tools for Teachers of Science," *Science Education* 96, no. 5 (2012): 879, doi:10.1002/sce.21027.
11. Shepard, "Classroom Assessment."
12. Jean Lave and Etienne Wenger, *Situated Learning: Legitimate Peripheral Participation* (Cambridge: Cambridge University Press, 1991).
13. Teaching Channel, "Conjecturing About Functions," https://www.teachingchannel.org/video/conjecture-lesson-plan.
14. National Research Council, *Education for Life and Work: Developing Transferable Knowledge and Skills in the 21st Century* (Washington, DC: National Academies Press, 2012), doi:10.17226/13398.
15. Elizabeth A. Van Es and Miriam Gamoran Sherin, "Learning to Notice: Scaffolding New Teachers' Interpretations of Classroom Interactions," *Journal of Technology and Teacher Education* 10, no. 4 (2002).
16. Margaret Heritage and Christine Harrison, *The Power of Assessment for Learning: Twenty Years of Research and Practice in UK and US Classrooms* (Thousand Oaks, CA: Corwin Press, 2020), 57.
17. Hanna Dumont, David Istance, and Francisco Benavides, eds., *The Nature of Learning: Using Research to Inspire Practice* (Paris: OECD, 2010); James G. Greeno, "Learning in Activity," in *The Cambridge Handbook of the Learning Sciences*, ed. R. Keith Sawyer (New York: Cambridge University Press, 2006); National Research Council, *How People Learn: Brain, Mind, Experience, and School*, expanded ed. (Washington, DC: National Academies Press, 2000), doi:10.17226/9853.
18. Lev Vygotsky, *Thought and Language*, trans. Eugenia Hanfmann and Gertrude Vakar (Cambridge, MA: MIT Press, 1962).
19. Heritage and Heritage, *Teacher Questioning*.
20. Lorrie A Shepard, William R Penuel, and James W Pellegrino, "Using Learning and Motivation Theories to Coherently Link Formative Assessment, Grading Practices, and Large-Scale Assessment," *Educational Measurement: Issues and Practice* 37, no. 1 (2018), doi:10.1111/emip.12189.
21. Windschitl et al., "Proposing a Core Set."
22. Paul Black et al., *Assessment for Learning: Putting It into Practice* (Buckingham, UK: Open University Press, 2003); Philip H. Scott, Eduardo F. Mortimer, and Orlando G. Aguiar, "The Tension Between Authoritative and Dialogic Discourse: A Fundamental Characteristic of Meaning Making Interactions in High School Science Lessons," *Science Education* 90, no. 4 (2006), doi:10.1002/sce.20131.
23. Robin Alexander, "Developing Dialogic Teaching: Genesis, Process, Trial," *Research Papers in Education* 33, no. 5 (2018), doi:10.1080/02671522.2018.1481140.

24. Margaret Heritage, "What Do Teachers Need to Know and Do," *Phi Delta Kappan* 89, no. 2 (2007).
25. Karen Littleton and Neil Mercer, *Interthinking: Putting Talk to Work* (London: Routledge, 2013).
26. Schleicher, "Educating Learners for Their Future."
27. Heather C. Hill, Stephen G. Schilling, and Deborah Loewenberg Ball, "Developing Measures of Teachers' Mathematics Knowledge for Teaching," *The Elementary School Journal* 105, no. 1 (2004): 11–30, doi:10.1086/428763; Margaret Heritage et al., "From Evidence to Action: A Seamless Process in Formative Assessment?" *Educational Measurement: Issues and Practice* 28, no. 3 (2009): 24–31, doi:10.1111/j.1745-3992.2009.00151.x; Deborah Loewenberg Ball, Mark Hoover Thames, and Geoffrey Phelps, "Content Knowledge for Teaching: What Makes It Special?," *Journal of Teacher Education* 59, no. 5 (2008), doi:10.1177/0022487108324554.
28. Lee Shulman, "Foreword," in *Disciplinary Styles in the Scholarship of Teaching and Learning: Exploring Common Ground*, ed. Mary Taylor Huber and Sherwyn Morreale (Merrifield, VA: AAHE Publications Orders, 2002), https://files.eric.ed.gov/fulltext/ED478800.pdf; Ball, Thames, and Phelps, "Content Knowledge for Teaching."
29. NRC, *How People Learn*.
30. Beverley Bell, Nigel Bell, and Bronwen Cowie, *Formative Assessment and Science Education*, Contemporary Trends and Issues in Science Education 12 (Dordrecht, Netherlands: Springer Science & Business Media, 2001); Paul Black and Dylan Wiliam, "Developing the Theory of Formative Assessment," *Educational Assessment, Evaluation and Accountability* (formerly *Journal of Personnel Evaluation in Education*) 21, no. 1 (2009); Connie Moss and Susan M. Brookhart, *Advancing Formative Assessment in Every Classroom* (Alexandria VA: ASCD, 2009); Gregory J. Cizek, Randy E. Bennett, and Heidi L. Andrade, "Formative Assessment: History, Definition, and Progress," in *Handbook of Formative Assessment in the Disciplines*, ed. Heidi L. Andrade, Randy E. Bennett, and Gregory J. Cizek (New York: Routledge, 2019); Siobhan Leahy et al., "Classroom Assessment: Minute by Minute, Day by Day," *Educational Assessment* 63, no. 3 (2005): 18–24.
31. *Revising the Definition of Formative Assessment* (Washington, DC: Council of Chief State School Officers, 2018), https://ccsso.org/resource-library/revising-definition-formative-assessment.
32. NRC, *Education for Life and Work*; *Synergies for Better Learning: An International Perspective on Evaluation and Assessment*, OECD Reviews of Evaluation and Assessment in Education (Paris: OECD, 2013), doi:10.1787/9789264190658-en.
33. Randy Bennett, "Integrating Measurement Principles into Formative Assessment," in Andrade, Cizek, and Bennett, *Handbook of Formative Assessment*.
34. E. Caroline Wylie and Christine J. Lyon, "The Fidelity of Formative Assessment Implementation: Issues of Breadth and Quality," *Assessment in Education: Principles, Policy & Practice* 22, no. 1 (2015): 140–60, doi:10.1080/0969594X.2014.990416.
35. Dale H. Schunk, Paul R. Pintrich, and Judith L. Meece, *Motivation in Education: Theory, Research, and Applications*, 3rd ed. (Upper Saddle River, NJ: Pearson/Merrill Prentice Hall, 2008); Edwin A. Locke and Gary P. Latham, "Building a Practically Useful Theory of Goal Setting and Task Motivation: A 35-Year Odyssey," *American Psychologist* 57, no. 9 (2002).

36. Luis C. Moll et al., "Funds of Knowledge for Teaching: Using a Qualitative Approach to Connect Homes and Classrooms," *Theory Into Practice* 31, no. 2 (1992), doi:10.1080/00405849209543534; Schunk, Pintrich, and Meece, *Motivation in Education*; Locke and Latham, "Building a Practically Useful Theory."
37. Lev S. Vygotsky, *Mind in Society: The Development of Higher Mental Process* (Cambridge, MA: Harvard University Press, 1978).
38. National Academies of Sciences, Engineering, and Medicine, *How People Learn II: Learners, Contexts, and Cultures* (Washington, DC: National Academies Press, 2018), doi:10.17226/24783.
39. NRC, *How People Learn: Brain, Mind, Experience, and School*; Charlotte Dignath, Gerhard Buettner, and Hans-Peter Langfeldt, "How Can Primary School Students Learn Self-Regulated Learning Strategies Most Effectively? A Meta-Analysis on Self-Regulation Training Programmes," *Educational Research Review* 3, no. 2 (2008), doi:10.1016/j.edurev.2008.02.003.
40. K. Anders Ericsson, Ralf T. Krampe, and Clemens Tesch-Römer, "The Role of Deliberate Practice in the Acquisition of Expert Performance," *Psychological Review* 100, no. 3 (1993).
41. Heidi L. Andrade, Ying Du, and Xiaolei Wang, "Putting Rubrics to the Test: The Effect of a Model, Criteria Generation, and Rubric-Referenced Self-Assessment on Elementary School Students' Writing," *Educational Measurement: Issues and Practice* 27, no. 2 (2008): 3–13, doi:10.1111/j.1745-3992.2008.00118.x; Catarina Andersson and Torulf Palm, "The Impact of Formative Assessment on Student Achievement: A Study of the Effects of Changes to Classroom Practice after a Comprehensive Professional Development Programme," *Learning and Instruction* 49 (2017): 92–102, doi:10.1016/j.learninstruc.2016.12.006; Black et al., *Assessment for Learning*; Paul Black and Dylan Wiliam, "Assessment and Classroom Learning," *Assessment in Education: Principles, Policy & Practice* 5, no. 1 (1998): 7–74, doi:10.1080/0969595980050102; Gavin Brown and Lois R. Harris, "Student Self-Assessment," in *The Sage Handbook of Research on Classroom Assessment*, ed. James H. McMillan (Thousand Oaks, CA: Sage, 2013), 367–93, doi:10.4135/9781452218649.n21; Jonathan A. Supovitz et al., *Experimental Impacts of the Ongoing Assessment Project on Teachers and Students*, CPRE Research Reports (Philadelphia: University of Pennsylvania Graduate School of Education, 2018), https://repository.upenn.edu/cpre_researchreports/107/.
42. Stefan Speckesser et al., *Embedding Formative Assessment: Evaluation Report and Executive Summary*, prepared for the Education Endowment Foundation (London: National Institute of Economic and Social Research, 2018), https://educationendowmentfoundation.org.uk/public/files/EFA_evaluation_report.pdf.
43. Margaret Heritage and E. Caroline Wylie, "Reaping the Benefits of Assessment for Learning: Achievement, Identity, and Equity," *ZDM Mathematics Education* (2018), doi:10.1007/s11858-018-0943-3.
44. Hongli Li, "How Is Formative Assessment Related to Students' Reading Achievement? Findings from Pisa 2009," *Assessment in Education: Principles, Policy & Practice* 23, no. 4 (2016): 473–94, doi:10.1080/0969594X.2016.1139543; Stuart S. Yeh, "Understanding and Addressing the Achievement Gap Through Individualized Instruction and Formative Assessment," *Assessment in Education: Principles, Policy & Practice* 17, no. 2: 169–82, doi:10.1080/09695941003694466.
45. William James Popham, personal correspondence, December 2018.

46. This teacher was observed and interviewed by the first author as part of a professional development opportunity.
47. Bronwen Cowie, Christine Harrison, and Jill Willis, "Supporting Teacher Responsiveness in Assessment for Learning Through Disciplined Noticing," *Curriculum Journal* 29, no. 4 (2018).
48. Brent Davis, "Listening for Differences: An Evolving Conception of Mathematics Teaching," *Journal for Research in Mathematics Education* 28, no. 3 (1997): 355–76, doi:10.2307/749785.
49. Jerome S Bruner, *Going Beyond the Information Given* (New York: Norton, 1973); Vygotsky, *Mind in Society*.
50. Norma González, Luis C. Moll, and Cathy Amanti, eds., *Funds of Knowledge* (New York: Routledge, 2005).
51. González, Moll, and Amanti.
52. Philippe Perrenoud, "From Formative Evaluation to a Controlled Regulation of Learning Processes: Towards a Wider Conceptual Field," *Assessment in Education: Principles, Policy & Practice* 5, no. 1 (1998): 85–102, doi:10.1080/0969595980050105.
53. Windschitl et al., "Proposing a Core Set," 886.
54. Heritage and Harrison, *Power of Assessment for Learning*.
55. Heritage and Harrison, *Power of Assessment for Learning*, 37.

Chapter 2

1. David C. Berliner, "In Pursuit of the Expert Pedagogue," *Educational Researcher* 15 (1986), doi:10.3102/0013189X015007007.
2. See Douglas Harris and Tim Sass, "Teacher Training, Teacher Quality, and Student Achievement," *Journal of Public Economics* 95 (2011), doi:10.1016/j.jpubeco.2010.11.009, and Matthew Wiswall, "The Dynamics of Teacher Quality," *Journal of Public Economics* 100 (2013), doi:10.1016/j.jpubeco.2013.01.006.
3. Thomas M. Smith and Richard M. Ingersoll, "What Are the Effects of Induction and Mentoring on Beginning Teacher Turnover?," *American Educational Research Journal* 41, no. 3 (2004): 705, doi:10.3102/00028312041003681.
4. Robert Glaser, "Changing the Agency for Learning: Acquiring Expert Performance," in *The Road to Excellence: The Acquisition of Expert Performance in the Arts and Sciences, Sports, and Games* (Hillsdale, NJ: Lawrence Erlbaum Associates, 1996).
5. Margaret Heritage and E. Caroline Wylie, "Teacher Preparation in Mathematics," in *Handbook of Formative Assessment in the Disciplines*, ed. Heidi L. Andrade, Randy E. Bennett, and Gregory J. Cizek (New York: Routledge, 2019).
6. Lev S. Vygotsky, *Mind in Society: The Development of Higher Mental Process* (Cambridge, MA: Harvard University Press, 1978).
7. Drew Polly et al., "Sociocultural Perspectives of Learning," in *Foundations of Learning and Instructional Design Technology*, ed. Richard E. West (Provo, UT: EdTech Books, 2018).
8. Polly et al.
9. Mayra Carrasco, interview with Margaret Heritage, 2017.
10. Vygotsky, *Mind in Society*.
11. David Wood, Jerome S. Bruner, and Gail Ross, "The Role of Tutoring in Problem Solving," *Journal of Child Psychology and Psychiatry* 17, no. 2 (1976),

doi:10.1111/j.1469-7610.1976.tb00381.x; Roland G. Tharp and Ronald Gallimore, *Rousing Minds to Life: Teaching, Learning, and Schooling in Social Context* (Cambridge: Cambridge University Press, 1988).

12. Deborah Loewenberg Ball, "Blurring the Boundaries of Research and Practice," *Remedial and Special Education* 16, no. 6 (1995), doi:10.1177/074193259501600605; Hilda Borko and Ralph Putnam, "Professional Development and Reform-Based Teaching: Introduction to Theme Issue," *Teaching and Teacher Education* 14, no. 1 (1998); Carol Sue Englert and Kathi L. Tarrant, "Creating Collaborative Cultures for Educational Change," *Remedial and Special Education* 16, no. 6 (1995), doi:10.1177/074193259501600602.
13. Gabriela Cárdenas, interview with Margaret Heritage, 2017.
14. Yrjö Engeström, "Developmental Work Research as Educational Research: Looking Ten Years Back and into the Zone of Proximal Development," *Nordisk Pedagogik* 16, no. 3 (1996).
15. Etienne Wenger, *Communities of Practice: Learning, Meaning, and Identity* (Cambridge: Cambridge University Press, 1998).
16. Etienne Wenger, Richard Arnold McDermott, and William Snyder, *Cultivating Communities of Practice: A Guide to Managing Knowledge* (Cambridge, MA: Harvard Business Press, 2002), 4.
17. Jean Lave and Etienne Wenger, *Situated Learning: Legitimate Peripheral Participation* (Cambridge: Cambridge University Press, 1991), 36.
18. This teacher worked with the first author in a variety of professional learning contexts over multiple years.
19. Linda Lambert, *Leadership Capacity for Lasting School Improvement* (Alexandria, VA: ASCD, 2003); Andy Hargreaves and Michael Fullan, *Professional Capital* (New York: Teachers College Press, 2012).
20. Geoffrey Gowlland, "Apprenticeship as a Model for Learning in and Through Professional Practice," in *International Handbook of Research in Professional and Practice-Based Learning*, ed. Stephen Billett, Christian Harteis, and Hans Gruber, Springer International Handbooks of Education (Dordrecht, Netherlands: Springer Science & Business Media, 2014), 760.
21. Lave and Wenger, *Situated Learning*.
22. Figure 2.1 is adapted from an earlier representation in Heritage and Wylie, "Teacher Preparation in Mathematics."
23. Andreas Schleicher, "Educating Learners for Their Future, Not Our Past," *ECNU Review of Education* 1, no. 1 (2018), doi:10.30926/ecnuroe2018010104.
24. Adapted from Heritage and Wylie, "Teacher Preparation in Mathematics."
25. Margaret Heritage and Christine Harrison, *The Power of Assessment for Learning: Twenty Years of Research and Practice in UK and US Classrooms* (Thousand Oaks, CA: Corwin Press, 2020).
26. Heritage and Harrison.
27. Margaret Heritage, "What Do Teachers Need to Know and Do," *Phi Delta Kappan* 89, no. 2 (2007).
28. Heritage and Harrison, *Power of Assessment for Learning*.
29. Heidi L. Andrade and Margaret Heritage, *Using Formative Assessment to Enhance Learning, Achievement, and Academic Self-Regulation* (New York: Routledge, 2017).
30. Brent Duckor and Carrie Holmberg, *Mastering Formative Assessment Moves: 7 High-Leverage Practices to Advance Student Learning* (Alexandria, VA: ASCD, 2017).

31. Olivia Lozano, interview with Margaret Heritage, 2017.
32. Lee Shulman, "Knowledge and Teaching: Foundations of the New Reform," *Harvard Educational Review* 57, no. 1 (1987): 7, doi:10.17763/haer.57.1.j463w79r56455411.
33. Deborah Loewenberg Ball, Mark Hoover Thames, and Geoffrey Phelps, "Content Knowledge for Teaching: What Makes It Special?," *Journal of Teacher Education* 59, no. 5 (2008), doi:10.1177/0022487108324554.
34. Margaret Heritage, *Learning Progressions: Supporting Instruction and Formative Assessment* (Washington, DC: Council of Chief State School Officers, 2008), https://www.csai-online.org/sites/default/files/Learning_Progressions_Supporting_2008.pdf.
35. Heritage and Wylie, "Teacher Preparation in Mathematics."
36. Meirav Arieli-Attali, E. Caroline Wylie, and Malcolm I. Bauer, "The Use of Three Learning Progressions in Supporting Formative Assessment in Middle School Mathematics" (paper presented at the annual meeting of the American Educational Research Association, Vancouver, Canada, April 2012).
37. Marie-Geneviève Séré, "Children's Conceptions of the Gaseous State, Prior to Teaching," *European Journal of Science Education* 8, no. 4 (1986), doi:10.1080/0140528860080408.
38. Paul Black, Mark Wilson, and Shih-Ying Yao, "Road Maps for Learning: A Guide to the Navigation of Learning Progressions," *Measurement: Interdisciplinary Research and Perspectives* 9, no. 2–3 (2011), doi:10.1080/15366367.2011.591654.
39. Brent Davis, "Listening for Differences: An Evolving Conception of Mathematics Teaching," *Journal for Research in Mathematics Education* 28, no. 3 (1997), doi:10.2307/749785.
40. K. Anders Ericsson, Ralf T. Krampe, and Clemens Tesch-Römer, "The Role of Deliberate Practice in the Acquisition of Expert Performance," *Psychological Review* 100, no. 3 (1993); Donald Schön, *The Reflective Practitioner: How Professionals Think in Action* (New York: Basic Books, 1983).
41. Alan Reid, *Towards a Culture of Inquiry in DECS*, Occasional Paper Series 1 (Adelaide: South Australian Department of Education and Children's Services, 2004).
42. Helen Timperley, *Teacher Professional Learning and Development*, International Academy of Education Educational Practices Series, no. 18, (Brussels: IAE, 2008).
43. This teacher worked with the first author in a variety of professional learning contexts over multiple years.
44. Reid, *Towards a Culture of Inquiry*.
45. John Dewey, *How We Think: A Restatement of the Relation of Reflective Thinking to the Educative Process* (Boston: D. C. Heath, 1933), cited in Reid, *Towards a Culture of Inquiry*, 7.
46. Deans for Impact, *Practice with Purpose: The Emerging Science of Teacher Expertise* (Austin, TX: Deans for Impact, 2016), https://deansforimpact.org/wp-content/uploads/2016/12/Practice-with-Purpose_FOR-PRINT_113016.pdf.
47. Olivia Lozano, interview with Margaret Heritage, 2017.
48. Olivia Lozano, interview with Margaret Heritage, 2017.
49. Jack C. Richards, "Towards Reflective Teaching," *The Teacher Trainer* 5, no. 3 (1991).
50. Leo Bartlett, "Teacher Development Through Reflective Teaching," in *Second Language Teacher Education*, ed. Jack C. Richards and David Nunan, Cambridge Language Teaching Library (New York: Cambridge University Press, 1990).
51. This teacher worked with the first author in a variety of professional learning contexts over multiple years.

Chapter 3

1. Robert Moses and Charles E. Cobb, *Radical Equations: Civil Rights from Mississippi to the Algebra Project* (Boston, MA: Beacon Press, 2002).
2. Moses and Cobb, 2.
3. "Lifelong Learning: How to Survive in the Age of Automation," special issue, *Economist*, January 14–20, 2017.
4. Lynn Arthur Steen, ed., *Mathematics and Democracy: The Case for Quantitative Literacy* (Princeton, NJ: National Council on Education and the Disciplines, 2001).
5. Steen, 8–9.
6. Margaret Heritage and John Heritage, "Teacher Questioning: The Epicenter of Instruction and Assessment," *Applied Measurement in Education* 26, no. 3 (2013), https://doi.org/10.1080/08957347.2013.793190.
7. *Common Core State Standards for Mathematics* (Washington, DC: National Governors Association Center for Best Practices and Council of Chief State School Officers, 2010), http://www.corestandards.org/wp-content/uploads/Math_Standards1.pdf.
8. National Research Council, *How Students Learn: Mathematics in the Classroom*, ed. M. Suzanne Donovan and John D. Bransford (Washington, DC: National Academies Press, 2005).
9. National Council of Teachers of Mathematics, *Principles and Standards for School Mathematics* (Reston, VA: NCTM, 2000).
10. NCTM, *Principles and Standards*.
11. Jeremy Kilpatrick, Jane Swafford, and Bradford Findell, eds., *Adding It Up: Helping Children Learn Mathematics* (Washington, DC: National Academies Press, 2001).
12. *Common Core State Standards for Mathematics*, 8.
13. Jaclyn Zubrzycki, "Teachers Say They Know More About the Common Core, but Challenges Linger," *Education Week*, December 22, 2016.
14. National Research Council, *How People Learn: Brain, Mind, Experience, and School*, expanded ed. (Washington, DC: National Academies Press, 2000), doi:10.17226/9853.
15. NRC, *How People Learn*, 14–18.
16. NRC, *How Students Learn*.
17. Mike Askew and Dylan Wiliam, *Recent Research in Mathematics Education*, Ofsted Reviews of Research (London: Office for Standards in Education, 1995).
18. The research reported here was supported by the Institute of Education Sciences, US Department of Education, through Grant Reference R305K040051 to Educational Testing Service; Joseph Ciofalo and E. Caroline Wylie, "Using Diagnostic Classroom Assessment: One Item at a Time," *Teachers College Record* (January 10, 2006), http://www.tcrecord.org/content.asp?contentid=12285; E. Caroline Wylie and Joseph Ciofalo, "Supporting Teachers' Use of Individual Diagnostic Items," *Teachers College Record* (September 5, 2008), http://www.tcrecord.org/content.asp?contentid=15363.
19. Wylie and Ciofalo, "Supporting Teachers' Use."
20. Rosalind Driver et al., *Making Sense of Secondary Science: Research into Children's Ideas*, 2nd ed. (London: Routledge, 2015); Ruth Stavy and Dina Tirosh, *How Students (Mis-) Understand Science and Mathematics: Intuitive Rules* (New York: Teachers College Press, 2000); Wylie and Ciofalo, "Supporting Teachers' Use."
21. E. Caroline Wylie, "A Role for Diagnostic Questions in Formative Assessment" (paper

presented at the Chief Council of State School Officers (CCSSO) National Conference on Student Assessment, Orlando, FL, June, 2008).

22. Linda Levi and Rebecca Ambrose, "Cognitively Guided Instruction and Formative Assessment," in *A Fresh Look at Formative Assessment in Mathematics Teaching*, ed. Valerie Mills and Edward Silver (Reston, VA: National Council of Teachers of Mathematics, 2018), 41–60.
23. Arkalgud Ramaprasad, "On the Definition of Feedback," *Behavioral Science* 28, no. 1 (1983): 4–13, https://doi.org/10.1002/bs.3830280103; Dylan Wiliam, "Keeping Learning on Track: Integrating Assessment with Instruction" (paper presented at the 30th annual conference of the International Association for Educational Assessment (IAEA), Philadelphia, PA, 2004).
24. Allan Collins, John Seely Brown, and Ann Holum, "Cognitive Apprenticeship: Making Thinking Visible," *American Educator* 15, no. 3 (1991); Lauren Resnick, ed., *Knowing, Learning, and Instruction: Essays in Honor of Robert Glaser* (Taylor & Francis, 2018), 32–42, ebook, doi:10.4324/9781315044408.
25. NRC, *How Students Learn*, 235.
26. This example of practice was provided by a district leader who observed and discussed the lesson with this teacher.
27. *Common Core State Standards for Mathematics*, 55.
28. *Common Core State Standards for Mathematics*, 8.
29. NRC, *How Students Learn*, 12.
30. Grace Kelemanik, Amy Lucenta, and Susan Creighton, *Routines for Reasoning: Fostering the Mathematical Practices in All Students* (Portsmouth, NH: Heinemann, 2016).
31. The first author was engaged in a project that captured videos of classroom practice and teacher interviews, including this teacher.
32. Malcolm Swan and Hugh Burkhardt, "Lesson Design for Formative Assessment," *Educational Designer* 2, no. 4 (2014).
33. Mathematics Assessment Resource Service, "Interpreting Multiplication and Division," *Classroom Challenges*, Mathematics Assessment Project (website), 2015, http://map.mathshell.org.
34. Magdalene Lampert, "Teaching Problems and the Problems of Teaching," *Journal of Mathematics Teacher Education* 5 (2001); Alan Schoenfeld, "Toward a Theory of Teaching-in-Context," *Issues in Education* 4 (1998); Deborah Loewenberg Ball, "With an Eye on the Mathematical Horizon: Dilemmas of Teaching Elementary School Mathematics," *Elementary School Journal* 93, no. 4 (1993); Jo Boaler and Cathleen Humphreys, *Connecting Mathematical Ideas* (Portsmouth, NH: Heinemann, 2005).
35. Mitchell J. Nathan and Eric J. Knuth, "A Study of Whole Classroom Mathematical Discourse and Teacher Change," *Cognition and Instruction* 21, no. 2 (2003).
36. Mary Kay Stein et al., "Orchestrating Productive Mathematical Discussions: Five Practices for Helping Teachers Move Beyond Show and Tell," *Mathematical Thinking and Learning* 10, no. 4 (2008), https://doi.org/10.1080/10986060802229675.
37. The first author was engaged in a project that captured videos of classroom practice and teacher interviews, including this teacher.
38. NRC, *How People Learn*.
39. Ramaprasad, "On the Definition of Feedback"; Wiliam, "Keeping Learning on Track."
40. Julie Whyte and Glenda Anthony, "Maths Anxiety: The Fear Factor in the Mathematics Classroom," *New Zealand Journal of Teachers' Work* 9, no. 1 (2012): 6–15.

Chapter 4

1. UNESCO, *The Plurality of Literacy and Its Implications for Policies and Programmes*, UNESCO Education Sector Position Papers (Paris: UNESCO, 2004), 13, https://unesdoc.unesco.org/ark:/48223/pf0000136246.
2. Richard Murnane, Isabel Sawhill, and Catherine Snow, "Literacy Challenges for the Twenty-First Century: Introducing the Issue," *The Future of Children* 22, no. 2 (2012), doi:10.2307/23317408.
3. UNESCO, *The Plurality of Literacy*, 13.
4. Terry Roberts and Laura Billings, "Thinking Is Literacy, Literacy Is Thinking," *Educational Leadership* 65, no. 5 (2008).
5. Roberts and Billings.
6. Fritz Mosher and Margaret Heritage, *Hitchhiker's Guide to Thinking About Literacy, Learning Progressions, and Instruction*, CPRE Research Reports (Philadelphia: Consortium for Policy Research in Education, 2017), https://www.cpre.org/hitchhikers-guide-thinking-about-literacy-learning-progressions-and-instruction.
7. *Common Core State Standards for English Language Arts* (Washington, DC: National Governors Association Center for Best Practices and Council of Chief State School Officers, 2010), http://www.corestandards.org/ELA-Literacy/.
8. Alison L. Bailey and Margaret Heritage, *Formative Assessment for Literacy, Grades K-6: Building Reading and Academic Language Skills Across the Curriculum* (Thousand Oaks, CA: Corwin Press, 2008); Alison L. Bailey and Margaret Heritage, *Progressing Students' Language Day by Day* (Thousand Oaks, CA: Corwin Press, 2018).
9. Bailey and Heritage, *Progressing Students' Language Day by Day*.
10. Mary J. Schleppegrell, "Linguistic Features of the Language of Schooling," *Linguistics and Education* 12, no. 4 (2001), doi:10.1016/S0898-5898(01)00073-0.
11. Schleppegrell.
12. Filip Dochy, Mien Segers, and Michelle M. Buehl, "The Relation Between Assessment Practices and Outcomes of Studies: The Case of Research on Prior Knowledge," *Review of Educational Research* 69, no. 2 (1999), doi:10.3102/00346543069002145; Amy M. Shapiro, "How Including Prior Knowledge as a Subject Variable May Change Outcomes of Learning Research," *American Educational Research Journal* 41, no. 1 (2004), doi:10.3102/00028312041001159.
13. Hemanth Kommuru et al., "Thoracic Part of Sympathetic Chain and Its Branching Pattern Variations in South Indian Cadavers," *Journal of Clinical and Diagnostic Research* 8, no. 12 (2014), doi:10.7860/JCDR/2014/9274.5246.
14. Marilyn Jager Adams, "Knowledge for Literacy," Albert Shanker Institute, http://www.shankerinstitute.org/blog/knowledge-literacy.
15. Luis C. Moll et al., "Funds of Knowledge for Teaching: Using a Qualitative Approach to Connect Homes and Classrooms," *Theory Into Practice* 31, no. 2 (1992): 132–41, doi:10.1080/00405849209543534.
16. The first author worked with this teacher on a professional development project focused on formative assessment. The teacher supplied this vignette illustrating how her teaching had changed as a result of the course.
17. Robert Gibbons, "Incentives in Organizations," *Journal of Economic Perspectives* 12, no. 4 (1998), doi:10.1257/jep.12.4.115.
18. *Common Core State Standards for ELA*, 3.

19. George C. Bunch, Amanda Kibler, and Susan Pimentel, "Realizing Opportunities for English Learners in the Common Core English Language Arts and Disciplinary Literacy Standards," Understanding Language Initiative (Stanford, CA: Stanford University, 2012), https://ell.stanford.edu/sites/default/files/pdf/academic-papers/01_Bunch_Kibler_Pimentel_RealizingOpp%20in%20ELA_FINAL_0.pdf.
20. Bunch, Kibler, and Pimentel.
21. Bunch, Kibler, and Pimentel, 3.
22. The video from which this vignette was transcribed was developed by the Michigan Association of Intermediate School Administrator General Education Leadership Network, the Early Literacy Task Force, and the 6–12 Disciplinary Literacy Task Force, https://www.michigan.gov/documents/mde/MAISA_Communication_Points_for_Early_Elementary_and_Disciplinary_Literacy_002_663214_7.pdf.
23. John Scieszka, *The True Story of the Three Little Pigs* (New York: Viking Books for Young Readers, 1989).
24. The first author worked with this teacher on a professional development project focused on formative assessment and was able to observe her teach.
25. *Common Core State Standards for ELA.*
26. Michigan Department of Education, "Michigan K–12 Standards: English Language Arts," https://www.michigan.gov/documents/mde/MDE_ELA_Standards_599599_7.pdf.
27. National Assessment of Educational Progress, "NAEP Reading Report Card," https://www.nationsreportcard.gov/reading_2017.
28. Annenberg Learner, "What Is Disciplinary Literacy?," *Reading and Writing in the Disciplines* (online course), https://www.learner.org/courses/readwrite/disciplinary-literacy/what-is-disciplinary-literacy/1.html.
29. Emily Rainey and Elizabeth B. Moje, "Building Insider Knowledge: Teaching Students to Read, Write, and Think Within ELA and Across the Disciplines," *English Education* 45, no. 1 (2012), https://www.jstor.org/stable/23365001.
30. Susan R. Goldman et al., "Disciplinary Literacies and Learning to Read for Understanding: A Conceptual Framework for Disciplinary Literacy," *Educational Psychologist* 51, no. 2 (2016), doi:10.1080/00461520.2016.1168741.
31. Grace Kena et al., *The Condition of Education 2014* (Washington, DC: US Department of Education National Center for Education Statistics, 2014), https://nces.ed.gov/pubs2014/2014083.pdf; Stella M. Flores, Jeanne Batalova, and Michael Fix, *The Educational Trajectories of English Language Learners in Texas* (Washington, DC: Migration Policy Institute, 2012), https://www.migrationpolicy.org/research/educational-trajectories-english-language-learners-texas.
32. Kena et al., *The Condition of Education 2014.*
33. Margaret Heritage, Aida Walqui, and Robert Linquanti, *English Language Learners and the New Standards* (Cambridge, MA: Harvard Education Press, 2015).

Chapter 5

1. National Research Council, *A Framework for K-12 Science Education: Practices, Crosscutting Concepts, and Core Ideas* (Washington, DC: National Academies Press, 2012), 278, doi:10.17226/13165.
2. NRC, *Framework*, 1.

3. National Research Council, *Next Generation Science Standards: For States by States*, vol. 1 (Washington, DC: National Academies Press, 2013), doi:10.17226/18290.
4. NRC, *Framework.*
5. NRC, *Framework.*
6. "Fruit and vegetable decomposition, Time-lapse," December 16, 2008, YouTube video, https://www.youtube.com/watch?v=c0En-_BVbGc.
7. NRC, *Framework.*
8. NRC, *Framework*, 31.
9. Joanna S. Gorin and Robert J. Mislevy, "Inherent Measurement Challenges in the Next Generation Science Standards for Both Formative and Summative Assessment" (paper presented at the Invitational Research Symposium on Science Assessment, Washington, DC, 2013).
10. National Research Council, *How People Learn: Brain, Mind, Experience, and School*, expanded ed. (Washington, DC: National Academies Press, 2000), 14–18, doi:10.17226/9853.
11. The first author met this teacher at a conference presenting on teaching and learning challenges and opportunities with NGSS and asked her to provide a more detailed example of her classroom practice.
12. E. Caroline Wylie and Joseph Ciofalo, "Supporting Teachers' Use of Individual Diagnostic Items," *Teachers College Record* (September 5, 2008), http://www.tcrecord.org/content.asp?contentid=15363.
13. Rosalind Driver et al., *Making Sense of Secondary Science: Research into Children's Ideas* (New York: RoutledgeFalmer, 1994); Ruth Stavy and Dina Tirosh, *How Students (Mis-)Understand Science and Mathematics: Intuitive Rules* (New York: Teachers College Press, 2000).
14. Wylie and Ciofalo, "Supporting Teachers' Use."
15. E. Caroline Wylie, "A Role for Diagnostic Questions in Formative Assessment" (paper presented at the Chief Council of State School Officers (CCSSO) National Conference on Student Assessment, Orlando, FL, 2008).
16. James Minstrell and Pamela Kraus, "Guided Inquiry in the Science Classroom," in *How Students Learn: History, Mathematics, and Science in the Classroom* (Washington, DC: National Academies Press, 2005).
17. Minstrell and Kraus, 486.
18. Driver et al., *Making Sense of Secondary Science*; Stavy and Tirosh, *How Students (Mis-) Understand.*
19. David C. Berliner, "In Pursuit of the Expert Pedagogue," *Educational Researcher* 15 (1986), doi:10.3102/0013189X015007007.
20. Lei Liu and Teresa Jackson, "A Recent Review of Learning Progressions in Science: Gaps and Shifts," *Educational Review* 3, no. 9 (2019), doi:10.26855/er.2019.09.001.
21. John D. Bransford and M. Suzanne Donovan, "Scientific Inquiry and How People Learn," in *How Students Learn: History, Mathematics, and Science in the Classroom* (Washington, DC: National Academies Press, 2005).
22. Grant P. Wiggins and Jay McTighe, *Understanding by Design* (Alexandria, VA: ASCD, 2005); The example of practice about Mr. Spencer was provided by one of the curriculum specialists with whom we consulted for the content chapters.
23. The example of practice about Mr. Rhodea was provided by one of the curriculum specialists with whom we consulted for the content chapters.

24. "Stomata Printing: Microscope Investigation," California Academy of Sciences, https://www.calacademy.org/educators/lesson-plans/stomata-printing-microscope-investigation.
25. Lee Shulman, "Foreword," in *Disciplinary Styles in the Scholarship of Teaching and Learning: Exploring Common Ground*, ed. Mary Taylor Huber and Sherwyn Morreale (Merrifield, VA: AAHE Publications Orders, 2002), https://files.eric.ed.gov/fulltext/ED478800.pdf.
26. Margaret Heritage, *Formative Assessment: A Process of Inquiry and Action* (Cambridge, MA: Harvard Education Press, 2013), 62.
27. Arkalgud Ramaprasad, "On the Definition of Feedback," *Behavioral Science* 28, no. 1 (1983), doi:10.1002/bs.3830280103;
28. Dylan Wiliam, "Keeping Learning on Track: Integrating Assessment with Instruction" (paper presented at the 30th annual conference of the International Association for Educational Assessment (IAEA), Philadelphia, PA, 2004).
29. Randy Bennett, "Integrating Measurement Principles into Formative Assessment," in *Handbook of Formative Assessment in the Disciplines*, ed. Heidi Andrade, Gregory Cizek, and Randy Bennett (New York: Routledge, 2019).

Chapter 6

1. Organisation for Economic Co-operation and Development, *The Future of Education and Skills: Education 2030* (Paris: OECD, 2018), https://www.oecd.org/education/2030/E2030%20Position%20Paper%20(05.04.2018).pdf.
2. National Council for the Social Studies, *National Curriculum Standards for Social Studies: Executive Summary* (Silver Spring, MD: NCSS, 2013), 1, https://www.socialstudies.org/standards/execsummary.
3. NCSS, *College, Career, and Civic Life (C3) Framework for Social Studies State Standards: Guidance for Enhancing the Rigor of K-12 Civics, Economics, Geography, and History* (Silver Spring, MD: NCSS, 2013), 6, https://www.socialstudies.org/c3.
4. NCSS, *C3 Framework.*
5. Susan Griffin, "Who, What, Where, How, and Now? The C3 Framework and the C3 Literacy Collaborative Project," *Social Education* 80, no. 6 (2016).
6. Michael Hansen et al., *The 2018 Brown Center Report on American Education: How Well Are American Students Learning?* (Washington, DC: Brown Center on Education Policy at Brookings, 2018).
7. Griffin, "Who, What, Where, How, and Now?"
8. Griffin, 330.
9. NCSS, *C3 Framework.*
10. S. G. Grant, "From Inquiry Arc to Instructional Practice: The Potential of the C3 Framework," *Social Education* 77, no. 6 (2013).
11. Stanford History Education Group, "Lunchroom Fight," Stanford University, https://sheg.stanford.edu/history-lessons/lunchroom-fight.
12. NCSS, *C3 Framework*, 29.
13. Grant, "From Inquiry Arc to Instructional Practice."
14. SHEG, "Reconstruction Structured Academic Controversy (SAC)," *Reading Like a Historian*, Stanford University, https://sheg.stanford.edu/sites/default/files/download-pdf/Reconstruction%20SAC.pdf.

15. SHEG, "Reconstruction SAC," 5.
16. Esri, *Geographic Inquiry: Thinking Geographically* (Redlands, CA: Esri Schools and Libraries Program, 2003), https://www.esri.com/Industries/k-12/education/~/media/Files/Pdfs/industries/k-12/pdfs/geoginquiry.pdf.
17. Charles Gilmore, personal correspondence, April 2019.
18. Daniel T. Willingham, "Ask the Cognitive Scientist: Students Remember . . . What They Think About," *American Educator* (Summer 2003), https://www.aft.org/periodical/american-educator/summer-2003/ask-cognitive-scientist.
19. Sam Wineburg, "Thinking Like a Historian," *TPS Quarterly* 3, no. 1 (2010).
20. Kathryn Au, "Isn't Culturally Responsive Instruction Just Good Teaching?," *Social Education* 73, no. 4 (2009).
21. NCSS, *National Standards for the Preparation of Social Studies Teachers* (Silver Spring, MD: NCSS, 2017).
22. Diana Cohn, *Si, se puede! Yes, We Can! Janitor Strike in L.A.* (El Paso, TX: Cinco Puntos Press, 2009); Cynthia Levinson, *The Youngest Marcher: The Story of Audrey Faye Hendricks* (New York: Atheneum, 2017).
23. NCSS, *Standards for Social Studies Teachers*, 59.
24. Gilmore, personal correspondence.
25. Philippe Perrenoud, "From Formative Evaluation to a Controlled Regulation of Learning Processes: Towards a Wider Conceptual Field," *Assessment in Education: Principles, Policy & Practice* 5, no. 1 (1998), cited in Bethan Marshall and Mary Jane Drummond, "How Teachers Engage with Assessment for Learning: Lessons from the Classroom," *Research Papers in Education* 21, no. 2 (2006): 134, doi:10.1080/02671520600615638.
26. Valerie Otero, "Moving Beyond the 'Get It or Don't' Conception of Formative Assessment," *Journal of Teacher Education* 57, no. 3 (2006), doi:10.1177/0022487105285963; Val Klenowski, "Assessment for Learning Revisited: An Asia-Pacific Perspective," *Assessment in Education: Principles, Policy & Practice* 16, no. 3 (2009), doi:10.1080/09695940903319646.
27. NCSS, *C3 Framework*.
28. NCSS, *Standards for Social Studies Teachers*.
29. Norma González, Luis C. Moll, and Cathy Amanti, eds., *Funds of Knowledge* (New York: Routledge, 2005), 4.
30. Margaret Heritage, *Learning Progressions: Supporting Instruction and Formative Assessment* (Washington, DC: Council of Chief State School Officers, 2008), https://www.csai-online.org/sites/default/files/Learning_Progressions_Supporting_2008.pdf.
31. Antonio J. Castro and Ryan T. Knowles, "Democratic Citizenship Education," in *The Wiley Handbook of Social Studies Research*, ed. Meghan McGlinn Manfra and Cheryl Mason Bolick (Malden, MA: John Wiley & Sons, 2017), doi:10.1002/9781118768747.ch13.
32. Lee Shulman, "Knowledge and Teaching: Foundations of the New Reform," *Harvard Educational Review* 57, no. 1 (1987): 7, doi:10.17763/haer.57.1.j463w79r56455411; Andreas Schleicher, "Educating Learners for Their Future, Not Our Past," *ECNU Review of Education* 1, no. 1 (2018), doi:10.30926/ecnuroe2018010104.

Chapter 7

1. Dan C. Lortie, *Schoolteacher: A Sociological Study* (Chicago: University of Chicago Press, 1975), 3.
2. Deborah J. Stipek et al., "Teachers' Beliefs and Practices Related to Mathematics Instruction," *Teaching and Teacher Education* 17, no. 2 (2001), doi:10.1016/s0742-051x(00)00052-4.
3. David K. Cohen and Deborah Loewenberg Ball, "Relations Between Policy and Practice: A Commentary," *Educational Evaluation and Policy Analysis* 12, no. 3 (1990), doi:10.3102/01623737012003331; Dona M. Kagan, "Implication of Research on Teacher Belief," *Educational Psychologist* 27, no. 1 (1992), doi:10.1207/s15326985ep2701_6.
4. Magdalene Lampert, "Learning Teaching In, From, and For Practice: What Do We Mean?," *Journal of Teacher Education* 61, no. 1–2 (2010), doi:10.1177/0022487109347321; Pamela Grossman, Karen Hammerness, and Morva McDonald, "Redefining Teaching, Re-Imagining Teacher Education," *Teachers and Teaching: Theory and Practice* 15, no. 2 (2009), doi:10.1080/13540600902875340; Pamela Grossman et al., "Teaching Practice: A Cross-Professional Perspective," *Teachers College Record* 111, no. 9 (2009), https://eric.ed.gov/?id=EJ858247; Pamela A. Moss, "Analyzing the Teaching of Professional Practice," *Teachers College Record* 113, no. 12 (2011), https://eric.ed.gov/?id=EJ988310; Mark Windschitl et al., "Proposing a Core Set of Instructional Practices and Tools for Teachers of Science," *Science Education* 96, no. 5 (2012), doi:10.1002/sce.21027.
5. Kathleen J. Sullivan, "Nathaniel Gage, 'Giant among Educational Researchers,' Dead at 91," *Stanford Report*, August 22, 2008.
6. Nathaniel L. Gage, "An Analytical Approach to Research on Instructional Methods," *Journal of Experimental Education* 37, no. 1 (1968).
7. Grossman et al., "Teaching Practice," 2058.
8. Grossman et al.
9. Grossman et al.
10. Grossman et al.
11. Lampert, "Learning Teaching," 21–34.
12. Grossman, Hammerness, and McDonald, "Redefining Teaching."
13. Grossman, Hammerness, and McDonald, 277.
14. Brent Duckor and Carrie Holmberg, *Mastering Formative Assessment Moves: 7 High-Leverage Practices to Advance Student Learning* (Alexandria, VA: ASCD, 2017).
15. Margaret Heritage and E. Caroline Wylie, "Teacher Preparation in Mathematics," in *Handbook of Formative Assessment in the Disciplines*, ed. Heidi L. Andrade, Randy E. Bennett, and Gregory J. Cizek (New York: Routledge, 2019).
16. FAST SCASS definition: Formative assessment is a planned, ongoing process used by all students and teachers during learning and teaching to elicit and use evidence of student learning to improve student understanding of intended disciplinary learning outcomes, and support students to become self-directed learners.

    Effective use of the formative assessment process requires students and teachers to integrate and embed the following practices in a collaborative and respectful classroom environment:

    - Clarifying learning goals and success criteria within a broader progression of learning
    - Eliciting and analyzing evidence of student thinking

- Engaging in self-assessment and peer feedback
- Providing actionable feedback
- Using evidence and feedback to move learning forward by adjusting learning strategies, goals, or next instructional steps from *Revising the Definition of Formative Assessment* (Washington, DC: Council of Chief State School Officers, 2018), https://ccsso.org/resource-library/revising-definition-formative-assessment.

17. Heritage and Wylie, "Teacher Preparation in Mathematics."
18. Valerie Mills and Edward Silver, eds., *A Fresh Look at Formative Assessment in Mathematics Teaching* (Reston, VA: National Council of Mathematics Teachers, 2018); Linda Levi and Rebecca Ambrose, "Cognitively Guided Instruction and Formative Assessment," Michael Steele and Margaret Smith, "The Mathematical Tasks Framework and Formative Assessment," and Megan Burton and Wanda Audrict, "Focusing on Formative Assessment to Improve Mathematics Teaching and Learning," all in Mills and Silver.
19. Thomasenia Lott Adams and Emily Bonner, "Distinguishing Features of Culturally Responsive Pedagogy Related to Formative Assessment in Mathematics Instruction," and Beth Kobett and Karen Karp, "Using Formative Assessment to Guide the Effective Implementation of Response to Intervention (RTI)," both in Mills and Silver.
20. Don Klinger et al., *Classroom Assessment Standards for PreK-12 Teachers* (Joint Committee on Standards for Educational Evaluation, Kindle Direct Press, 2015); E. Caroline Wylie and Christine J. Lyon, "Supporting Teacher Assessment Literacy: A Proposed Sequence of Learning," *Teachers College Record*, no. 22193 (October 30, 2017), http://www.tcrecord.org/content.asp?contentid=22193.
21. National Research Council, *Knowing What Students Know: The Science and Design of Educational Assessment* (Washington, DC: National Academies Press, 2001).
22. E. Caroline Wylie and Christine Lyon, *Using the Formative Assessment Rubrics, Reflection and Observation Tools to Support Professional Reflection on Practice* (Washington, DC: Formative Assessment for Teachers and Students State Collaborative on Assessment and Student Standards of the Council of Chief State School Officers (CCSSO), 2015).
23. E. Caroline Wylie, "Supporting Teacher Learning Through Self and Peer Observation" (paper presented at the CCSSO National Conference on Student Assessment, Philadelphia, PA, 2016); Kathleen Brinko, "The Practice of Giving Feedback to Improve Teaching," *Journal of Higher Education* 64, no. 5 (1993), doi:10.1080/00221546.1993.11778449.
24. Christine Lyon, "Preliminary Findings on How Teachers Use Observation Protocols" (paper presented at the CCSSO National Conference on Student Assessment, Orlando, FL, 2019).
25. Heidi L. Andrade, Ying Du, and Kristina Mycek, "Rubric-Referenced Self-Assessment and Middle School Students' Writing," *Assessment in Education: Principles, Policy & Practice* 17, no. 2 (2010), doi:10.1080/09695941003696172; David Fontana and Margarida Fernandes, "Improvements in Mathematics Performance as a Consequence of Self-Assessment in Portuguese Primary School Pupils," *British Journal of Educational Psychology* 64, no. 3 (1994); Barbara Y. White and John R. Frederiksen, "Inquiry, Modeling, and Metacognition: Making Science Accessible to All Students," *Cognition and Instruction* 16, no. 1 (1998).

26. Alison L. Bailey and Margaret Heritage, "The Role of Language Learning Progressions in Improved Instruction and Assessment of English Language Learners," *TESOL Quarterly* 48, no. 3 (2014), doi:10.1002/tesq.176.
27. Paul Black and Dylan Wiliam, "Assessment and Classroom Learning," *Assessment in Education: Principles, Policy & Practice* 5, no. 1 (1998): 37, https://doi.org/10.1080/0969595980050102.
28. Paola Sztajn et al., "Learning Trajectory Based Instruction: Toward a Theory of Teaching," *Educational Researcher* 41, no. 5 (2012), doi:10.3102/0013189X12442801; Meirav Arieli-Attali, E. Caroline Wylie, and Malcolm I. Bauer, "The Use of Three Learning Progressions in Supporting Formative Assessment in Middle School Mathematics" (paper presented at the annual meeting of the American Educational Research Association, Vancouver, Canada, April 2012); Marge Petit, "Learning Trajectories and Adaptive Instruction Meet the Realities of Practice," in *Learning Trajectories in Mathematics: A Foundation for Standards, Curriculum, Assessment, and Instruction*, ed. Phil Daro, Frederic Mosher, and Tom Corcoran (Philadelphia: Consortium for Policy Research in Education, 2011), http://www.ogapmath.com/wp-content/uploads/2014/01/OGAP-Chapter1.pdf; Carol Smith et al., *Implications of Research on Children's Learning for Assessment: Matter and Atomic Molecular Theory* (paper commissioned by the Committee on Test Design for K-12 Science Achievement, Center for Education, National Research Council, 2004).
29. Heritage and Wylie, "Teacher Preparation in Mathematics."
30. Common Core Standards Writing Team, "Progressions Documents for the Common Core Mathematics Standards," University of Arizona Institute for Mathematics and Education (2013), http://ime.math.arizona.edu/progressions/#products.
31. CCSWT, "Progressions Documents for Mathematics."
32. Heritage and Wylie, "Teacher Preparation in Mathematics."
33. "Appendix E—Progressions Within the Next Generation Science Standards," Next Generation Science Standards (website), https://www.nextgenscience.org/sites/default/files/resource/files/AppendixE-ProgressionswithinNGSS-061617.pdf.
34. "New Hampshire College and Career Ready K–8 English Language Arts Model Competencies," New Hampshire Department of Education (website), https://www.education.nh.gov/innovations/hs_redesign/documents/english-k-8-2016.pdf.
35. Lei Liu, Aaron Rogat, and Maria Bertling, *A CBAL(tm) Science Model of Cognition: Developing a Competency Model and Learning Progressions to Support Assessment Development*, ETS Research Report Series (Princeton, NJ: Educational Testing Service, 2013).
36. Heritage and Wylie, "Teacher Preparation in Mathematics."
37. Jean Lave and Etienne Wenger, *Situated Learning: Legitimate Peripheral Participation* (Cambridge: Cambridge University Press, 1991).
38. Jon R. Star and Sharon K. Strickland, "Learning to Observe: Using Video to Improve Preservice Mathematics Teachers' Ability to Notice," *Journal of Mathematics Teacher Education* 11, no. 2 (2008), doi:10.1007/s10857-007-9063-7; Jon R. Star, Kathleen Helen Lynch, and Natasha Perova, "Using Video to Improve Mathematics Teachers' Abilities to Attend to Classroom Features: A Replication Study," in *Mathematics Teacher Noticing: Seeing Through Teachers' Eyes*, ed. Miriam G. Sherin, Victoria R. Jacobs, and Randolph A. Philipp (New York: Routledge, 2011).

39. Traci Bliss and Anne Reynolds, "Quality Visions and Focused Imagination," in *Using Video in Teacher Education*, ed. Jere Brophy (Boston: Elsevier, 2003).
40. Burton and Audrict, "Focusing on Formative Assessment."
41. Duckor and Holmberg, *Mastering Formative Assessment Moves*.
42. Duckor and Holmberg.
43. Grossman, Hammerness, and McDonald, "Redefining Teaching."
44. Brent Duckor and Carrie Holmberg, "Exploring How to Model Formative Assessment Trajectories of Posing-Pausing-Probing Practices: Toward a Teacher Learning Progressions Framework for the Study of Novice Teachers," *Journal of Educational Measurement* (published ahead of print, September 12, 2019), doi:10.1111/jedm.12239.
45. Jamie N. Mikeska, Heather Howell, and Carrie Straub, "Using Performance Tasks Within Simulated Environments to Assess Teachers' Ability to Engage in Coordinated, Accumulated, and Dynamic (CAD) Competencies," *International Journal of Testing* 19, no. 2 (2019), doi:10.1080/15305058.2018.1551223.
46. Deborah Loewenberg Ball et al., "Combining the Development of Practice and the Practice of Development in Teacher Education," *Elementary School Journal* 109, no. 5 (2009); Daniel Chazan and Patricio Herbst, "Animations of Classroom Interaction: Expanding the Boundaries of Video Records of Practice," *Teachers College Record* 114, no. 3 (2012), https://eric.ed.gov/?id=EJ1000012; Elizabeth A. Davis and Timothy Boerst, "Designing Elementary Teacher Education to Prepare Well-Started Beginners" (working paper, Teaching Works, University of Michigan School of Education, 2014); Benjamin Dotger et al., "Exploring Iconic Interpretation and Mathematics Teacher Development Through Clinical Simulations," *Journal of Mathematics Teacher Education* 18 (2014).
47. Jamie N. Mikeska, Heather Howell, and Andrew Croft, "Simulations as Practice-Based Spaces to Support Elementary Science Teachers in Learning How to Facilitate Argumentation-Focused Science Discussions" (unpublished manuscript, 2019).
48. "Mathematics Common Core Study Guide Preview," Talking Teaching Network, http://talkingteaching.org/cc-mathematics/#toggle-id-3.
49. Brent Davis, "Listening for Differences: An Evolving Conception of Mathematics Teaching," *Journal for Research in Mathematics Education* 28, no. 3 (1997), doi:10.2307/749785.
50. Deborah Loewenberg Ball, Mark Hoover Thames, and Geoffrey Phelps, "Content Knowledge for Teaching: What Makes It Special?," *Journal of Teacher Education* 59, no. 5 (2008), doi: 10.1177/0022487108324554.
51. James Hiebert et al., "Preparing Teachers to Learn from Teaching," *Journal of Teacher Education* 58, no. 1 (2007), doi:10.1177/0022487106295726.
52. James Hiebert, Anne K. Morris, and Brad Glass, "Learning to Learn to Teach: An 'Experiment' Model for Teaching and Teacher Preparation in Mathematics," *Journal of Mathematics Teacher Education* 6, no. 3 (2003), doi:10.1023/A:1025162108648.
53. Dylan Wiliam, *Embedded Formative Assessment* (Bloomington, IN: Solution Tree, 2011).
54. Matt Bromley, "Teaching Practice: Hinge Questions," Teaching Practice Series, *SecEd* 2017, no. 4, doi:10.12968/sece.2017.4.4.
55. Caroline Ebby and Marjorie Petit, "Using Learning Trajectories to Elicit, Interpret, and Respond to Student Thinking," in Mills and Silver, *Fresh Look at Formative Assessment*.
56. Levi and Ambrose, "Cognitively Guided Instruction."

57. Neal M. Kingston and Angela Broaddus, "The Use of Learning Map Systems to Support Formative Assessment in Mathematics," *Education Sciences* 7, no. 1 (2017), doi:10.3390/educsci7010041.
58. Sandy Buczynski and C. Bobbi Hansen, "Impact of Professional Development on Teacher Practice: Uncovering Connections," *Teaching and Teacher Education* 26, no. 3 (2010); Joan Heller et al., "Differential Effects of Three Professional Developments Models on Teacher Knowledge and Student Achievement in Elementary Science," *Journal of Research in Science Teaching* 49, no. 3 (2012), doi:10.1002/tea.21004.
59. Heritage and Wylie, "Teacher Preparation in Mathematics."
60. Heritage and Wylie.
61. Christine J. Lyon and E. Caroline Wylie, *How Structure and Focus Support Teacher Learning*, ETS Research Memorandum RM-09-02 (Princeton, NJ: Educational Testing Service, 2009); E. Caroline Wylie, Christine J. Lyon, and Elia Mavronikolas, *Effective and Scalable Teacher Professional Development: A Report of the Formative Research and Development*, ETS Research Report RR-08-65 (Princeton, NJ: ETS, 2008).
62. Marilyn Strutchens and Edward Silver, "Formative Assessment and Equitable Mathematics Classrooms: Probing the Intersection," in Mills and Silver, *Fresh Look at Formative Assessment*; Valerie Otero, "Moving Beyond the 'Get It or Don't' Conception of Formative Assessment," *Journal of Teacher Education* 57, no. 3 (2006), doi:10.1177/0022487105285963.
63. Heritage and Wylie, "Teacher Preparation in Mathematics."
64. Hiebert, Morris, and Glass, "Learning to Learn to Teach," 207; Duckor and Holmberg, *Mastering Formative Assessment Moves*.
65. Heritage and Wylie, "Teacher Preparation in Mathematics."
66. David Tripp, *Critical Incidents in Teaching: Developing Professional Judgment* (New York: Routledge, 1993); David Allen and Joseph McDonald, "Tuning Protocol: A Process for Reflection on Teacher and Student Work," *Horace* 13, no. 2 (1997); Glenda Moss, Terry Springer, and Karol Dehr, "Guided Reflection Protocol as Narrative Inquiry and Teacher Professional Development," *Reflective Practice* 9, no. 4 (2008), doi:10.1080/14623940802431739.
67. Tennessee State University, "Strengthening Instruction in Tennessee Elementary Schools–Focus on Mathematics," http://www.tnstate.edu/sitesm/index.aspx.

Chapter 8

1. Steven A. Melnick and Denise G. Meister, "A Comparison of Beginning and Experienced Teachers' Concerns," *Educational Research Quarterly* 31, no. 3 (2008), https://eric.ed.gov/?id=EJ788428.
2. Melnick and Meister.
3. Dan C. Lortie, *Schoolteacher: A Sociological Study* (Chicago: University of Chicago Press, 1975).
4. Robert Glaser, "Changing the Agency for Learning: Acquiring Expert Performance," in *The Road to Excellence: The Acquisition of Expert Performance in the Arts and Sciences, Sports, and Games* (Hillsdale, NJ: Lawrence Erlbaum Associates, 1996), cited in David C. Berliner, "Comment: Educational Research: The Hardest Science of All," *Educational Researcher* 31, no. 8 (2002), doi:10.3102/0013189X031008018.

5. Note that some states require teachers to complete a second tier of credentialing after induction; other states do not. Our focus in this chapter is on how to structure learning opportunities for beginning teachers during the induction phase rather than on subsequent, consequential assessment of teachers.
6. Lev S. Vygotsky, *Mind in Society: The Development of Higher Mental Process* (Cambridge, MA: Harvard University Press, 1978).
7. Thomas M. McCann, Larry Johannessen, and Bernard Ricca, "Responding to New Teachers' Concerns," *Educational Leadership* 62, no. 8 (2005); "Common Problems and Concerns for New Teachers," Leicester Learning Institute, University of Leicester, https://www2.le.ac.uk/offices/lli/recognition-for-teaching/peers/preparing-to-teach/new-teachers-faqs.
8. Melnick and Meister, "A Comparison."
9. Rebecca Alber, "6 Opening and Closing Routines for New Teachers," Edutopia website, George Lucas Educational Foundation, August 17, 2016, https://www.edutopia.org/blog/6-opening-and-closing-routines-new-teachers-rebecca-alber; Harry K. Wong, Rosemary T. Wong, and Chelonnda Seroyer, *The First Days of School: How to Be an Effective Teacher* (Mountain View, CA: Harry K. Wong Publications, 2005); Paula Denton and Roxann Kriete, *The First Six Weeks of School*, Strategies for Teachers Series (Greenfield, MA: Northeast Foundation for Children, 2000).
10. Richard M. Ingersoll and Thomas M. Smith, "The Wrong Solution to the Teacher Shortage," *Educational Leadership* 60, no. 8 (2003); Lucinda Gray and Soheyla Taie, *Public School Teacher Attrition and Mobility in the First Five Years: Results from the First Through Fifth Waves of the 2007–08 Beginning Teacher Longitudinal Study*, First Look series (Washington, DC: National Center for Education Statistics, 2015), http://ies.ed.gov/pubsearch/pubsinfo.asp?pubid=2015337.
11. Eric A. Hanushek et al., *The Market for Teacher Quality* (Cambridge, MA: National Bureau of Economic Research, 2005); Richard M. Ingersoll and Michael Strong, "The Impact of Induction and Mentoring Programs for Beginning Teachers: A Critical Review of the Research," *Review of Educational Research* 81, no. 2 (2011), doi:10.3102/0034654311403323.
12. Ruth Chung Wei, Linda Darling-Hammond, and Frank Adamson, *Professional Development in the United States: Trends and Challenges* (Dallas, TX: National Staff Development Council, 2010), https://learningforward.org/docs/default-source/pdf/nsdcstudytechnicalreport2010.pdf.
13. The scope and power of state boards of education varies from state to state. Typically they are responsible for statewide curriculum standards, high school graduation requirements, qualifications for professional education personnel, state accountability and assessment programs, standards for accreditation of local school districts and of preparation programs for teachers and administrators, the administration of federal assistance programs, and the development of rules and regulations for the administration of state programs. See http://www.nasbe.org/about-us/state-boards-of-education/.
14. Chris Sun, *Teacher Induction: Improving State Systems for Supporting New Teachers*, National Association of State Boards of Education Discussion Guide (Arlington, VA: NASBE, 2012).
15. Thomas Smith and Richard M. Ingersoll, "What Are the Effects of Induction and Mentoring on Beginning Teacher Turnover?," *American Educational Research Journal* 41, no. 3 (2004): 685, doi:10.3102/00028312041003681.

16. Smith and Ingersoll.
17. Tara Kini and Anne Podolsky, *Does Teaching Experience Increase Teacher Effectiveness? A Review of the Research* (Palo Alto, CA: Learning Policy Institute, 2016), https://learning-policyinstitute.org/product/does-teaching-experience-increase-teacher-effectiveness-review-research.
18. Smith and Ingersoll, "What Are the Effects?," 705.
19. Alliance for Excellent Education, *Tapping the Potential: Retaining and Developing High Quality New Teachers* (Washington, DC: All4Ed, 2004), https://all4ed.org/reports-fact-sheets/tapping-the-potential-retaining-and-developing-high-quality-new-teachers/.
20. Geoffrey Gowlland, "Apprenticeship as a Model for Learning in and Through Professional Practice," in *International Handbook of Research in Professional and Practice-Based Learning*, ed. Stephen Billett, Christian Harteis, and Hans Gruber, Springer International Handbooks of Education (Dordrecht, Netherlands: Springer Science & Business Media, 2014), 760.
21. New Teacher Center, *High Quality Mentoring and Induction Practices* (Santa Cruz, CA: New Teacher Center, 2007); Steven Glazerman et al., *Impacts of Comprehensive Teacher Induction: Final Results from a Randomized Controlled Study*, NCEE 2010-4027 (Washington, DC: National Center for Education Evaluation and Regional Assistance, 2010): xxv.
22. Paula Rutherford, "Challenges and Concerns of New Teachers," *Mentoring in the 21st Century* (September 2006), https://justaskpublications.com/just-ask-resource-center/mentoring-in-the-21st-century/challenges-and-concerns-of-new-teachers.
23. Ikujiro Nonaka and Hirotaka Takeuchi, The Knowledge-Creating Company: How Japanese Companies Create the Dynamics *of Innovation* (Oxford: Oxford University Press, 1995).
24. Liam Goldrick, *Support from the Start: A 50-State Review of Policies on New Educator Induction and Mentoring* (Santa Cruz, CA: New Teacher Center, 2016).
25. McCann, Johannessen, and Ricca, "Responding to New Teachers' Concerns."
26. Goldrick, *Support from the Start.*
27. Rutherford, "Challenges and Concerns of New Teachers."
28. Megan Burton and Wanda Audrict, "Focusing on Formative Assessment to Improve Mathematics Teaching and Learning," in *A Fresh Look at Formative Assessment in Mathematics Teaching*, ed. Valerie Mills and Edward Silver (Reston, VA: National Council of Mathematics Teachers, 2018).
29. Laura Hullinger, email correspondence with E. Caroline Wylie, August, 2019.
30. Miriam Gamoran Sherin, Rosemary S. Russ, and Adam A. Colestock, "Accessing Mathematics Teachers' In-the-Moment Noticing," in *Mathematics Teacher Noticing: Seeing through Teachers' Eyes*, ed. Miriam Gamoran Sherin, Victoria R. Jacobs, and Randolph A. Philipp (New York: Routledge, 2011).
31. Judith Warren Little et al., "Looking at Student Work for Teacher Learning, Teacher Community, and School Reform," *Phi Delta Kappan* 85, no. 3 (2003); Tina Blythe, David Allen, and Barbara Schieffelin Powell, *Looking Together at Student Work*, 3rd ed. (New York: Teachers College Press, 2015).
32. "NSRF Protocols and Activities . . . From A to Z," National School Reform Faculty (website), https://nsrfharmony.org/protocols/.
33. Stacy Wenzel et al., *Documentation of the 1996–2002 Chicago Annenberg Research Project Strand on Authentic Intellectual Demand Exhibited in Assignments and Student*

Work: A Technical Process Manual (Chicago: Consortium on Chicago School Research, 2002), https://eric.ed.gov/?id=ED499376.

34. Wenzel et al.
35. Sun, "Teacher Induction" 8.
36. Sun.
37. Anders Jonsson, Christian Lundahl, and Anders Holmgren, "Evaluating a Large-Scale Implementation of Assessment for Learning in Sweden," *Assessment in Education: Principles, Policy & Practice* 22, no. 1 (2015), doi:10.1080/0969594X.2014.970612; Christine J. Lyon et al., "Formative Assessment and the Role of Teachers' Content Area," *School Science and Mathematics* 118, no. 5 (2018); Michael O'Leary, Zita Lysaght, and Larry Ludlow, "A Measurement Instrument to Evaluate Teachers' Assessment for Learning Classroom Practices," *International Journal of Educational and Psychological Assessment* 14, no. 2 (2013); E. Caroline Wylie and Christine J. Lyon, "The Fidelity of Formative Assessment Implementation: Issues of Breadth and Quality," *Assessment in Education: Principles, Policy & Practice* 22, no. 1 (2015), doi:10.1080/0969594X.2014.990416.
38. E. Caroline Wylie and Christine Lyon, *Using the Formative Assessment Rubrics, Reflection and Observation Tools to Support Professional Reflection on Practice* (Washington, DC: Formative Assessment for Teachers and Students State Collaborative on Assessment and Student Standards of the Council of Chief State School Officers (CCSSO), 2015).
39. Helen F. Ladd and Lucy C. Sorensen, "Returns to Teacher Experience: Student Achievement and Motivation in Middle School," *Education Finance and Policy* 12, no. 2 (Spring 2017), doi:10.1162/EDFP_a_00194; Kini and Podolsky, *Does Teaching Experience Increase Teacher Effectiveness?*, 1.
40. Kini and Podolsky, 1.
41. Mark Windschitl et al., "Proposing a Core Set of Instructional Practices and Tools for Teachers of Science," *Science Education* 96, no. 5 (2012), doi:10.1002/sce.21027.

Chapter 9

1. See David Berliner, "Learning About and Learning From Expert Teachers," *International Journal of Educational Research* 35, (2001), doi:10.1016/S0883-0355(02)00004-6, for an extended discussion of the development of expertise; Malcolm Gladwell, *Outliers: The Story of Success* (New York: Little, Brown, 2008).
2. Tara Kini and Anne Podolsky, *Does Teaching Experience Increase Teacher Effectiveness? A Review of the Research* (Palo Alto, CA: Learning Policy Institute, 2016), 15, https://learningpolicyinstitute.org/product/does-teaching-experience-increase-teacher-effectiveness-review-research.
3. Milbrey W. McLaughlin and Joan E. Talbert, *Contexts That Matter for Teaching and Learning: Strategic Opportunities for Meeting the Nation's Educational Goals* (Stanford, CA: Center for Research on the Context of Secondary School Teaching, 1993); David Cohen and Heather C. Hill, "Instructional Policy and Classroom Performance: The Mathematics Reform in California," *Teachers College Record* 102, no. 2 (2000), https://www.tcrecord.org/content.asp?contentid=10377, cited in Berliner, "Learning About and Learning From Expert Teachers."

4. Berliner, 446.
5. John Hattie, "What Are the Attributes of Excellent Teachers?" in *Teachers Make a Difference: What Is the Research Evidence?* (Wellington, New Zealand: Council for Educational Research, 2002), http://www.educationalleaders.govt.nz/Pedagogy-and-assessment/Building-effective-learning-environments/Teachers-Make-a-Difference-What-is-the-Research-Evidence.
6. John Hattie, *Visible Learning for Teachers: Maximizing Impact on Learning* (New York: Routledge, 2012).
7. Lloyd Bond et al., *The Certification System of the National Board for Professional Teaching Standards: A Construct and Consequential Validity Study* (Greensboro, NC: Center for Educational Research and Evaluation, 2000).
8. David C. Berliner, "Comment: Educational Research: The Hardest Science of All," *Educational Researcher* 31, no. 8 (2002), doi:10.3102/0013189X031008018.
9. TNTP, *The Opportunity Myth: What Students Can Show Us About How School Is Letting Them Down—and How to Fix It* (New York: TNTP, 2018), https://tntp.org/publications/view/student-experiences/the-opportunity-myth.
10. Paul Black and Dylan Wiliam, "Assessment and Classroom Learning," *Assessment in Education: Principles, Policy & Practice* 5, no. 1 (1998): 7–74, doi:10.1080/0969595980050102.
11. Thomas M. Smith and Richard M. Ingersoll, "What Are the Effects of Induction and Mentoring on Beginning Teacher Turnover?" *American Educational Research Journal* 41, no. 3 (2004), doi:10.3102/00028312041003681.
12. Margaret Heritage, Nancy Gerzon, and Marie Mancuso, *Necessary Conditions for Successful Implementation of Formative Assessment* (San Francisco: WestEd, 2017).
13. Heritage, Gerzon, and Mancuso.
14. Alison L. Bailey and Margaret Heritage, *Progressing Students' Language Day by Day* (Thousand Oaks, CA: Corwin Press, 2018).
15. Linda Darling-Hammond, Maria E. Hyler, and Madelyn Gardner, *Effective Teacher Professional Development* (Palo Alto, CA: Learning Policy Institute, 2017), https://learningpolicyinstitute.org/product/teacher-prof-dev.
16. Darling-Hammond, Hyler, and Gardner, v.
17. Laurie Calvert, "The Power of Teacher Agency," *Learning Professional* 37, no. 2 (2016): 4, https://learningforward.org/docs/default-source/jsd-april-2016/the-power-of-teacher-agency-april16.pdf.
18. Laura Goe et al., *State of the States' Teacher Evaluation and Support Systems: A Perspective from Exemplary Teachers*, ETS Research Report series (Princeton, NJ: Educational Testing Service, Council of Chief State School Officers, and National Network of State Teachers of the Year, 2017), doi:10.1002/ets2.12156.
19. Olivia Lozano, interview with Margaret Heritage, 2017.
20. Jean Lave and Etienne Wenger, *Situated Learning: Legitimate Peripheral Participation* (Cambridge: Cambridge University Press, 1991).
21. Etienne Wenger, Richard Arnold McDermott, and William Snyder, *Cultivating Communities of Practice: A Guide to Managing Knowledge* (Cambridge, MA: Harvard Business Press, 2002).
22. Bailey and Heritage, *Progressing Students' Language.*
23. Goe et al., *State of the States' Teacher Evaluation.*

24. Cindy Ziker, *FASTER Grant Summary Report of the Use of the Hewlett Funding to CCSSO*, unpublished report submitted to the CCSSO Formative Assessment State Collaborative (Menlo Park, CA: SRI International, 2017).
25. WestEd, "Student Agency in Assessment and Learning (SAAL) Materials," https://fa-insights.wested.org/saal/.
26. *Revising the Definition of Formative Assessment* (Washington, DC: CCSSO, 2018), https://ccsso.org/resource-library/revising-definition-formative-assessment.
27. *Revising the Definition of Formative Assessment*.
28. Lee Shulman, "Knowledge and Teaching: Foundations of the New Reform," *Harvard Educational Review* 57, no. 1 (1987): 7, doi:10.17763/haer.57.1.j463w79r56455411.
29. National Research Council, *How People Learn: Brain, Mind, Experience, and School*, expanded ed. (Washington, DC: National Academies Press, 2000), doi:10.17226/9853.
30. Gabriela Cárdenas, interview with Margaret Heritage, 2017.
31. Valerie Otero, "Moving Beyond the 'Get It or Don't' Conception of Formative Assessment," *Journal of Teacher Education* 57, no. 3 (2006), doi:10.1177/0022487105285963.
32. Jim Minstrell, Ruth Anderson, and Min Li, "Assessing Teacher Competency in Formative Assessment," *Annual Report 2009* (Seattle, WA: FACET Innovations, 2009), 15.
33. Margaret Heritage, *Formative Assessment: Making It Happen in the Classroom* (Thousand Oaks, CA: Corwin Press, 2010), 52.
34. Black and Wiliam, "Assessment and Classroom Learning," 37.
35. Alison L. Bailey and Margaret Heritage, "The Role of Language Learning Progressions in Improved Instruction and Assessment of English Language Learners," *TESOL Quarterly* 48, no. 3 (2014), doi:10.1002/tesq.176.
36. Jason Riley, "Learning Progressions" (paper presented at the National Student Assessment Conference, Detroit, MI, June 26, 2010).
37. Margaret Heritage, *Formative Assessment: A Process of Inquiry and Action* (Cambridge, MA: Harvard Education Press, 2013).
38. Luis C. Moll et al., "Funds of Knowledge for Teaching: Using a Qualitative Approach to Connect Homes and Classrooms," *Theory Into Practice* 31, no. 2 (1992), doi:10.1080/00405849209543534.
39. Norma González, "Beyond Culture: The Hybridity of Funds of Knowledge," in *Funds of Knowledge: Theorizing Practices in Households, Communities, and Classrooms*, ed. Norma González, Luis C. Moll, and Cathy Amanti (New York: Routledge, 2006).
40. Bronwen Cowie, Christine Harrison, and Jill Willis, "Supporting Teacher Responsiveness in Assessment for Learning Through Disciplined Noticing," *Curriculum Journal* 29, no. 4 (2018): 7.
41. Margaret Heritage and Christine Harrison, *The Power of Assessment for Learning: Twenty Years of Research and Practice in UK and US Classrooms* (Thousand Oaks, CA: Corwin Press, 2020).
42. Jennifer Hauver James, Jessica F. Kobe, and Xiaoying Zhao, "Examining the Role of Trust in Shaping Children's Approaches to Peer Dialogue," *Teachers College Record* 119, no. 10 (2017), http://www.tcrecord.org/Content.asp?ContentId=21898.
43. Bhaskar Raj Upadhyay, "Using Students' Lived Experiences in an Urban Science Classroom: An Elementary School Teacher's Thinking," *Science Education* 90, no. 1 (2006), doi:10.1002/sce.20095.

Chapter 10

1. John M. Holland, Jon Eckert, and Megan M. Allen, "From Preservice to Teacher Leadership: Meeting the Future in Educator Preparation," *Action in Teacher Education* 36, no. 5–6 (2014), doi:10.1080/01626620.2014.977738; Center for Comprehensive School Reform and Improvement, "The Role of Principal Leadership in Improving Student Achievement," news release, 2005; Jennifer York-Barr and Karen Duke, "What Do We Know About Teacher Leadership? Findings from Two Decades of Scholarship," *Review of Educational Research* 74, no. 3 (2004), doi:10.3102/00346543074003255.
2. Teacher Leadership Exploratory Consortium, *Teacher Leader Model Standards* (Carrboro, NC: TLEC, 2011), https://www.ets.org/s/education_topics/teaching_quality/pdf/teacher_leader_model_standards.pdf.
3. Center for Comprehensive School Reform and Improvement, *What Does the Research Tell Us About Teacher Leadership?* Research Brief (Washington, DC: CCSRI, 2005).
4. Ann Lieberman, "Teachers at the Forefront: Learning to Lead," in *The Power of Teacher Leaders: Their Roles, Influence, and Impact*, ed. Nathan Bond (New York: Routledge, 2015).
5. Valeri R. Helterbran, "Teacher Leadership: Overcoming 'I Am Just a Teacher' Syndrome," *Education* 131, no. 2 (2010).
6. Katherine Bassett et al., "Re-Imagining Teaching: Five Structures to Transform the Profession," (Philadelphia: National Network of State Teachers of the Year, 2013), https://eric.ed.gov/?id=ED581423.
7. Bradley Portin, "The Roles That Principals Play," *Educational Leadership* 61, no. 7 (2004), https://eric.ed.gov/?id=EJ716732.
8. TLEC, *Teacher Leader Model Standards.*
9. Norma Silva, personal correspondence, August 17, 2019.
10. This second-grade teacher leader has worked with the first author for many years and provided her a description of what she valued about her role as a teacher leader.
11. Jane Coggshall, Molly Lasagna, and Sabrina Laine, *Toward the Structural Transformation of Schools: Innovations in Staffing* (Naperville, IL: Learning Point Associates, 2009), https://eric.ed.gov/?id=ED509963; Teresa Jackson et al., *Teacher Leadership: An Assessment Framework for an Emerging Area of Professional Practice*, ETS Research Report Series (Princeton, NJ: Educational Testing Service, 2010), https://www.ets.org/Media/Research/pdf/RR-10-27.pdf; Bassett et al., "Re-Imagining Teaching."
12. CCSRI, *What Does the Research Tell Us?*"; Tim Waters, Robert J. Marzano, and Brian McNulty, *Balanced Leadership: What 30 Years of Research Tells Us About the Effect of Leadership on Student Achievement* (Denver, CO: McREL International, 2008).
13. Laura Goe et al., *State of the States' Teacher Evaluation and Support Systems: A Perspective from Exemplary Teachers*, ETS Research Report series (Princeton, NJ: Educational Testing Service, Council of Chief State School Officers, and National Network of State Teachers of the Year, 2017), doi:10.1002/ets2.12156.
14. Goe et al., 14.
15. Goe et al.
16. Goe et al., 13.
17. Jo R. Blase and Joseph J. Blase, *Teachers Bringing Out the Best in Teachers: A Guide to Peer Consultation for Administrators and Teachers* (Thousand Oaks, CA: Corwin Press, 2006).

18. Marilyn Katzenmeyer and Gayle Moller, *Awakening the Sleeping Giant: Helping Teachers Develop as Leaders* (Thousand Oaks, CA: Corwin Press, 2001), 2.
19. Bassett et al., "Re-Imagining Teaching."
20. Rachelle Feiler, Margaret Heritage, and Ronald Gallimore, "Teachers Leading Teachers," *Educational Leadership* 57, no. 7 (2000), https://eric.ed.gov/?id=EJ609648.
21. Cindy Harrison and Joellen Killion, "Ten Roles for Teacher Leaders," *Educational Leadership* 65, no. 1 (2007).
22. E. Caroline Wylie and Margaret Heritage, "Developing and Deepening Formative Assessment Practice," in *Formative Assessment: Making It Happen in the Classroom*, ed. Margaret Heritage (Thousand Oaks, CA: Corwin Press, 2010).
23. Organisation for Economic Co-operation and Development, *Education at a Glance 2018* (Paris: OECD, 2018).
24. Frederic A. Mosher, "Learning Progressions," in *Routledge Encyclopedia of Education*, ed. Douglas Fisher (Abingdon, UK: Routledge, in press).
25. Mosher.
26. E. Caroline Wylie and Joseph Ciofalo, "Supporting Teachers' Use of Individual Diagnostic Items," *Teachers College Record* (September 5, 2008), http://www.tcrecord.org/content.asp?contentid=15363.
27. This teacher leader has worked with the first author for many years and provided her a description of what she valued about her role as a teacher leader.
28. Paul Black, Mark Wilson, and Shih-Ying Yao, "Road Maps for Learning: A Guide to the Navigation of Learning Progressions," *Measurement: Interdisciplinary Research and Perspectives* 9, no. 2–3 (2011), doi:10.1080/15366367.2011.591654.
29. E. Caroline Wylie and Christine Lyon, *Using the Formative Assessment Rubrics, Reflection and Observation Tools to Support Professional Reflection on Practice* (Washington, DC: Formative Assessment for Teachers and Students State Collaborative on Assessment and Student Standards, Council of Chief State School Officers, 2015).
30. "The Role of the Facilitator," University of Virginia Process Simplification (archive), https://www2.virginia.edu/processsimplification/resources/Facilitator.pdf.
31. Linda Darling-Hammond, Maria E. Hyler, and Madelyn Gardner, *Effective Teacher Professional Development* (Palo Alto, CA: Learning Policy Institute, 2017), https://learningpolicyinstitute.org/product/teacher-prof-dev.
32. Educational Testing Service, *TLC Leader Handbook* (Portland, OR: ETS, 2009).
33. Vicki Collet, "ReVisioning Teachers' Professional Development Through Collaborative Lesson Study," Teachers College Press blog, July 29, 2019, https://www.tcpress.com/blog/collet-collaborative-lesson-study/; Catherine C. Lewis and Jacqueline Hurd, *Lesson Study Step by Step: How Teacher Learning Communities Improve Instruction* (Portsmouth, NH: Heinemann, 2011).
34. Wylie and Heritage, "Developing and Deepening Formative Assessment Practice."
35. Harrison and Killion, "Ten Roles for Teacher Leaders."
36. Teacher Leadership Institute, *The Teacher Leadership Competencies* (Carrboro, NC: Center for Teaching Quality, National Board for Professional Teaching Standards, and National Education Association, 2014), https://www.nbpts.org/wp-content/uploads/teacher_leadership_competencies_final.pdf.
37. TLI, *Teacher Leadership Competencies*.
38. Jackson et al., *Teacher Leadership*.
39. Jackson et al.; TLI, *Teacher Leadership Competencies*.

40. Jackson et al., *Teacher Leadership.*
41. Charlotte Danielson, *Teacher Leadership That Strengthens Professional Practice* (Alexandria, VA: ASCD, 2006);
42. TLI, *Teacher Leadership Competencies.*
43. Danielson, *Teacher Leadership That Strengthens Professional Practice.*
44. American Federation of Teachers, *Leadership in Teaching*, Teacher Leaders Series (Washington, DC: American Federation of Teachers, AFL-CIO, 2016), 4, https://www.aft.org/sites/default/files/leadershipinteaching.pdf.

Conclusion

1. Lev S. Vygotsky, *Mind in Society: The Development of Higher Mental Process* (Cambridge, MA: Harvard University Press, 1978).
2. E. Caroline Wylie and Margaret Heritage, "Developing and Deepening Formative Assessment Practice," in *Formative Assessment: Making It Happen in the Classroom*, Margaret Heritage (Thousand Oaks, CA: Corwin Press, 2010).
3. American Federation of Teachers, *Leadership in Teaching*, Teacher Leaders Series (Washington, DC: American Federation of Teachers, AFL-CIO, 2016), https://www.aft.org/sites/default/files/leadershipinteaching.pdf.

Acknowledgments

This book has its origins in our coauthored chapter for the Handbook of Formative Assessment in the Disciplines, and we are grateful to the Handbook's editors, Heidi Andrade, Randy Bennet, and Greg Cizek for their invitation to contribute and stimulate our thinking about professional learning in discipline-based formative assessment.

We owe a huge debt of thanks to the many teachers whose classroom practice is illustrated in the examples throughout the book, and whose quotes help illuminate how teachers develop skills in formative assessment. In particular, we offer our gratitude to Monica Brennan, Gabriela Cárdenas, Mayra Carrasco, Katie Closs, Julie Eilertsen, Wendy Johnson, Hilary Johannes, Olivia Lozano, Mark Martino, and Chris Wilson, who have willingly shared their practice with us, and from whom we have learned so much about ambitious teaching and formative assessment. In addition, we thank Norma Silva for showing us exemplary leadership for formative assessment.

Our grateful thanks to the subject matter experts from the Sacramento County Office of Education who provided feedback on the chapters and contributed examples of practice they have seen in the field: Becky Sullivan, David Chun, Fran Gibson, Jonathan Rhodea, and Charles Gilmore.

We are extremely grateful to colleagues at Educational Testing Service for their review and feedback on each of the book's chapters. There is no doubt that this is a better book for it.

Our warm thanks to Eowyn Winchester for her gracious assistance in the preparation of our manuscript.

We have a special word of thanks for the members of the Formative Assessment State Collaborative in the US, whose definition of formative assessment we use in the book. This group has been steadfast in its commitment to advancing formative assessment across the nation and has contributed so much to the development of our thinking.

We express countless thanks to Caroline Chauncey, our editor from Harvard Education Press, whose guidance from our initial thinking about a book proposal has been invaluable. She is a peerless editor and we have benefited beyond measure from her feedback and encouragement during our writing process.

Finally, Margaret thanks her husband, John, who has lived this book with her, for his unwavering encouragement, support, and patience. Caroline thanks her husband, Craig, for his supportive cheerleader role when the writing got tough and all-consuming.

About the Authors

Margaret Heritage is an independent consultant in education. For her entire career, her work has spanned both research and practice. In addition to spending many years in her native England as a practitioner, a university teacher, and an inspector of schools, she had an extensive period at UCLA, first as principal of the laboratory school of the Graduate School of Education and Information Studies and then as an assistant director at UCLA's National Center for Research on Evaluation, Standards, and Student Testing. She has also taught in the departments of education at UCLA and Stanford. Her recent books, both coauthored with Alison Bailey, are *Progressing Students' Language Day by Day* (Corwin Press) and *Self-Regulation in Learning: The Role of Language and Formative Assessment* (Harvard Education Press).

E. Caroline Wylie is a research director at Educational Testing Service. Having completed her preservice teacher education with a focus on mathematics in Belfast, Northern Ireland, her focus shifted to classroom-based research. Those interests include issues related to balanced assessment systems, with a focus on the use of formative assessment to improve classroom teaching and learning. She has led studies related to the creation of effective, scaleable, and sustainable teacher professional development focused on formative assessment; on the formative use of diagnostic questions for classroom-based assessment; on assessment literacy; and on the role of learning progressions to support formative assessment in mathematics and science. She is currently the principal investigator on a grant (funded by the Institute of Education Sciences) that is examining classroom observations with a formative assessment focus and the relationship between observations, feedback, and changes to practice.

Authorship is listed alphabetically. Margaret Heritage and Caroline Wylie contributed equally to the conceptualization and writing of this book.

Index